CLAIMS OF REINCARNATION

An Empirical Study of Cases in India

PRAISE FOR
CLAIMS OF REINCARNATION

Dr. Satwant Pasricha is a giant in the field of empirical investigation of past-life claims. Here she presents—clearly and concisely—a fascinating look at more than fifteen years of her research in India. *Claims of Reincarnation* is an important work that will give readers new insights into that most basic human question: Do we survive death?

~ **JIM B TUCKER, MD,** DIRECTOR OF THE DIVISION OF PERCEPTUAL STUDIES, BONNER-LOWRY PROFESSOR OF PSYCHIATRY AND NEUROBEHAVIORAL SCIENCES, UNIVERSITY OF VIRGINIA USA. AUTHOR OF *LIFE BEFORE LIFE*

In an area where the general level of reporting ranges from the sensational to the incompetent, it is refreshing to find a book that commands considerable critical respect, regardless of what one thinks of the subject matter. Such a work is Pasricha's *Claims of Reincarnation*, perhaps the most intelligent book to appear on the subject since the publication of Ian Stevenson's classic series of cases studied.

~ **ROGER I. ANDERSON,** VINITA, OKLAHOMA, *THE JOURNAL OF THE AMERICAN SOCIETY FOR PSYCHICAL RESEARCH*

This book is a careful, thorough report of the author's investigations of claims of young children who seemed to recall events of a previous life on earth. The book presents a wealth of information ... is a fine addition to the literature on the subject. I enjoyed reading it, and I recommend it without reservation to any one who is interested in this phenomenon.

~ **PAUL ROBB,** PALO ALTO, CALIFORNIA, *JOURNAL OF SCIENTIFIC EXPLORATION*

Claims of Reincarnation: An Empirical Study of Cases in India contains references, a general and name index and many tables. The book is well organized and edited and offers a sound and valuable contribution to the study of children who claim memories of previous life.

~ **ERLENDUR HARALDSSON,** UNIVERSITY OF ICELAND, *JOURNAL OF SOCIETY FOR PSYCHICAL RESEARCH*

Reincarnation is a subject that arouses as much interest as controversy. It is not easy to come by a book that keeps to facts, reports objectively the findings of research without sensationalism or embellishment for the benefit of curious readers. Dr. Pasricha is a serious researcher whose decades of painstaking examination of reports of reincarnation has culminated in this book. Dr. Pasricha is perhaps the only Clinical Psychologist of the country, who based her reports strictly on field work, meticulously weeding out numerous fake claims from scientifically verifiable instances. Considered a giant in the field of empirical investigation of claims of past life memories, she has presented a fascinating report that gives new insights into this phenomenon as well as the needed thrust to further research in this area.

~ **DR. INDIRA JAI PRAKASH, M.A; D.M &S.P; PH.D.** FORMER PROFESSOR AND CHAIRPERSON, DEPARTMENT OF PSYCHOLOGY, BANGALORE UNIVERSITY, BANGALORE.

CLAIMS OF REINCARNATION

An Empirical Study of Cases in India

Satwant K. Pasricha, Ph.D.

WHITE
CROW

www.whitecrowbooks.com

Dedicated
To the memory of my Bapuji

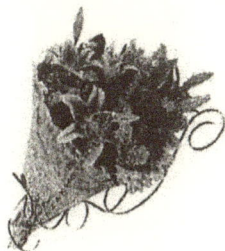

Contents

List of Tables

An Appeal

In order to have a better understanding of the phenomenon of reincarnation and related areas, namely possession and near- death experiences (NDEs), I request readers to write to me as soon as they learn about a case in their family, circle of friends and acquaintances, or neighborhood. In cases of claims of past life memories (reincarnation and possessions type) persons concerned should avoid taking the subject (child) to the other family till we have completed our studies. In case of NDEs, they should inform us soon after the episode occurs. In this way they will make a big contribution to our understanding of the nature of man, his personality development, and some questions concerning life after death.

I, on my part, would like to assure readers, as they would learn while reading the book, that our techniques of investigation do not cause any distress or harm to the subjects, their family or any other informant. If desired, the identities of persons concerned in a case, or informing me about one, can be kept confidential.

Readers are requested to write to me at the following address giving (i) their own names and addresses, and (ii) the names and addresses of the subjects of cases they know of. (It would be helpful if they could write a brief summary of the case in any language.)

Dr. Satwant K. Pasricha

Department of Clinical Psychology

National Institute of Mental Health and Neurosciences,

Bangalore 560 029

INDIA

Foreword

This is the first book on cases of the reincarnation type to be published in India in more than thirty years. And its author is the best qualified person to write it. She has been investigating these cases in India for more than fifteen years and has more knowledge of them than anyone else. Through numerous articles in scientific journals Dr. Satwant Pasricha has become well known for her research among scientists interested in the field of parapsychology. However, her work is still insufficiently known by members of the general public and this book will help to remedy that deficiency.

I have worked closely with Dr. Pasricha since 1973 and can take some credit for drawing her into the research reported in this book. I can also testify to the great contribution that she has made toward improving our methods of research. As a woman she was able to hear from female informants details they might never have told to male investigators. However, Dr. Pasricha's skill as an interviewer goes far beyond feminine gentleness. Her sensitivity to the persons with whom she is talking has made men just as willing as women to share details of their experiences with her and children just as willing as adults.

Good research requires more than the gathering of information. What the investigator learns through interviews and from other sources has to be carefully appraised and then competently reported. In this side of her work also Dr. Pasricha has shown outstanding abilities. Some of the cases she describes may seem difficult to believe for a reader encountering them for the first time. I agree to that. The reader can, however, believe this: that everything in this book has been set out as carefully and accurately as could possibly be.

The subject of reincarnation nearly always arouses interest and often strong feelings. Much has been written about it, but most that has been written is secondhand, inaccurate, or sensational. I am happy to recommend unreservedly this book on reincarnation that the reader can regard with complete trust.

Ian Stevenson, M.D.
Carlson Professor of Psychiatry
University of Virginia, USA

Acknowledgements

This book is based on my Ph.D. thesis submitted to the Bangalore University in 1978. Many had helped in different measures at various stages of its preparation and I had recorded my gratitude to them at the time.

Over the next ten years of further research, I have incurred debts from many persons who deserve a special mention in this book.

I am grateful to the following for accompanying me to various places, at different times, during my field investigations:

Allahabad: Dr. Jamuna Prasad, Dr. L.P. Mehrotra, and Mr. K.S. Rawat

Delhi: Mr. M.S. Arora, Mr. P. Tanwar, and Mr. H.S. Kalra

Fatehabad, Agra: Mr. Mahavir Singh

University of Virginia, USA: Prof. Ian Stevenson, U Win Maung, and Dr. McClean Rice

I am deeply indebted to Prof. Ian Stevenson for providing generous help in the preparation of this book in more than one way. He accepted to write the foreword in spite of his own commitments, participated in the research of several cases, read some parts of the book more than once and offered valuable suggestions for their improvement. However, I assume full responsibility for the deficiencies that still remain.

I express my deep sense of gratitude to Prof. H.N. Murthy (Bangalore), and Prof. Ian Stevenson for being continuous sources of inspiration and encouragement throughout the conduct of my research and preparation of the book.

I warmly thank Mr. Punkaj Tanwar for his selfless involvement and untiring assistance at various stages of the work reported in this book. He also arranged a microcomputer and ably handled various technical problems that arose while preparing the manuscript. But for his heip this book would not have taken its present shape.

Ms. Harpal Kaur Pasricha, and Ms. Jagjit Kaur Khurana gave much of their time and patiently sat through the final readings of the manuscript. I warmly appreciate their help.

My research was supported by the National Institute of Mental Health and Neurosciences (NIMHANS), Bangalore, India, and the University of Virginia, U.S.A. I gratefully acknowledge the help of both these institutions. I thank Prof. G.N. Narayana Reddy, Director, and Prof. G.G.Prabhu, Head of the department of Clinical Psychology, NIMHANS, Bangalore for their interest in my research and administrative help in facilitating it.

Recently M/s Jindal Aluminium Ltd. have contributed generously for the support of my continuing research, for which I am sincerely grateful to them.

I also thank Mr. Manjit Singh for bearing with me for several alterations during the publication of this book.

Last, but not least, I am indebted to my subjects, their family members, and several other informants for their enduring cooperation and hospitality.

Bangalore   S.K.P.

CHAPTER ONE

Introduction

Throughout recorded history in every culture and period, many persons have believed that they could perceive or influence events at a distance without known physical means of communication or action. These abilities now called paranormal were either rejected by skeptics as "recrudescence of superstition" or accepted by believers as "evidence of the supernatural" without an objective basis for doing so (Barrett, 1911).

Scientific investigation of such claims began over a hundred years ago. A number of eminent scientists from various fields, including the physicists Sir William Barrett (1844-1925) and Sir Oliver Lodge (1851-1940), the chemist Sir William Crookes (1832-1919), and the biologist Alfred Russel Wallace (1823-1913) gave serious thought to the subject. They felt that the reports of such occurrences had much more to offer than conventional scientists had recognized. After a few unsuccessful attempts to bring these matters to the serious attention of the scientific world, a group of scholars, mostly of Cambridge University, decided to investigate those faculties of man, real or supposed, that appeared inexplicable to science. For this purpose they founded in 1882 the Society for Psychical Research in London, England.

In its first phase, psychical research (which is now often known as parapsychology) was largely conducted by individual investigators. Some of them had academic appointments, but their work in this field was usually carried on outside their regular duties in teaching and research. Gradually however, some faculty members of colleges and universities took up the work more or less on a full-time basis, and for a time during the 1960s and 1970s a considerable amount of research was conducted within universities. However, on the whole, studies of paranormal phenomena have not been either encouraged or supported except in a few universities. Investigations of apparent paranormal events are, nevertheless, in progress in several university departments.

Paranormal phenomena have long presented a serious challenge to science. But scientists even today are trying to understand and come to grips with them. The great and even revolutionary developments in modern science make the previously unthinkable phenomena of parapsychology now appear somewhat less preposterous than they seemed to an earlier generation (Koestler, 1972/1973; Hardy, Harvie and Koestler, 1974). As a result, some scientists of the "official sciences" have started recognizing, although often only implicitly, certain affinities between what they think and do and research in the field of parapsychology.

Parapsychology has two main branches: the study of ostensibly paranormal phenomena that occur spontaneously in everyday life; and the study of whatever phenomena of the kind in question can be elicited under the more controlled conditions of laboratories. (The investigation of the unusual abilities of mediums and sensitives occupies a somewhat intermediate position, half way between spontaneous occurrences and experiments.)

Investigators of the first period in psychical research—up to about 1930—strongly emphasized the study of spontaneous cases. Then from about 1930 to about 1960 experimental research in laboratories received the most attention and spontaneous cases were relatively neglected. During the past three decades, spontaneous cases have again received more attention from parapsychologists.

Among all the different types of spontaneous cases, claimed memories of previous lives received, at least until recently, the least attention of any group of cases. Scientists who became aware of such claims were inclined to attribute them to mental abnormalities, superstitions, or at best to culture-bound beliefs. Persons living in cultures where the belief in reincarnation prevailed, on the other hand, were inclined often to accept the idea of reincarnation solely on the basis of their religious teachings. Thus members of neither group had any incentive to examine seriously and empirically specific claims of memories of previous lives.

It is a major task of scientists to observe events, especially unusual ones, to consider different interpretations for them, and to communicate their observations and findings to other persons. In this way the benefit of experiences that only rare persons may have can be shared with other persons who do not have such experiences.

Human beings acquire knowledge in two ways: from their own experiences and from those of others. The first, a universal method of obtaining knowledge, suffices for many persons. What they know derives exclusively from their own experiences. Some persons of this group are uneducated or mentally ill equipped to learn from other persons. But this group also includes persons who possess unusual gifts or powers of self-penetration and who can, from within themselves, acquire profound knowledge of many things. According to some traditions and claims, such persons may even attain knowledge of the highest truths. Members of the other group, who are persons without either the handicaps or the gifts of the first group, derive their knowledge from external sources. This is to say that they benefit

3

from the experiences of other people.

This categorization of knowledge into two types is far from new. In the ancient philosophy of India, the distinction has been made for centuries between direct or primary knowledge (*shruti*) and indirect knowledge (*smriti*).

The experiences studied by parapsychologists illustrate the distinction between these two types of knowledge well; and this is particularly true of claims to remember a previous life. A person who says that he remembers a previous life rarely has any doubt that he has in fact remembered one. For him, his memories of the previous life are matters of which he claims to have direct, reliable knowledge, and they have the status of certainty, just as memories of childhood have for other persons. Although people sometimes misremember their own childhoods, it is unusual for a person to doubt the accuracy of his childhood memories. It is unusual also for other persons to deny that a person who says he remembers his childhood can actually do so. To challenge another person's memories of his childhood could undermine a person's confidence in the accuracy of his memories of his own childhood. But some persons claim that they can remember their early infancy and these persons, being rather rare, encounter varying degrees of skepticism on the part of other persons. Even rarer are persons who claim to remember a previous life; and they understandably encounter even more skepticism.

Claims to remember previous lives have been reported under a variety of conditions. Such memories may occur during the normal waking state and also in altered states of consciousness. The latter condition may lead to some difficulty of interpretation. Two conditions that are radically different may resemble each other closely in outward aspects. For example, persons having parapsychological experiences may behave in unusual ways that cause other persons to consider them mentally ill, when they are not. Similarly, some persons who are mentally ill may claim to have paranormal experiences when they do not have them; or they may actually have some paranormal abilities, which are masked by their mental illness. Or a justifiable claim of paranormal powers may be dismissed as only a part of their delusions or hallucinations. Thus confusion can easily occur between the paranormal and the abnormal (or psychopathological). The difference deserves a careful examination of the pertinent phenomena.

A scientific study of the evidence for reincarnation consists in examining, to whatever extent this is possible, the claims of persons who say that they have direct knowledge of previous lives and in communicating the findings to others. But the task of the scientist in parapsychology, as in most other branches of science, goes far beyond that of merely reporting observations. Analysis is no less important than observing and recording.

The earliest available reports of rebirth cases appeared sometime in the late nineteenth century. However, up to the 1960s cases were published only in single reports, occasionally in small groups of reports. A major turn was made in the history of parapsychological investigations in the 1960s by Professor Ian Stevenson of the University of Virginia. He objectively examined the claims of persons who spontaneously recalled previous lives, subjected his data to group analysis for possible recurrent features in the cases; and weighed individual cases against several plausible hypotheses. He thus brought the phenomenon of reincarnation as a legitimate subject for study in the realm of scientific investigations.

Claims of reincarnation have been reported from numerous cultures, and Stevenson has extended his investigations to many of them, including India. A considerable body of data has been gathered by him enough to begin understanding the similar and different features of such cases in various cultures. In fact,

5

Stevenson's is the only scientific study available on the subject. His techniques of examining such claims are an important improvement over the methodology that was used previously. I have enumerated his major contributions to the advancement of methodology in Chapter Two on the Review of Previous Work.

I have used the same working definition of reincarnation in the present study which is consistent with that established by Stevenson. I have modified his techniques and have used them in the present investigation according to the objectives described in the chapter on Present Study (Chapter Three). I have made the modifications (described in Chapter Four) by adding some more tools without distorting or deleting from those used by Stevenson.

I have presented the Results obtained in the present investigation in Chapter Four. The statistical treatment of the data is relevant only to the material collected at this stage. Many inferences cannot be drawn, but the analysis will help in the understanding of the data obtained.

I have discussed the data of individual case reports and features noted in all the cases considered together in Chapter Five. I have discussed the merits and demerits of both normal and paranormal interpretations that may account for the claims of previous life memories. I have included the hypotheses of fantasy, fraud, genetic memory, paramnesia, and cryptomnesia under normal interpretations of the case material. Under paranormal interpretations, I have considered the hypotheses of extrasensory perception and personation, possession, and reincarnation.

It is conjectured that these memories may be a defect rather than a gift to the person who experiences them. An understanding of the phenomenon may contribute to improved knowledge of deviant behavior of children that cannot be explained on the basis of available hypotheses. I have summarized the findings of the present investigation and enumerated the implications of this research in Chapter Six of this book. Most of the work presented in these six chapters, I had submitted in the form of a doctoral thesis to the Bangalore University.

Subsequently, I have continued investigation of cases of the reincarnation type up to the present. Simultaneously, I have also been studying cases of the possession type as well as experiences of persons who come closer to death but do not die because they revive with or without medical intervention. I have summarized my research activities after the submission of the thesis in Chapter Seven, and my current interests for future research, in Chapter Eight.

I must add here that I do not pretend to have dealt with all the interpretations finally, or even adequately, in the present study. However, I have discussed the results not in abstraction but with reference to the evidence that is actually available. Information on each case has varied widely among the different details; but I have made every effort to treat each case cited entirely on its merits or demerits without prejudging it.

CHAPTER TWO

Review of Previous Work

The subject of reincarnation has been dealt with from various angles since the beginning of civilization. Claims of reincarnation, like those of other paranormal happenings, have occurred all through the ages and in nearly every part of the world. Paranormal experiences of this and other types have played important roles in the development and practice of esoteric and religious systems and were usually viewed within this context as supernormal. Largely for this reason paranormal phenomena were not subjected to scientific investigation until the development, in the late nineteenth century, of that branch of science which is now called parapsychology. Volumes of literature from philosophical and spiritual points of view have been written about the subject. A review of all these writings is beyond the scope of the present study, since its principal aim is to deal with claims about reincarnation from a scientific point of view.

Definition and Brief History of Parapsychology

A paranormal phenomenon, by definition, is any experience of a person who can perceive or influence events at a distance without known physical means of communication or action. The history of scientific investigation into these paranormal claims is of fairly recent origin. It is usually said to have begun with the founding in 1882 (in London, England) of the Society for Psychical Research. This was the first organization established for the scientific investigation of the phenomena now called parapsychological.

An increasing acceptance of parapsychology is evident from the surveys of American psychologists. The younger members of the profession seem to be more inclined toward accepting it (Warner and Clark, 1938; Warner, 1952, 1955). A recent survey by New Scientist in London (Evans, 1973) reported that more than 70 percent of the respondents regarded extrasensory perception as either "an established fact" or a "likely possibility." This outcome was apparently unexpected. The increased serious attention to the field is perhaps due in part to the admission in December 1969 of the Parapsychological Association as an affiliate of the American Association for the Advancement of Science (Dean, 1970).

As psychical research (parapsychology) developed, it became divided into two main branches. The first consisted of the investigation of apparently paranormal events occurring spontaneously in what may be called everyday life. The second consisted of investigations conducted in laboratories. Proponents of the first group of investigations claimed, and still claim, that they are studying important experiences as they occur naturally. Those who prefer laboratory investigations maintain that they can control conditions and can also introduce variables, two features that are rarely possible in the study of spontaneous cases. In the early years of psychical research, the investigators emphasized spontaneous cases, but they also conducted some experiments. Later, experimentalists dominated the field, and spontaneous cases were rather neglected, although not completely forgotten. Today, spontaneous cases are again being investigated, and the field seems to have a better balance between its two main branches.

Brief History of Various Approaches to the Evidence of Reincarnation

On the basis of theoretical assumptions and logical thinking the concept of reincarnation has been treated by some as primitive magical thinking or as an expression of a massive denial of man's impermanence and an attempt to overcome his fears of death and the unknown. But since the late nineteenth century the claims of reincarnation have attracted the attention of some serious scientists who have conducted various experiments and studied the phenomenon in several different ways. Some of them prefer to study it under controlled situations —by inducing altered states of consciousness where the person experiences or recollects events of his "previous life"; others prefer to study the evidence that manifests itself under natural conditions. Approaches have been made from time to time to understand the phenomenon by the use of various techniques that I shall briefly discuss here.

Use of drugs. Memories of apparent previous lives have been reported to occur to persons under a variety of conditions. They have been reported both under natural and controlled situations. Under controlled situations, they have sometimes occurred as vivid images, such as during intoxication with certain drugs, for example, LSD (lysergic acid diethylamide). Reports of experiences of individuals who survive clinical death and death-bed observations by physicians and nurses have shown great similarity to ancient descriptions of the phenomena of death. Research with psychedelic drugs has brought important additional data of a phenomenological and neurophysiological nature suggesting that experiences involving complicated mythological, religious, and mystical sequence before, during, and after death might well reflect an aspect of reality (Grof and Grof, 1976).

Carl Gustav Jung, as a result of his extensive studies in comparative mythology, unusual intuitive capacity, and his own personal near-death experience recognized the value of the *Tibetan Book of the Dead* and similar texts describing the after death experiences for the understanding of the human mind. He saw them as manifestations of archetypes, transindividual matrices in the unconscious, that form an integral part of the human personality and that can, under certain conditions, find expression in powerful individual experiences (Jung, 1963). Aldous Huxley suggested that such concepts as hell and heaven represent subjective realities that are experienced very convincingly in the states of mind induced by drugs or other techniques (Huxley, 1954). Systematic clinical research with LSD has brought ample evidence supporting the ideas of Jung and Huxley.

Detailed phenomenological analysis of the content of LSD sessions of a larger number of individuals reveals that their experiences are not only identical with those found in eschatological mythologies but are frequently expressed in terms of specific symbolisms of culture areas basically alien to the experience (Grof and Grof, 1976). Psychedelic drugs have made it possible to study the deep parallels and unusual interrelations among actual near death and death experiences, make maps of the post-mortem journey developed by various cultures, and examine other aspects of death and rebirth. It has also been reported that some subjects under the influence of psychedelic drugs describe detailed sequences similar to aspects of Hindu, Buddhist, or Jain mythology; they may experience complex scenes, like those of the *Tibetan Book of the Dead*, of cultures to which they do not belong but of which they have some knowledge.

Experiments with drugs for the study of reincarnation phenomena suffer from important weaknesses. Individuals under the influence of drugs respond to suggestions, whether implicit or explicit. Their experiences usually match the text with which they are familiar; they are not necessarily imaged memories of a real previous life. No doubt these experiences are helpful to an individual in preparing him to accept death more calmly, but they add little to the evidence of reincarnation, since they rarely give any verifiable details about a previous life.

Recall of previous life memories during meditation, and through hypnotic regression, has also been claimed, and I shall deal with these in the following passages.

"Life Readings" by Yogis and Mediums. Many persons have been reported to claim a new sense of hope, rejuvenation, and "reincarnation" on emerging from certain profound alterations of consciousness; for example, psychedelic experiences, abreactions, hypnotic regression, religious conversion, spiritistic possession fits, primitive puberty rites, and transcendental and mystical states (La Barre, 1962; Bucke, 1961; Ebin, 1961; Ludwig and Levine, 1966).

The next category of experiences bearing on the evidence of reincarnation comes from yogis who with certain practices not only can (or claim to) recall their own previous lives, but also claim sometimes to see those of others. There have been clear allusions to these capacities in the Indian scriptures, such as in Patanjali's yoga-sutras and the Bhagavad Gita.

However, no formal investigations have been reported in this area to verify the assertions about reincarnation made by these yogis. The difficulty with experiments concerning such claims is that of finding suitable subjects. Those who are "true yogis" do not like to indulge in practices that may induce paranormal powers, because they consider them interference in natural processes and a hindrance in their spiritual progress; and other yogis may make claims that they cannot justify even if they are willing to be tested.

The claims of some yogis that they know about other persons' previous lives are similar to those made by some mediums or sensitives. Some persons have attributed importance to statements made by mediums and sensitives concerning "previous lives" of other persons. In nearly all instances of this type the statements of the persons claiming to have such powers consist mostly of unverifiable assertions about the allegedly perceived events (Sugrue, 1942/1974; Cerminara, 1950). However, occasionally a few sensitives have made the same (or very similar) statements about a presumed previous life of one person; and, also very rarely, mediums have made statements concerning the previous life of a person that are concordant with spontaneous memories of that person himself. Such cases, in Stevenson's opinion, provide (assuming no normal leak of information) "evidence of extrasensory perception on the part of the medium or sensitive making the statements; but they are not necessarily evidence of reincarnation, although harmonious with that interpretation (Stevenson, 1977a)." In his opinion, this has by far the weakest evidential value in support of the reincarnation hypothesis.

Use of hypnosis. Hypnosis, in its different forms, has been practiced for thousands of years and has interested scientifically oriented researchers for the past over two hundred years beginning with Franz A. Mesmer in 1774 and his theory of "magnetic currents."

By about 1880, hypnosis had been recognized as primarily psychological in nature, largely through the experiments of French scientists of the late nineteenth century.

The technique of hypnotic regression is accepted by some hypnotists as a method having some value for investigating certain mental processes and aspects of memory.

Research in reincarnation by the use of hypnotic regression

technique was probably an accidental development with some hypnotists. In 1893, de Rochas, in the sixth experiment with the first of his subjects, accidentally hit upon the possibility of regressing a subject to a possible earlier life; but it was not until 11 years later (1904) that, having regressed an 18 year-old girl to the time of her birth, the idea occurred to him to continue the longitudinal passes so as to take her back to a possible previous life (de Rochas, 1911, cited by Ducasse, 1961). Experiments with hypnosis have shown that a tremendous recall of childhood memories sometimes occurs with the recovery of unusual details of previously forgotten events which on verification are found to be correct (Reiff and Scheerer, 1959).

Professor A.D. Wiersman regressed a young woman of 25 to the age of eight. Under his suggestions she behaved "exactly" like an eight-year-old child. Von Kraft-Ebbing, in the late nineteenth century, regressed his subjects further back, to a still earlier stage of life. De Rochas carried Kraft-Ebbing's work further and, as mentioned above, regressed his subjects back by stages to a "previous life." But he met with the usual failures in such experiments. Either he could not identify the previous personalities mentioned by his subjects, or the subjects had some knowledge of the persons they identified themselves with, even though they had no conscious memory of this.

Several other difficulties arise in such experiments. The subject under hypnosis is in a condition of increased suggestibility and one wonders whether, when a subject is regressed to the age of a young child, he or she actually behaves as he (or she) originally did at that age or simply behaves as he imagines he would have behaved then. Similarly, when a hypnotist regresses the subject back to a previous life the subject will attempt to make up a "previous life" to the best of his ability; it matters little how explicit the instructions are because the subject responds almost as obediently to implied suggestions as he does to verbalized ones (Stevenson, 1979a).

The hypnotic state facilitates the mobilization of memories of all kinds that ordinarily remain unconscious. These may include forgotten memories of books read, films seen, or facts heard about the lives of other persons. Subjects under hypnosis may construct "previous lives" that are quite plausible and impressive, but completely imaginary. In some instances the previous lives may contain a mixture of fact and fiction. In a number of instances, the content of a hypnotically induced previous life has been traced to a book or some other normal source of information to which the subject has been exposed. The subject is usually completely unaware of such exposure and hence such instances are indicative of cryptomnesia rather than conscious deception or fraud. In some cases, subjects under hypnosis even show appropriate emotions for the "previous life" they describe, but which has no verifiable details. This probably shows the dramatizing powers of the mind that ordinarily are not displayed but remain unconscious.

However, in a small number of investigations with hypnotic regression, the subjects have come up with some interesting information (Bernstein, 1956; Blythe, 1957). Stevenson (1965-70) has conducted experiments in hypnotic regression with several subjects. Results were mostly negative (Stevenson, 1976a). The previous personalities that emerged during these experiments were usually fictitious. However, two good cases of responsive xenoglossy have emerged during experiments with hypnotic regression, and they may throw considerable light on our understanding of the phenomenon of reincarnation (Stevenson, 1974a, 1976b).

Spontaneous memories claimed to be of reincarnation
The most important evidence bearing on reincarnation comes from

the claims of certain persons, nearly always young children, who say that they spontaneously remember details of a previous life, or, rarely, details of two or more previous lives. In the following section I shall briefly summarize the efforts of investigators who made important contributions to the investigation of such cases.

Early Reports of Spontaneous Memories of Previous Lives

Most of the case reports published between the 1890s and 1960s were included in books written for the general public or from the point of view of spiritualists. Hence, they fell outside the literature and growing tradition of psychical research, which eventually developed into modern parapsychology.

Over a hundred books have been written on the subject of reincarnation since the late nineteenth century. However, the purpose of the present review is not simply to list or outline every mention of the subject, but to describe the efforts of scientists who have contributed significantly toward the establishment of a scientific inquiry into the phenomenon of rebirth. Thus, I shall not include the literature in the present review that deals with the subject from a fictitious or a nonscientific viewpoint.

Fielding Hall (1898), an English civil servant, who lived for many years among the Burmese people, published six brief case histories of Burmese children who recalled previous lives.

Gabriel Delanne (1924) published a book that included an extraordinary collection of reports about Asian and European cases of the reincarnation type. He reproduced in his book many original letters, newspaper reports, and other documents. This was a significant contribution toward the documentation of such cases that added to the authenticity of them. Unfortunately, his work has never been translated into English.

Shirley published a book around 1932 that included many cases cited by Delanne. He also included the case of Nellie Foster that was first reported in the St. Louis Globe-Democrat in September 1892; his book also described some other cases that were not mentioned by Delanne.

Rao Bahadur Shyam Sunderlal (1922-23) began the first systematic investigation of rebirth cases in India. In 1924 he published reports of four cases in the Revue Metapsychique published in France. One of his case reports appears to be quite strong, because it included a written record of the statements made by the subject about his previous life before verifications were attempted. The subject of one of his cases also had a severe deformity apparently related to the previous life he recalled.

In 1927 K.K.N. Sahay, a lawyer of Bareilly, U.P., published a little booklet containing reports of seven cases that he had personally investigated. One of the reports was that of his own son Jagdish Chandra.

A notable feature of three of the Indian cases published in the 1920s (Sahay, 1927; Shyam Sunderlal, 1924), was that a written record of what the subject had said was made before any attempt at verifying his statements was begun.

S.C. Bose published a book of case reports (in Bengali) in 1959 (translated into English in 1960). This included reports of 14 cases that he had studied in the late 1930s.

Professor B.L. Atreya (1957) of Benares Hindu University published a book on parapsychology. He included in it a section on reincarnation and a rather full account of one case of the reincarnation type that he had investigated (the case of Pramod Sharma). Stevenson later investigated this case and included a report of it in his first book of case reports (Stevenson, 1974b).

In 1960, Stevenson published a two-part paper in which he surveyed the writings of scholars on the question of reincarnation from antiquity down to modern times. He included in this article summaries of several cases from different cultures. Through this article he was able to show that the numbers and quality of at least some reports of cases suggestive of reincarnation justified a systematic investigation of any additional cases that could be located (Stevenson, 1960).

In the following year (1961), Stevenson began his field investigations in India and Sri Lanka and gradually extended them to many other parts of the world. The first results of his scientific endeavor were published in 1966 (Stevenson, 1966/1974b) with further articles and books following in subsequent years (Stevenson, 1970,1974c, 1975a, 1977b; Stevenson and Story, 1970; Story and Stevenson, 1967; Pasricha and Stevenson, 1977).

Stevenson (1966/1974b) published a book reporting cases suggestive of reincarnation that he himself had investigated. This book included seven cases from India, three from Ceylon, two from Brazil, seven from Alaska, and one from Lebanon. The 20 cases he presented in this book represented the range of cases he had encountered and the different facets of evidence they offered. The cases ranged from weak to strong with regard to the evidence they presented for reincarnation.

The most noteworthy feature of Stevenson's research was that he systematically recorded and investigated a large number of cases (about 600 by the time he published his first reports) and took a greater number of explanatory factors into account than his predecessors had considered. The study of a large number of cases helped him to discern some recurrent features in cases of different cultures; these may give clues to underlying processes. The numerous details that he elicited in his inquiries helped in weighing each case with regard to different plausible hypotheses that may account for such claims. Although Stevenson did not arrive at any final conclusions on the basis of the evidence obtained from these cases, he considered reincarnation the best explanation for the stronger cases. He thought it preferable to the alternative hypotheses for these claims, namely, fraud, cryptomnesia, paramnesia, genetic memory, extrasensory perception and personation, and possession. (I shall explain these terms in detail in the chapter on Discussion.)

In support of the reincarnation hypothesis Stevenson laid stress on some other evidential aspects. First, the unusual behavioral aspects of the cases. The subject of a case of this type often behaves in a manner that is strange for his family, but that corresponds well with the life and personality of the deceased person he claims to have been. This unusual behavior may include similar eating and clothing habits, likes and dislikes, and phobias apparently derived from the previous life.

A second kind of evidence shown by these subjects is their demonstration of special skills or aptitudes similar to ones the related previous personalities possessed (Stevenson, 1974b, 1977c).

Third and finally, special importance has been attached to the occurrence in the subject of birthmarks, deformities, and diseases for which there is no obvious normal explanation. When these correspond, as they often do, to wounds or diseases of the concerned previous personality they add considerably to the evidence for reincarnation. In Stevenson's opinion, these physical correspondences between the subject and the related previous personality are probably the most important feature of the cases in which they occur.

Gradually Stevenson's investigations and findings led him to isolate patterns of cases in several cultures (Stevenson, 1966, 1970, 1973, 1975b) and to compare these with each other (Stevenson, 1970). For instance, he compared the characteristics of Turkish cases with those from Ceylon with regard to various factors such as predominant sex of the subjects, the familial relationships, the circumstances of death of related previous personalities, and the occurrence of various other features. He began to correlate those features with the beliefs in reincarnation held by people in different cultures.

Since the investigation of these cases is mainly dependent on the testimony of the informants, the information may be defective and at times unreliable. To overcome this weakness Stevenson tried the modified techniques of more careful recording of data obtained from a large number of firsthand informants and interviews with the same informants at different occasions. He also proposed to follow these cases up to observe the later development of the subjects and in some cases to elicit further evidence bearing on the authenticity of the cases. In 1974, he revised his work on 20 cases published in 1966 (Stevenson, 1974b). The new edition included a chapter that summarized the results of follow-up interviews with 18 of the 20 subjects of the cases included in the book.

In subsequent years it has been possible for him to publish reports of cases in various cultures separately (Stevenson, 1975a, 1977b, 1980, 1983b).

With the expansion of his investigations and his increased confidence in the hypothesis of reincarnation, Stevenson has presented a comprehensive article on the explanatory value of the idea of reincarnation (Stevenson, 1977c) that has received considerable recognition by its publication in a widely circulated and highly reputed academic journal. The same journal devoted much of another, later number to the study of paranormal phenomena. The first mentioned article suggests a new approach in understanding various aspects of human personality that are not adequately understood in the light of currently available theories. The author suggests the idea of reincarnation as a "potentially unifying theory that can make intelligible a number of disparate and seemingly unrelated observations in the fields of psychology, psychiatry, biology and medicine" (Stevenson, 1977c). However, he offers reincarnation as a supplement to existing knowledge and not the only solution to all the incomprehensible aspects of human behavior. For example, it might help to understand the presence of infantile phobias, philias, and attitudes of vengefulness in children for which no apparent obvious factors available in the immediate environment can account.

Improved Methodological Features of Recent Investigations

The methodology of investigation into the claims of reincarnation advanced very slowly from simple verification of statements of the children of these cases to a fully developed scientific inquiry. The early investigators, even when they were careful in documentation, were mainly concerned with verifying the statements made by the subjects. On the basis of these verifications, they would either accept a case as that of reincarnation or reject it as a hoax without considering other possible interpretations for such claims. Secondly, the number of cases investigated up to 1960 by all these investigators put together did not exceed 50. It was therefore difficult to look for any particular patterns in such a small number of cases studied by different investigators using different techniques. Although their cases did have some of the features found in later investigations, such as a high incidence of violent death and birthmarks (Shyam Sunderlal, 1924), these were not emphasized particularly by the investigators themselves.

The credit of lifting the subject of reincarnation out of the realm of anecdote to that of responsible scientific inquiry goes to Stevenson, who has been investigating such cases since 1960

(Ducasse, 1961). The crux of the problem lies in the verification of cases that depend on the oral testimony of the informants, which may lead to grave errors of recording and invalidity of the whole information if proper measures are not taken. For the first time, he introduced scientific precautions to consider the reliability and validity of information obtained through various sources. The advances made in the methodology of investigation of rebirth cases since 1960 can be summarized as follows:

1. The more systematic collection and recording of data from a large number of cases. This has permitted the search for recurrent features in the cases that may give clues to underlying processes

2. The more careful recording of data obtained from firsthand informants. This includes also appraisal of the competence of informants and the reliability of documents

3. The analysis of each case with regard to interpretations alternative to reincarnation

4. The increased attention given to observations of the physical and behavioral resemblances between subjects and related previous personalities of the cases

5. Follow-up interviews (when feasible) with the subjects and some other informants for the cases. These have permitted observations of the subjects' later development and also (in some instances) further accumulation of evidence bearing on the authenticity of the cases

Through the present investigation I have made an effort to make possible some further methodological improvements. I shall mention these in the following chapter on Present Study.

Surveys of Belief in Reincarnation

The belief in reincarnation has existed down the ages in

various parts of the world at different periods. In certain cultures it still continues strongly and in others it seems to have ceased although it may once have existed there at some stage. The belief has usually been associated with the southeast Asian countries, but many persons, even educated ones, do not know that even in modern times numerous groups of people outside southeast Asia have believed in reincarnation, and still do so. The subject has attracted the attention of modern thinkers and a comprehensive compilation of such beliefs has been published (Head and Cranston, 1967, 1977).

Islamic sects of western Asia, such as the Alevis (Stevenson,1970) and Druses (Stevenson, 1966/1974b); certain natives in North America, especially of the north-west territories of Canada (Slobodin, 1970; Stevenson, 1966/1974b); several tribes of east and west Africa (Beals and Hoijer, 1965; Besterman, 1968; Noon, 1942; Parrinder, 1954, 1956; Uchendu, 1964); the Trobriand Islanders of the South Pacific (Malinowski, 1954); the northern tribes of Central Australia (Spencer and Gillen, 1904; Durkheim, 1965); and the Ainu of northern Japan (Munro, 1963) are some of the groups among which the belief in reincarnation has been reported.

The above reports suggest that in spite of lack of physical communications and geographical segregation, similar beliefs in reincarnation have been sometimes reported in widely geographically separated cultures. It has also been observed that the belief in reincarnation is sometimes absent among people living close to those who believe in it. For example, recent inquiries have revealed that the Alevis of Anatolia do not believe in reincarnation (Bayer, 1970-71), although other Alevis who live in south central Turkey do. Similarly, the Ismailis, (an Islamic sect of Shiite Muslims) do not believe in reincarnation (Makarem, 1972,1973) although their ancestors are said to have earlier believed in it. The Cunas of Panama also do not believe in reincarnation (Van de Castle, 1973).

The occurrence of similar in widely geographically isolated countries suggests that the belief originated independently in various regions of the world.

Approaches to Reincarnation by Western Philosophers

India is said to have been one of the greatest sources of religious and philosophical developments for at least the last four millennia, and it has significantly contributed toward various concepts that deal with life after death (Parrinder, 1976). The idea of reincarnation is generally associated with Southeast Asia, but it is important to note that a large number of Western philosophers have also approached the subject through philosophical reasoning. They have come to think that reincarnation is at least sensible, and perhaps even necessary. The German Philosopher Schopenhauer was a leader in this respect. He argued that it was impossible to think that the soul was immortal without also thinking that it had had an existence (and hence, terrestrial life or lives) before its present life. (It appears that Schopenhauer was influenced by the Eastern writings that were beginning to come to Europe during his lifetime.)

Several other western philosophers, notably Hume (1881), McTaggart (1915), Ducasse (1961), and Broad (1962/1971) have taken reincarnation seriously and defended it.

David Hume, a skeptical philosopher, argued for the reasonableness of the idea of reincarnation. He emphasized the weakness of the metaphysical and moral arguments for the immortality of the soul, as well as drew attention to the strength of the physical arguments for its mortality. He concluded that, "metempsychosis is therefore the only system of this kind that philosophy can hearken to."

John McTaggart, another British philosopher, pointed out that the doctrine of reincarnation would be in any case the most probable form of the doctrine of immortality. He further argued that if both pre-existence and immortality are true, then, "each man would have at least three lives, his present one, one before it, and one after it." In his opinion this doctrine of pluralities of life is more probable even on a theory of immortality that did not include pre-existence.

C.D. Broad, a distinguished Cambridge philosopher, considered the theory of pre-existence and plurality of lives as one, "which is of sufficient theoretical interest and *prima facie* plausibility to deserve considerably more attention from psychical researches and from philosophers who concern themselves with the nature and destiny of human beings than it has hitherto received."

C.J. Ducasse, another eminent philosopher, in his book on life after death, devoted a full section containing seven chapters to the doctrine of reincarnation. At the end of his discussion of the empirical arguments which may be presented in support of the reincarnation hypothesis, he states: "If the reports [of the claimed reincarnation cases] are accurate, which we have of them and of other cases where memory likewise spontaneously extends to a period earlier than the birth or conception of the present body they provide the best conceivable evidence that the person having those memories is a reincarnation of one who had died earlier."

Allusions to Reincarnation in Indian Scriptures

In India, where I conducted the present study, there is a long history of belief in reincarnation. Scholars debate about the date of the earliest Indian scriptures in which reference is made to reincarnation. Some find passages of Rig Veda that can be interpreted as referring to reincarnation (Ranade, 1926;

Radhakrishnan, 1953); others believe the first clear allusions to the subject occur in the Upanishads (Schweitzer, 1957). Definite mentions of reincarnation occurred in the Aitareya, Chandogya, Brihadaranyaka, Katha, Mundaka and Prasna Upanishads. One also finds in some of the Upanishads definite allusions to the concept that is now generally known as that of karma, the idea that good or bad conduct in one life will influence the conditions and circumstances of a person in another life.

Scriptures have the authority derived from their ascription to Divine inspiration. They are said to be based on the direct knowledge of the perceiver. The Upanishads assert truths about reincarnation; they are the records of empirical facts based on the personal experiences of the ancient seers. They, however, contain nothing that modern scientists would call "evidence."

In some other ancient scriptures (Puranas, for example) one occasionally finds a story about some experiences that appeared to influence the next life of a person. These examples might be considered a type of case history, but they contain little detail and are hardly more than anecdotes. Their main value today lies in telling about the duration and depth of the belief in reincarnation among Indians of two thousand or more years ago.

It appears that the belief has been carried to modern ages through various systems which believed in rebirth and pre-existence. When Indian thinkers of various schools began to develop their own notions of survival, diverse opinions were expressed and there was no imposed orthodoxy. The belief in reincarnation served different purposes. The concepts of rebirth and karma have been used as a moral or social law in Manu's *Dharamshastra.*

Gradually heterodox schools of Indian philosophy and religion arose with their own scriptures, but some of their basic doctrines concerning life after death parallel or supplement Hindu teachings. Buddhism and Jainism, now small in numbers in India, profess ancient and in some ways divergent beliefs. The Sikhs arose much later, but in their concepts of life after death, they share much with their Hindu neighbors (Parrinder, 1976).

The belief in reincarnation among Jain and Buddhists is considered to have existed even during the pre-Aryan Indus Valley civilization. Both these religions reject the gods (of the Hindus); or may include them as secondary figures but they do not believe in a creator God. They believe that the world goes round in endless cycles till salvation is attained. Both, however, believe in reincarnation.

The Jains believe in countless souls in human beings, animals, and plants. Like Hindus, Jains also believe that one goes through a cycle of rebirths till he attains liberation. They believe that the soul cannot exist without a physical body until it has become purified and has attained moksh (Radhakrishnan, 1923). However, their belief regarding interval between a person's death and rebirth differs from Hindus. The Jains believe that at the very moment of death, a discarnate soul associates itself with a new physical body at the time of conception which will be born after the usual period of gestation. According to Hinduism, however, the interval differs according to one's karma; although the Jains believe in the philosophy of karma, they do not attribute the interval between death and rebirth to karma.

Buddhists, especially of the Theravada branch, not only deny or ignore God but also deny the existence of a soul. According to Buddhism, when a person dies, the accumulated effects of his actions set in motion a further train of events which leads to other consequences, one of which may be the birth of another terrestrial personality. Different schools of Buddhists subscribe to somewhat different concepts regarding what persists after death, but they agree among themselves in believing that the conduct of one personality can affect events in the life of another, later personality that is related to the first one through the process of rebirth. The Buddha himself is said to have passed through hundreds of births. One of the most popular books in Asia is the Jataka (birth stories), which contains some 550 accounts of previous births of the Buddha in various human and animal forms, in each of which he performed his role perfectly.

The Sikh religion was founded by Guru Nanak in the fifteenth century A.D. Sikhs are monotheists, but although perhaps in some ways they were influenced by Muslim monotheism and mysticism, they are within the Indian (Hindu) tradition. In Sikhism also, the theory of karma explains the present sad or happy lot of man, although it can be changed by good deeds and the grace of God (Adi Granth).

From the study of patterns of belief in India it appears that they have been diverse in nature and the diversity has been increased from time to time. There could be several factors responsible for this change. First, different people have different experiences relating to reincarnation, and these may add to or modify existing beliefs. Second, long after writing had come into use, the Samhitas, Brahamanas and Upanishads were only handed down orally. (It was felt that as sacred matters they must not be published or uttered before members of lower castes.) By great feats of memory they were retained until eventually they were written sometime in the Christian era. It is likely that in the process of passing down the messages the doctrines were modified and took different forms.

So far, I have dealt with the concept of rebirth from an historical point of view. Now I shall review some of the existing beliefs that have been inquired into by some earlier students of reincarnation.

The Hinduism of Indian villages differs markedly from what

a scholar consulting the Hindu scriptures might expect. Dube (1955) pointed out that the Hinduism in villages is markedly different from that of the educated classes in the towns and cities. He showed that "the religious practices of Indian villages have deviated from the classical philosophical systems of India and have become reduced to only fasts, feasts, and festivals in which prescribed rituals cover all the major crises of life. Worship and propitiation of gods and spirits follow the annual round of festivals and rituals of the human life cycle. Diseases and other difficulties may also necessitate invoking assistance from these sources."

Several field workers from different disciplines have carried out systematic inquiries concerning the religious beliefs and practices of their informants, including their acquaintance with the traditional Hindu teachings on reincarnation.

Carstairs (1957), who worked in a village of Rajasthan, found that high caste villagers had a thorough familiarity with the doctrines of reincarnation and karma; but the lower caste groups seemed to him to know much less about the belief in reincarnation.

Elder (1959) made inquiries in a village of Uttar Pradesh and reported that 88 percent of the persons he interviewed believed in reincarnation; the percentage of believers in reincarnation in his group was higher among the low caste people than among the higher ones.

Other surveys have revealed much lower incidences of belief in reincarnation among the lower castes. Lewis (1958) interviewed 25 villagers in a village near Delhi. Only 14 of his respondents expressed a belief in reincarnation. He reported that the belief was stronger among the extreme social classes (i.e., Brahmins and Sudras) and was weaker among the intermediate ones.

Cohn (1959) made similar observations in a village of Uttar Pradesh. While discussing the matter of life after death with chamars, he found they were absolutely ignorant about the traditional Hindu concepts of life after death and rebirth.

Harper (1959) reported from his observations in a village of Mysore that lower caste people showed complete unfamiliarity with the concept of rebirth.

Kolenda (1964) carried out an inquiry with sweepers (low caste villagers) in Uttar Pradesh. They were familiar with the concept of rebirth and karma but did not relate their present status (low caste) to any sinful deeds in past lives.

There have been some surveys of the belief in reincarnation in Western countries. For example, in 1968 a Gallup Poll showed that an average of 18 percent of respondents in eight countries of West Europe believed in reincarnation. In the United States, a similar survey showed that 20 percent of the respondents believed in reincarnation. And a survey in Canada showed that 26 percent of the respondents believed in reincarnation (Gallup International, 1969).

In a survey of a wide range of paranormal experiences conducted by Palmer (1979) in a small city of the United States, 12.3 percent of the respondents claimed that they had had what they believed were memories of a previous life. (Examination of their statements suggested that these were almost certainly fantasies and not similar to the cases of the reincarnation type with which the present study is concerned; some such cases do occur in the United States, but none were elicited in the survey by Palmer.)

The above mentioned surveys in Western countries were conducted by sampling methods different from those used by the investigators, mostly anthropologists, who made inquiries about the belief in reincarnation in Indian villages. The results obtained in India and in the Western countries should therefore be compared only with an awareness of these methodological differences. So far as the results from the two regions are comparable, however, they show that the percentage of persons believing in reincarnation is appreciably greater in India than in the West. (A later section of this book will contribute further support to this conclusion.)

The Belief in Reincarnation and Its Importance to the Study of Cases

It has been suggested, and probably rightly so, that cases of the reincarnation type nearly always—but there are exceptions—have been reported in cultures and families having a strong belief in reincarnation. This appears to be an important aspect that has not been dealt with scientifically. It is necessary, therefore, to examine and understand this belief, its strength, and its variations, in order to evaluate the cases themselves. In the present study I had also aimed at examining the claims of persons, who say they can recall spontaneously a previous life, in relation to the strength of the belief in reincarnation.

A major assumption of this work, for which I shall present some evidence, is that the belief in reincarnation promotes the cases or at least facilitates their development and expression; at the same time the cases strengthen the belief in reincarnation among persons exposed to them, either directly or through reports of them published in news media.

In the present investigation I have included a study of the belief in reincarnation (in India) by means of a questionnaire on this subject to which 137 persons responded.

CHAPTER THREE

Present Study

The study reported in this chapter was aimed at "An investigation into reported cases of persons who claim to have reincarnated." I have made an attempt at understanding and examining objectively the phenomenon that manifests itself through the cases of persons who say that they can recall previous lives. For this, I had set the following objectives:

1) To verify the claims of persons who say that they spontaneously recall previous lives on earth

2) To study various factors interacting with the phenomenon of apparent reincarnation

3) To examine the evidence for reincarnation against various alternative hypotheses

4) To study the extent of belief in reincarnation and its relationship with the occurrence and patterns of cases of claimed reincarnation

5) To study the value and possible implications of these claims in understanding deviant behavior

In planning such an investigation it was necessary to take care of the lacunae in the previous studies. The most systematic investigations in this field have been carried out by Stevenson (1966, 1974b, 1975a, 1975b, 1977b). However, there have been some weaknesses in his methods of investigation of these cases, of which the most important are:

1) The frequent occurrence of a long interval between the receipt of the first information regarding a rebirth case and the start of its investigation
2) The use of interpreters
3) Shorter and more superficial interviews with the mothers of the subjects
4) Shorter and more superficial interviews with the subjects

I tried to avoid these weaknesses by going to the cases as soon as possible after I received information about them. I was able to contact most (98%) of the cases within one year; fifty-eight of these within six months of receipt of their addresses. It was possible for me to conduct more extensive interviews with subjects and their mothers, since the mothers of most of the subjects were available and cooperative for interviews. I did not use any interpreters since the investigations were carried out in north India, and I am well versed in most of the languages spoken there.

Explanation of Important Terms

I have used certain words and phrases so often in this book that it will be helpful to explain them in this section. I shall offer explanations of certain other terms either in the later sections of the text where they are first introduced or in an appendix (see Appendix A). Most of these definitions are similar to the ones used by Stevenson.

Reincarnation. The term reincarnation has a broad meaning, but for the present study it refers to the concept that human beings consist of two separate components — a physical body and a psychical entity, soul, or mind. At the death of the physical body the other component (psyche, soul, or mind) persists and after a variable interval becomes associated with a new physical body. This is merely a short working definition that does not take account of varying ideas. (For a further description of the term, see Appendix A.) I have used the words "rebirth" and "reincarnation" interchangeably in the present study, although in Hinduism "reincarnation" is often used in a different sense, the manifestation of God in human form as an avatar.

Karma. The concept of reincarnation is closely associated with the concept of karma in south Asian countries where the belief in reincarnation is widely held by most people.

Etymologically, the word karma means "action." In common usage, however, it has come to mean the effects of actions and particularly, the effects in one life, of actions in a previous life. It is often used more narrowly in reference to the consequences of moral conduct, good or bad, that are incurred in a life later than the life in which the moral conduct occurs.

Karma is often analyzed in terms of time. According to W.Q. Judge (in his Aphorisms on Karma) karma may be of three types: a) presently operative in this life through the appropriate instruments, b) that which is being made or stored up to be exhausted in the future, and c) karma held over from past life or lives and not yet operating because inhibited by inappropriateness of the instrument in use by the ego or by the force of karma now operating (Humphreys, 1943).

Subject of the case. Refers to persons in the present sample who have been reported to have claimed to recall events of their previous lives on earth. The subjects of this series all first made these claims when they were children, usually young ones. I have referred them as the cases of the "reincarnation type" as they are reported by the informants, without any commitment to this interpretation. Occasionally I have used the term "present personality" to refer to these subjects, especially when I have made a comparison between their characteristics and those of the claimed previous personalities.

Previous personality. The deceased person with whom the subject identifies himself or claims to have been. This term has been used for convenience to refer to the person whose life the subject claims to recall. The reader should note that the term has been used whether or not an actual deceased person has been found whose life corresponded to the child's statements. Also, its use does not imply any commitment to any interpretation of the case, including a particular explanation as to how the subject obtained any correct knowledge he showed about the person identified.

Some other terms used in this book have been defined in Appendix A.

Sample

In the study reported here I had included two samples, one for the main study in which I have attempted a verification of claims of persons who say that they spontaneously recall previous lives on earth and the second one for the assessment of belief in reincarnation.

The original sample for the main study consisted of 60 subjects from different parts of north India. I restricted the investigation to north India for two reasons. First, the spontaneous cases of the reincarnation type were mainly reported to me from that part of the country and secondly, I was well versed in the north Indian languages. The cases have come from different places. Table 3.01 shows the geographical distribution of the cases reported and contacted for the present study.

Of the 76 cases reported, one subject had moved from the address communicated to me and his present address was not available; in two cases the family of the subjects of the cases denied that the cases ever existed; and in one case the address

TABLE 3. 01		
Geographical Distribution of the Sample		
Name of State	No. of Cases Reported N = 76	No. of Cases Contacted N = 60
Uttar Pradesh	43	37
Rajasthan	18	16
Delhi	4	4
Punjab	11	3

was incomplete and hence it could not be traced. Twelve cases were still on the list for investigation in the future.

Mode of Selection

Since the phenomenon manifests itself spontaneously and follows so far as is known uptil now no definite distribution patterns, I had used no fixed criterion for selection of cases. I investigated all cases that were reported to me as and when feasible.

In all, I studied 60 cases. On the basis of a preliminary review of case histories and analysis of data I had to exclude 15 of the cases from the present analysis of data for the following reasons.

Two of the subjects were very old (aged 70 and 76 respectively) and were the sole informants for their own cases. I felt that much reliance could not be placed on their testimony since they themselves did not remember anything at the time of the interview. Whatever information they gave me was secondhand. They had learned from their parents or others that they (the subjects) used to make statements or had made recognitions related to previous lives when they were young. Secondly, the concerned events had occurred many years earlier, and it was difficult to get any reliable information from the surviving relatives of the related previous personalities. So I did not include these cases in the final analysis.

In one case the subject was getting married (at the age of 14 years); her parents refused to cooperate and completely denied the existence of the case.[1]

Two of the subjects of the cases gave very little information; what they gave was insufficient even to attempt tracing the previous families. One of them (who lives in Farrukhabad) just said that she had been the Queen of Bhutan. Another one (who lived in Mathura) said that she (he in the presumed previous life) had a wife in Delhi and that she had a dog and a cat.[2]

Five of the cases appeared to be of the Parakayapravesh[3] rather than of the rebirth type.

Two other cases did not fall in the category of rebirth type cases. One of the subjects was clinically declared dead and revived after some time. The other one had some kind of communication from spirits.

One case appeared to be a possible hoax.

1. Later, I was informed through another source that the subject did make statements about a previous life and also recognized places and persons associated with the previous personality's life. But her parents were afraid that if they acknowledged the case, the subject's marriage might be affected.

2. If her statements are taken as true (not fantasy, which is not completely unlikely) then it could be taken as a "sex change" case.

3. The term Parakayapravesh is explained in the "Explanation of the Terms Used" in Appendix A.

I had contacted two more cases briefly but they did not provide enough information for analysis.

After examination of the cases a residue of 45 cases remained. I have provided a list of these subjects included in the final analysis, together with their respective geographical locations in Appendix B. I have arranged them in the order of my initial contact with them as and when they were first brought to my notice. The following analysis is based on these 45 cases.

Source of Data

Initially I sent a request to Dr. Stevenson of the University of Virginia to send me the list of addresses of fresh, uninvestigated rebirth cases in India. The information on these cases had reached the University of Virginia either through newspapers or from private sources. I planned a field trip as soon as the first list of these cases reached me at Bangalore. During the course of my investigation, several more cases were reported. I made every effort to contact these subsequent cases as soon as they were reported.

I contacted one case on the very day that I received information about it; nine of the cases within a month of receipt of information of these cases; 16 cases within six months; 18 cases within one year; I approached one case only 17 months after the receipt of information. In all, I was able to contact 44 (98%) out of 45 of the "fresh cases"[4] within one year of their reporting.

As I have stated earlier, during the course of investigation several new cases were notified to me. In addition, persons

4. By a "fresh case" is meant a case that had not been investigated by other scientists

who were aware of my research informed me about those cases that they knew personally or through other sources. At a later stage (in August 1976) we made an appeal to the public, through regional newspapers, to inform me about rebirth cases. In response to this appeal I received letters about eight cases out of which I have contacted two cases in Punjab; the remaining six cases had already been studied by other investigators.

Once I had started the investigation, information about fresh cases kept coming through different sources. Sometimes persons related to the subject of a case knew of another case, or persons who were present at an interview gave me information on some new cases. Thus study of one case often led to the discovery of another case, or several other cases. Most of these cases were not known to the public, or had never received any press publicity. I investigated these cases (with assistance from other colleagues) as and when it was possible for me to do so. We could gather preliminary information on over 150 cases during the field trips, but could contact and investigate only 60 cases up to 1978 (the stipulated time for submission of my thesis). I have mentioned earlier how 15 cases were eliminated after the preliminary review of the data. I classified the remaining cases geographically and studied several more cases after the submission of the thesis (I have summarized my research activities since 1978 in Chapter Seven).

In a later section of this book (under Results) I will present a comparison of the 45 cases that I studied myself with 50 cases studied by Stevenson. It will be helpful if I say something here about the criteria I used for identifying the cases of these two groups. I examined a group of 113 cases and divided them into three categories: "S.P.," "I.S.," and

"Joint."

An "S.P. Case" was defined as one for which I myself obtained the principal information about the case without the presence or assistance of Prof. Stevenson. (A partial exception to this occurred in one case; for it I interviewed members of the family of the previous personality concerned in the case; it happened that Prof. Stevenson and I were together when I met the subject and his family for the first time.) In two other cases Prof. Stevenson obtained a small amount of information about the case from the subject's side of the case; but this information was so insubstantial compared with the much fuller information that I later obtained, that it was judged appropriate to include these cases among the "S.P. Cases."

An "I.S. Case" was defined similarly as one for which Prof. Stevenson without my assistance obtained the principal information about the case.

A "Joint Case" was defined as one for which we both (Prof. Stevenson and myself) obtained the principal information about the case together.

In interviews following those during which the principal information was obtained, Dr. Stevenson accompanied me for interviews in 17 "S.P. Cases." Similarly, I accompanied Dr. Stevenson for further interviews, especially follow-up interviews, on 16 of the "I.S. Cases."

From these considerations 45 cases were identified as "S.P. Cases," 50 as "I.S. Cases," and 18 as "Joint cases." (Dr. Stevenson has also studied a considerable number of other Indian cases that were not included in the cases under consideration here because they were older cases, ones only partly investigated, or ones about which insufficient information had been obtained for their inclusion in the analyses that were intended.)

Characteristics of the Sample

In the following section I shall present the characteristics of the sample supplemented by some tables. In order to facilitate comparisons in various situations between present and previous personalities, I have provided the characteristics of both the personalities and wherever changes have occurred, I have indicated these.

I had worked out most of the characteristics for all of the 45 cases, but since the information was not available on certain items, for various reasons (discussed in Chapter Four), the number (N) has not been constant throughout the presentation.

Ages of the subjects at the time of first interview. Thirty- two (71%) of the subjects were first contacted when they were below the age of 15 years; four (9%) of these subjects were below the age of four years. Six (13%) of the remaining 13 subjects were between the ages of 15 and 19. Only seven (16%) of them were 20 and above at the time of my first interview. However, all of them were below the age of 40.

Sex distribution. Table 3.02 provides information about the sex distribution of the present and the related previous personalities.

TABLE 3. 02				
Sex Distribution of Present and Related Previous Personalities				
Sex	Present Personality		Previous Personality	
	N=45	%	N=45	%
Male	30	66.7	29	64.4
Female	15	33.3	16	35.6

The reader will notice that there is a preponderance of males in the sample reported here. I have discussed the possible reasons of this finding in Chapter Five. There was only one "sex change" case reported and the direction of change was from female to male.

Religion. Table 3.03 shows data on religion of the present and the related previous personalities.

TABLE 3.03				
Religion of the Present and Related Previous Personalities				
Religious Community	Present Personality N=45	%	Previous Personality N=45	%
Hindu	41	91.1	40	89.0
Sikh	2	4.4	2	4.4
Muslim	2	4.4	0	-
Jain	0	-	2	4.4
Zoroastrian	0	-	1	2.2

Note: Change of religion from previous to present personality was reported in five cases. The direction of change was as folows:

Hindu to Muslim	-	2 cases
Jain to Hindu	-	2 cases
Zoroastrian to Hindu	-	1 case

Occupation of the subjects. Most (84%) of the subjects when first contacted were of school age or students. Only seven (16%) of them were in some business or occupation. Of the seven non-student group subjects, one was a carpenter, one a policeman, one had his own business, two were farmers, and two were employed in government jobs. Two of these subjects were dead by the time I received information about them. Since so few of the subjects had reached adulthood, a comparison of their occupations with those of the related previous personalities did not seem fruitful; but such a comparison may be of great interest after the subjects have chosen their life's work.

Marital status. Table 3.04 shows the marital status of the subjects and the related previous personalities. Only five subjects were married when I conducted my investigation.

TABLE 3. 04
Marital Status of Present and Related Previous Personalities

Marital Status	Present Personality N=45	%	Previous Personality N=45	%
Single	40	88.9	11	24.4
Married	5	11.1	34	75.6

Social status of present and previous personalities. Social status was subdivided into different categories on the basis of caste. All Brahmins were classified under upper; Kshatriya and Vaishya under middle; Sudra and other lower castes were classified under lower status categories. Their further categorization, namely high upper, medium upper, and lower upper, etc., was done according to their status in the community.

Although cases have been reported from all social strata, most of the cases were from lower upper and middle strata in both the groups. Cases in the extreme categories, i.e., high upper and lowest, were missing in present personalities. Only one case belonged to high upper class in the previous life.

Table 3.05 shows the distribution of the subjects (present personalities) and the previous personalities among the different social classes, both in numbers and in percentages of the totals.

Change in social status. If the subject claimed to have lived in a higher social status in his previous life the social change was taken as "downward"; if the subject was born into a social class that was higher than his claimed previous personality the direction of movement in social status was considered "upward." If the circumstances of social position were the same for both personalities, there was considered to be "no change" in social status between the two personalities.

TABLE 3.05				
Social Status of Present and Related Previous Personalities				
Status Category	Present Personality N = 44	%	Previous Personality N = 37	%
High Upper	0	-	1	2.7
Medium	5	11.4	3	8.1
Lower Upper	9	20.5	4	10.8
High Middle	7	15.9	14	37.8
Middle	7	15.9	7	18.9
Lower Middle	4	9.1	2	5.4
High Lower	5	11.4	1	2.7
Middle	7	15.9	5	13.5
Lowest	0	-	0	-

Information about the change in the social status was available for 37 cases for both the personalities. In nine (24%) subjects an upward movement and in 15 (41%) subjects a downward movement was reported. In the remaining 13 (35%) cases there was no change in the social status between the two personalities concerned.

Degree of social change. The degree of change in social status between the two personalities was considered *small* if the change occurred within the same class. For example, if the previous personality belonged to middle class and the present one belonged to high middle or lower middle; it was considered *moderate* if there was a shift in status from previous to present personality or vice versa by one major category, i.e., if the previous personality belonged to middle class and the present one belonged to either upper or lower class. The change was considered as *great* if the shift from previous personality to the present one was by two major categories on either side; for example, from lower to upper or vice versa.

Information on this variable was available for 37 cases. As stated above, there was no change in the social status between the two personalities in 13 (35%) cases. In seven (19%) cases there was a great degree of change; in 12 (32%) cases a moderate degree and in five (14%) cases a small degree of change in social status was reported.

Economic status of present and previous personalities. For arriving at a socioeconomic status index, Kuppuswami's (1962) and Udai Pareek's (1964) scales were used for urban and rural population respectively. Further categorization was done on the basis of my own judgment of the social position and the material possessions of the informants.

Table 3.06 summarizes the data concerning the economic status of the subjects and the concerned previous personalities. Most of the cases came from the middle and lower middle classes of economic status in both groups. Extreme categories were almost nil.

The same criterion has been used to assess the degree and direction of change for the economic status as was used for the social status.

TABLE 3. 06
Economic Status of Present and Related Previous Personalities

Status Category	Present Personality N=44	%	Previous Personality N=37	%
High Upper	0	-	1	3.0
Medium Upper	2	4.6	2	6.1
Lower Upper	2	4.6	3	9.1
High Middle	13	30.2	10	30.3
Middle	10	23.3	10	30.3
Lower Middle	6	14.0	3	9.1
High Lower	6	14.0	3	9.1
Middle Lower	4	9.3	1	3.0
Lowest	0	-	0	-

Note : Most of the cases fall in middle and lower middle classes of economic status in both groups. Extreme categories are almost nil.

Change in economic status from previous to present personality. As is evident from Table 3.06, information about the economic status of the previous personalities was available for 33 cases. In 12 (36%) cases an upward movement, and in 16 (49%) cases a downward movement was reported. In five (15%) cases there was no change in the economic circumstances from the previous to the present life.

Degree of economic change. Of the 28 (85%) cases in which a change in the economic circumstances was reported, the degree of change was ascertained to be great in seven (21%) cases, moderate in 12 (36%) cases, and a small degree of change in nine (27%) cases.

Population of the Geographical Area of Residence of Present and Previous Personalities

Table 3. 07 shows the geographical area of residence of

the present and previous personalities with regard to the population.

Thirty (67%) subjects came from geographical areas with a population of·upto 10,000 people and 15 (33%) from with a population above 10,000 people. Similarly, 23 (58%) of the related previous personalities resided in areas with a population of less than 10,000; and 17 (42%) from places with a population of more than 10,000.

TABLE 3.07 Population of the Geographical Area of Residence Of Present and Related Previous Personalities				
Population	Present Personality N = 44	%	Previous Personality N = 37	%
Up to 1,000	6	13.3	5	12.5
1,000–2,500	17	37.8	13	32.5
2,500–10,000	7	15.6	5	12.5
10,000–250,000	8	17.8	14	35.0
250,000–1,000,000	1	2.2	1	2.5
Over a Million	6	13.3	2	5.0

Distribution of Sample with Respect to State and District

Table 3.08 provides information about the geographical locations of the subjects. Most of the cases came from Uttar Pradesh (24), followed by Rajasthan (15), Delhi (four), and Punjab (two).

In five cases a difference in state of residence between present and the related previous personalities was reported.

In two cases the previous personalities who lived in Madhya Pradesh, were born as subjects in Rajasthan; in one

TABLE 3.08
Distribution of Sample with Respect to State and District

State / District	No. of Cases	State / District	No. of Cases
Uttar Pradesh (24)		**Union Territory (4)**	
Mainpuri	7	Delhi	4
Agra	2	**Rajasthan (15)**	
Etah	2	Jhalawar	9
Mathura	1	Kota	1
Budaun	5	Bundi	1
Bareilly	1	Ajmer	2
Shahjahanpur	1	Udaipur	1
Moradabad	1	Alwar	1
Farrukhabad	2	**Punjab (2)**	
Lucknow	1	Sangrur	1
Bulandshahar	1	Gurdaspur	1

case a change in state of residence occurred from Rawal Pindi (Pakistan) to Gurdaspur (Punjab, India); and in two cases the previous personalities lived in Bihar and Punjab respectively and were reported to have been reborn in Delhi.

Sample for the Study of the Belief in Reincarnation

The sample for the study of the belief in reincarnation consisted of 137 respondents. I have further divided this sample into two groups based on the knowledge of a rebirth case. Group I consisted of 71 respondents who were either related to the subjects of the main study sample or had a firsthand knowledge of a case; Group II consisted of 66 respondents who were neither related to a subject nor knew of a rebirth case at firsthand. The majority of Group II were students at the National Institute of Mental Health and Neurosciences (NIMHANS), Bangalore.

It will be seen that the respondents in Group I gave answers on the questionnaire that were often markedly different from those given by the members of Group II. Some of these differences appear to be attributable to an influence that exposure to an actual case may have on the belief in reincarnation. The differences between the two groups should, however, be interpreted cautiously, because it happened that the groups were not matched with regard to socioeconomic status and education. Most members of Group II had had at least a high school education, and many had gone beyond; most of them also came from moderately prosperous urban families of south India. In contrast, Group I contained a large number of uneducated or even illiterate persons of humble backgrounds living in small towns and villages of north India.

These important differences indicate the need for the Belief in Reincarnation Questionnaire to be administered to larger numbers of persons suitably matched with regard to the above-mentioned factors. At the same time, the present study has some value. First, it shows that the belief in reincarnation is widely held among different groups of persons drawn from widely differing socioeconomic and geographical sections of Indian society. And second, notwithstanding the differences in back ground of the respondents in the two groups, the results of the questionnaire appear to show an important influence on belief from exposure to an actual case of the reincarnation type.

Characteristics of the Sample for Study of Belief in Reincarnation

In the preceding section, I have described some of the general characteristics of the sample for the study of belief in reincarnation. In the following section I shall present the characteristics of this sample in more detail.

For the study of belief in reincarnation, I have worked out most of the characteristics for all the 137 respondents. However, in some instances information was not available for all the items; therefore the number (N) has been reduced for those items.

Age distribution. One hundred and twenty-one (88%) of the respondents were between 21 and 50 years of age. Only 16 (12%) of them fell above (11 respondents) or below (five respondents) this age range.

Sex distribution. Seventy-one (52%) of the respondents were males and 66 (48%) were females. Although for group I the questionnaire was mostly administered to the mothers of the subjects and the mothers or other relatives of the related previous personalities, the sample balanced out for the total group because there were more male respondents who were not related to a subject or who otherwise had no firsthand knowledge of a rebirth case. Hence, the distribution of sex is almost equal in the entire sample.

Religion. Table 3.09 shows that the percentage of the Hindu community in the present sample is closer to the census figures of religious communities in India. However, Muslims have a lower percentage and Christians have a higher percentage in my sample than in the general population.

The data were collected between 1975 and 1978; therefore

the figures were compared with the 1971 census figures, which were the latest available at the time.

TABLE 3.09 Religion of Respondents			
Religious Community	N=137	%	Census Figures* %
Hindu	114	83.2	82.72
Christian	9	6.6	2.60
Muslim	6	4.4	11.21
Sikh	4	2.9	1.89
Jain	3	2.2	0.70
Zoroastrian	1	0.7	-

* Major religious communities in India (1971)
Total population 547, 949, 809.

Educational status. Since about 50 percent of the sample consisted of respondents from NIMHANS, the percentage of

TABLE 3.10 Educational Status of Respondents		
Educational Status	N = 135	%
Professional or Advanced Degree	60	44.4
College Degree	11	8.1
Intermediate or Post High School	13	9.6
High School	5	3.7
Middle School	14	10.4
Primary or Literate	16	11.9
Illiterate	16	11.9

"professional or advanced degree" is high. Table 3.10 summarizes data on the respondents' education.

Other Demographic Features of the Respondents

Caste. Out of the 114 Hindus, information on caste was available for only 67 respondents. Thirty-two (48%) were Brahmins, 13 (19%) Kshatriyas, 17 (25%) Vaishyas and five (7%) belonged to the Sudra caste.

Marital status. Information for this variable was available for 131 respondents. Seventy-five (57%) of the respondents were married, 51 (39%) single, and five (4%) were either widowed (three respondents) or separated (two respondents) from their spouses.

Population of area of residence of respondents. The majority of the respondents (54%) came from communities with a population of above 250,000; 43 (31%) from ones with a population up to 10,000 and 20 (15%) from ones with a population between 10,000 and 250,000.

Urban-Rural background of respondents. Of the 137 respondents 108 (79%) came from an urban and 29 (21%) from a rural background.

Geographical distribution of respondents. Seventy-one (52%) of the respondents were from different parts of northern India namely, Uttar Pradesh (50 respondents), Rajasthan (13 respondents), Punjab (three respondents), and Delhi (five respondents). Sixty-six (48%) of the respondents gave their present address in Karnataka. Some of the respondents of the latter group did not belong to Karnataka; they were visitors or students at NIMHANS, mostly from southern India, at the time when I administered the questionnaire to them.

Procedure of Data Collection for the Main Study

Once I received the information regarding addresses of the subjects of these cases, I planned the field trips to investigate them as economically as possible. All those cases that fell within a radius of approximately 50 miles of a particular district town from where I could reach the cases in all directions, and where reasonably safe accommodation was available, I grouped them together. Thus, I studied cases out of, for example, Bareilly, Kanpur, Allahabad, and Agra.

Since research of this kind mainly depends on the oral testimony of the informants, major importance was attached to the precision of description of the events about which the claims were made. And since the cases were scattered all over north India, it was felt that a team of at least two or more persons would be helpful from various points of view: first, a group of persons studying a case together could get more reliable information than a single person. It usually happens in the villages that when a stranger enters the village a big crowd gathers around him and more so if one has to conduct an interview. Under such circumstances, a single person cannot take cognizance of all the events happening around him or make notes of everything. In addition, he has to interview a number of informants and also observe their non-verbal behavior in order to see if their testimony adequately corresponds with their expressions or not. Second, a team would reduce the number of errors caused during recording of the information and also would offer an important control over the "personal equation" of the observer's bias. Thirdly, the investigation involves a great deal of traveling in all types of areas, including dacoit-infested areas, so that it becomes sometimes unsafe for a single person to carry out research in such areas; one would not even be able to concentrate on the investigation properly for he would be apprehensive of these and other kinds of dangers.

Hence keeping in view the quality of the research, and personal safety I was always accompanied by one or more experienced investigators.

Number of informants interviewed. For each case the number of informants varied from one to nine on the subject's side, and from one to eleven on the previous personality's side, depending upon their availability. (A very small number of potential informants, for various reasons, declined to cooperate with my investigations.) I interviewed a total of 319 informants: 174 on the subject's side and 145 on the previous personality's side. In all, 382 interviews were held, as I interviewed 47 informants twice and another eight informants three times.

Among subjects who were potential informants for their own cases, 31 gave me at least some information of value; of the remaining 14, two had died at the time of my investigation, two (very young at the time) did not cooperate, and ten said they no longer remembered anything about the previous life.

Number of visits. The number of my visits for investigation also varied in each case. On both the sides it ranged between one and six visits for each case. In all, I made 196 visits to contact informants related to the subject's side and 88 visits to the informants connected with the previous personality's side of the case.

In two cases on the previous personality's side, no informants were available. Thus I contacted informants for 37 cases in 39 visits. In addition to the visits at the informants' places of residence, I made five visits to different hospitals and police stations to get precise information regarding the dates and circumstances of the previous personalities' deaths.

Techniques of Investigation Used

In most of the cases, the main events had already occurred and the experiences of recall had already been communicated by the subjects to their parents or other relatives before we reached the scene of the case. Therefore, we gathered the information through various sources. In order to ascertain the conditions and circumstances, under which the claims were made for the first time, we employed the usual clinical methods of case studies, including interview techniques. There have been controversies regarding these methods of inquiry. Some authorities suggest that leading questions cause more errors than non-leading ones. Yet some experiments have shown that leading questions were a harmless procedure for getting information regarding a case (Marshall, 1969; Marshall, Marquis and Oskamp, 1971). Leading questions increased completeness of information by about 25 percent in comparison to those who were given free recall, although it decreased the accuracy by 11 percent (Marston, 1924). Richardson (1960) and Richardson, Dohrenwend, and Klein (1965) experimentally proved that leading questions stimulated answers that were slightly more accurate than non-leading ones.

I adopted an eclectic approach in the present study. I first allowed the informants to give information spontaneously and then geared the interviews toward the required information on the case. I carried out structured, semistructured, and unstructured types of interviews as and when the situation demanded. Methods of direct observation of the behavior were also employed whenever the opportunity was available for me to do so.

In any scientific inquiry where the accuracy of an event cannot be empirically tested by checking with the facts or by applying logical tests of correctness, validity must be based on consensual agreement. What everyone testifies must be true (Festinger, 1950). In each case I recorded the testimony of as many witnesses as were available. Also, I conducted a second interview (or more) with as many witnesses as possible in the available time. I carried out interviews with many different informants, and repeated interviews with the same informants, in order to check the reliability of the information by comparing the information furnished by different persons at the same time, and that of one person furnished on different occasions.

We did not give prior notice of our visits to the informants, although this was a little risky and a time-consuming process. It was risky in the sense that sometimes the informants would not be available at home if they did not know about our visits in advance. On the other hand, this policy was thought to be more fruitful, because different witnesses had no prior knowledge of our visit and therefore no scope for comparing memories or preparing the information. Also, those who wanted to avoid meeting with us would not get an opportunity to do so. On reaching the spot, we made an effort to interview the informants separately so that they would not get a chance to influence each other's testimony, contaminate each other's memories, or harmonize their narrations falsely. In some cases, however, the informants who had already furnished the information could not be sent away since they insisted that they would not interfere with the interview. We requested each informant to tell what he himself had heard from the subject at firsthand or describe the events that he himself had witnessed. We also recorded their initial reaction, response, and attitude toward the claims of the subject whether they regarded these claims as healthy, harmless, or morbid.

We placed an equal importance on the observation of the non-verbal behavior of the witnesses and the subjects as they communicated various details to us. Observation of the non-verbal behavior proved useful in establishing the reliability of the witnesses; and it also gave clues to the corresponding emotions related to the events narrated by the subjects. All this proved helpful in establishing the validity and reliability of the information furnished. We employed methods of cross-questioning within the time available and the informants' level of cooperation and tolerance for it. We also tried to assess the apparent reliability of the informants with regard to accuracy of perception and memory for the events they were describing; and to evaluate their motives to exaggerate or reduce the information and any indications of less conscious influences that might bias their testimony in one way or another.

I made every effort to record the statements of the subjects whenever they themselves were still talking about the events of their past lives. This might have been colored since the two families concerned had already met. Nevertheless it was important for consideration of other hypotheses such as fraud, fantasy, etc. It also reflected on the reliability of other informants.

In addition to the subject's immediate family, whenever other "neutral" informants were available, we immediately sought their testimony. The following were the sources of information on the subject's side:

1. Parents, aunts, uncles, grandparents, and neighbors
2. Schoolteachers
3. Municipality records of births and deaths

4. Diaries, horoscopes, or other written or printed documents pertaining to the precise dates of birth or other important events related to the subject

After gathering as much information as possible, at least in the initial stage, from the subject's family, I used the same techniques to verify the information from the family of the deceased person about whom the child had been talking and with whom he had identified himself. We also made an independent verification of the subject's statements. Here again, we placed the emphasis on the fact that the informant should state what he personally knew about the previous personality or, if he had met the subject, what he himself had heard the subject say; or if he witnessed any recognitions the subject had made, exactly what he had observed. Although the recognitions may not have much importance among all the evidence (since they are often crudely conducted with grossly leading questions or other cues given to the subject), they have some bearing on the interpretation of these cases.

Sometimes the parents or other informants on the subject's side offered to accompany us to the place of residence of the previous personality. We always discouraged them politely for it was felt that their presence might affect the testimony of informants for various reasons. However, in one case we had to take a member of the previous family to the subject's village since it was not possible to reach the place unaided from the information given. It was in the interior and had to be approached through the fields. We requested the person who accompanied us to stay away from the interview. He gladly accepted the request and waited away from the subject's house. The following sources provided information on the previous personality's side:

1. Parents, aunts, uncles, brothers, sisters, wife, husband,

or children, friends and neighbors

2. Other independent informants not related to the previous personality but who had firsthand information about the case or related events

3. Municipality records of births and deaths

4. Police stations (cases where murder or accidental deaths were involved)

5. Hospitals for the exact date of death, cause of death, autopsy reports, etc.

I took care to see that the family of the deceased person concerned did not compliantly, even if unintentionally, furnish false information that gave more credit to the subject for his statements or recognitions than he actually deserved. These biases could not always be avoided; I made efforts to notice them when they occurred and to take them into account in evaluating the case.

The standard procedure I adopted for the present investigation was to interview the subject's family first and then go to the family of the related previous personality for verification of the information received from the subject's family. However, owing to different conditions, we approached ten cases in the present series first through the previous personality's side. In seven of these cases, the preliminary information for tracing the case was available only for the previous personality's family. (The subject's address had not been furnished.) In the remaining three cases, it was physically convenient for us to reach the cases from the previous personality's side, since these persons lived closer to the places where we were studying other cases.

Methods of recording information. I was usually accompanied by one or two other persons who had already had experience in this kind of fieldwork. I took sufficient care to make verbatim written records of the statements given by each informant. Each and every word spoken by the informant was recorded in written notes. Occasionally, however, we recorded the testimony on a tape recorder. The use of tape recording was kept limited for the following reasons:

1. The amount of time available with the informants was usually very limited. They could not overcome the initial inhibitions or would not have developed sufficient confidence in us to allow the recording of their testimony

2. The informants sometimes became nervous and forgetful. They did not feel as free as they were initially when the notes were being written

3. Tape recorders pick up considerable irrelevant talk that enters into the interview. One can not conveniently switch tape recorders off and on when omitting such irrelevant talk, but one can quietly put down one's pen

4. Handwritten notes are much easier to review for gaps in information than are tape recordings. This is important in reviewing the information of a case in the hotel any time before leaving the area

5. In addition, the handwritten notes get the spellings of proper names correctly

However, we *did* use tape recordings under the following special circumstances:

1. With a subject who was still talking of the previous life to record exactly what he had to say in the subject's own words

2. When time was extremely short, for example, when we were a long way from our base city and could open an "office" just as the sun was setting

3. As an occasional check on the accuracy of note taking.

Sometimes we took independent notes, and these were often compared after the interviews when time permitted. In cases where an important discrepancy could not he resolved among ourselves, we would sometimes return back to the informants concerned for clarification of the doubtful details.

Types of data Collected During the Investigation of Cases

We had available lists of the types of data we hoped to obtain for each case. I used a registration form in data collection and a coding sheet in data analyses, respectively. In the actual conduct of interviews I used the registration form with the informants when appropriate. It provides space for the recording of all essential vital statistics. In addition, it has a checklist of many of the most important items to be covered during the interviews. The coding sheet could be consulted to check after an interview for any omissions during an interview, but I rarely consulted 'it in the presence of informants.

I inquired about the following types of data for the cases and obtained for most of them.

Demographic Data

A. *Subject's Side of Case*

1. Age (his birthdate; from this I derived his age at the time of the first interview)
2. Sex
3. Birth order
4. Religion
5. Occupation
6. Marital status
7. Socioeconomic status

8. Place of main residence
9. Population of main residence
10. Educational Level of parents

B. *Previous Personality's Side of Case*

Similar data were obtained for the related previous personality. In addition, further information about him was obtained as follows:

1. Date of death
2. Place of death
3. Cause of death

Personal Data of the Subjects

1. Desires, cravings, etc., of the subject's mother during her pregnancy with the subject
2. Announcing dream
3. Complications of pregnancy
4. Subject's age of first speaking coherent phrases
5. Subject's age when first speaking of previous life
6. Play preferences
7. Special skills and aptitudes
8. Adjustments
9. Unusual food and clothing habits
10. Unusual attachments and animosities
11. Unusual fears and phobias
12. Other unusual habits or interests
13. Maturity level

Scholastic History of the Subjects (Wherever Applicable)

1. Age at entering school
2. Relation and adjustment at school
3. Rank in class

4. Other unusual features noticed by the teachers
5. Level achieved

Other Factors Associated with the Phenomenon of Reincarnation

A. Factors Associated with Normal Knowledge of Communication of Information: Interactions and Associations between Two Families Concerned before the Development of the Case

1. Biological relationship
2. Marital relationship
3. Connection of subject's parents to the area of previous personality
4. Social relations in each other's area of residence
5. Commercial relations in each other's area of residence
6. Geographical distances

B. Memory Stimulants Associated with previous Personality's Life

1. Meeting with persons connected with the previous personality
2. Visit to places connected with the previous personality
3. Events similar to those of the life recalled
4. Strikingly different circumstances from the claimed previous life

C. Principal Events and Topics Recalled by the Subject

1. Recall of previous name
2. Recall of circumstances and mode of death of previous personality

3. Recall of other realms
4. Recall of places and persons as they appeared during the previous personality's lifetime

D. Condition of Subject While Narrating Events of Previous Life

1. Evidence of emotions
2. Evidence of physical symptoms
3. Evidence of extrasensory perception
4. Evidence of personality change
5. Unusual behavior patterns
6. Strong desire or reluctance to go to previous family

E. Other Features

1. Birthmarks
2. Intermission between death and rebirth
3. Change in religion
4. Change in caste/class
5. Change in sex

F. Status of Case After its Development

1. Parents' initial attitude toward claims
2. Identification of related previous personality
3. Exchange of visits between two families concerned
4. Exchange of gifts between two families concerned
5. Support or rejection of the subject's claims by the family of previous personality
6. Support or gains from outside the two families concerned

Period of Data Collection

I collected the data for the present study from April 14, 1975 to March 23, 1977 at suitable periods of the years.[5]

Altogether I made four field trips, each one extending over a period of 12 weeks except for the last one that lasted for two weeks.

First trip	:	April 14, 1975 to July 2, 1975	(12 weeks)
Second trip	:	September 1, 1975 to December 13, 1975	(15 weeks)
Third trip	:	September 16, 1976 to December 15, 1976	(13 weeks)
Fourth trip	:	March 13, 1977 to March 23, 1977	(02 weeks)

By the end of the period earmarked for data collection, information was available on the 45 cases, which formed the final sample for the main study. Since in the final analysis some information was found missing, I made two more field

---

5. Before I began collecting data independently I had a period of preliminary training in the methods of field investigations used. This was under the supervision of Dr. Stevenson and largely with him. Four days were spent with him in October 1973. In December 1973 I toured for investigations with Dr. L.P. Mehrotra of Allahabad, who had earlier assisted Dr. Stevenson in the investigation of cases. I again toured for investigations with Dr. Stevenson for four weeks in autumn of 1974. After I began collecting data for the present investigation, I continued training under Dr. Stevenson by accompanying him on four more field trips during 1975, 1976, and 1977. Approximately 14 weeks were passed on these later tours with Dr. Stevenson. During the remaining 37 weeks of field investigations, after the period of data collection began, I toured with other persons. They assisted helpfully in various arrangements necessary for the tours; they participated in the interviews and occasionally assisted with some note taking; they did not, however, have any responsibility for actual data collection.

trips from October 13, 1977 to November 11, 1977 (four weeks) and from February 4, 1978 to March 11, 1978 (five weeks). Thus I spent a total of 51 weeks on field investigations during the years 1975 through 1978.

Difficulties Encountered During Data Collection

In any field of study one encounters a number of problems that crop up during data collection; there are perhaps more of these in the type of investigation that I had undertaken for the present study. The chief problems that arose in the present investigation can be broadly classified under two sections: (1) Difficulties experienced in tracing a case; and (2) Difficulties that arose after a case had been traced.

Difficulties in Tracing a Case

Inadequate knowledge of the informants while informing about a new case. As I have pointed out earlier, one common source of information regarding fresh cases has been a person who says he has heard about a case of the type under study. Such informants are usually connected with a case, or unrelated to it but happening to be present during an investigation of one. We always note down the information supplied by them on the Preliminary Information Forms with as much information as is available on the addresses of the subjects of the case and/or their related previous personalities. The address of the person who furnishes the information is also noted down. Mostly the informants know the correct address of at least one side of the case, namely the subject's family or that of the related previous personality. However, in some cases the informants do not know the exact address of the case, but cannot resist the temptation of showing their knowledge of such a case if they had seen one or heard about one. On the basis of their information, it is not always possible for us to judge the reliability of the information since it mainly consists of one or two addresses.

The informants do not give wrong information with the intention of harassing us; but probably they do not realize the consequent difficulties that we may have to face due to their carelessness. Great difficulties thus occurred in two cases (the case of Naresh Kumar Verma and one other case that still could not be traced).

In the first of these two cases, we received the information at Shikohabad, U.P., during the investigation of another case in that area. When we went to locate the new case in the village mentioned by the informant, the villagers told us that no such case had ever existed in their village. First we thought that probably the villagers were hiding the case (as sometimes happens); but later, after further inquiries, we felt that in fact no such case had existed there. So we went back to the informant (who lived about 60 kilometers away from the supposed village of the subject) to ask for more details and an exact address of the case. (There were at least four villages by the same name!) He showed a rather careless attitude at this time saying that he was not the only person to give information and added, "If this is not his correct address, it may be elsewhere, but he (the subject) had come to visit his previous family here. I myself had seen the boy." That gave us some hope. So we took down the address of the previous personality's family who happened to be in the same locality where the informant was.

Therefore, we started the investigation from the previous personality's side. Since the subject had visited the family of the previous personality, we had hoped that they would know the address of the subject; but unfortunately that was not the case. The subject had moved from that locality and the family of the previous personality had no idea of his present address. So we took the subject's old address in the hope of knowing something about the subject from the neighbors or present occupants of the house.

The present occupants were quite cooperative but they did not know more about the subject's location than that his family had moved to Delhi. However, after great effort one informant remembered one family who might know the subject's address since they were the "caste-brothers" of the subject's family. We reached that family who were also not aware of the subject's exact address; but they had a son-in-law in Delhi and gave his address in the care of his employees. So I contacted this person on a third visit, since on two previous occasions he was on leave. This person knew the subject's family, but did not have their postal address; he promised that he will either take me to the subject's residence or bring the address the next day, since on that particular day he could not get leave from his work and also was not sure of the address. He had to obtain it from another common acquaintance. Finally I obtained the address and approached the subject and then investigated the case.

The address given for the second case was also wrong and the informant had moved away from his previous address; hence the case could not be traced. This case was in district Budaun, U.P.

Inaccessibility of some places. In some cases, there was no direct road communication either to the place of residence of the subjects (the cases of Brijendra Singh, Bachan Singh, Pramod Kumar Sharma, Parmanand, and Brijesh) or to that of the related previous personalities (the cases of Manju Sharma (of Mathura, U.P.), Bhagwan Das, Nasaruddin Shah, Mihi Lal Yadav, Bachan Singh, and Manju Sharma (of Salawad, Rajasthan). So we covered the distance by walking a minimum of three kilometers and a maximum of 16 kilometers. (But inspite of this, in the instance of walking 16 kilometers the case could not be traced.) The need to walk considerably reduced the time available for interviews with the informants. On other occasions, after the monsoons, road communications had been blocked due to the sudden collapse of a bridge; we then had to wade through water (the case of Parmanand, and a "Joint case"). In the first of these cases, there was a small river on the way to the subject's village that we could not avoid.

Long distances and dacoit infested areas. In a number of cases, the death of the related previous personalities had occurred as a result of murder or involved some kind of riot or scuffle. We had to approach the informants concerned with such cases in these areas also for the investigation of cases reported there. Since some of these areas are well known for their high incidence of murders and other crimes due to the presence of dacoits (some areas around Farrukhabad, U.P., and some in Rajasthan), we sometimes had to return back from such areas with little or no information, especially if there was much traveling involved. For example, it used to take us about four hours each way to travel by a taxi between Kanpur and Farrukhabad. Some of the cases were located beyond Farrukhabad, so another hour or two were needed to get to these cases. We were invariably discouraged by the residents of these places from staying in those areas after sunset.

There were two cases in the same direction in Farrukhabad area about 28 kilometers apart, but we had to come back after getting some information on one case only and return back to the other the next day (the cases of Mahesh Shakya and Sahdeo Singh).

We also faced this type of difficulty in the Jhalawar District of Rajasthan. One village was located in the extreme interior in District Jhalawar. It was between nine and 13 kilometers from the road and was remarkably inaccessible. After having tried three different routes, we found that the jeep could go only half the way, after which there was a small river. So we continued on foot and walked to the village after crossing the river. By the time we got into the village it was already 5 p.m. in the month of October. There was hardly any time left for us to explain the purpose of our visit and conduct the interview. Unfortunately, there was no one at the home of the subject except his mother, who was hesitant (probably rightly so) to give us any information in the absence of male members of the family, since she had never seen us before. We sent word to the subject's father and grandfather who were working in the fields; meanwhile, on persuasion of others in the village, the subject's mother gave us some information. We ourselves started going towards the fields to interview the subject's father, since it was already getting dark. The subject's father was not available, so we hurriedly interviewed his grandfather (whom I had met once). Fortunately, this man remembered our previous meeting, so no time was wasted for another introduction.

The interview had to be terminated shortly since we had to walk back about three to four kilometers, wade through the river, and get to the jeep, which was about five to six kilometers away from the main road, from where it took us another three hours to get back to the place where, we had lodged ourselves. The other side of the same case (the case of Parmanand) was very close to the subject's village, but due to lack of time and poor road conditions, we had to leave it for some future visit.

Difficulties after Reaching a Case

The problems do not stop after a case has been located. First, we have to spend some time in introducing ourselves, explain the purpose of our visit, and convince the persons concerned (or even unconcerned sometimes) that we are harmless people. Investigations of any kind are usually associated in the villages with police inquiries or Family Planning. The present investigations did not pose many problems where the cases were located in towns or cities, or even villages where the family members or informants themselves were educated or had some knowledge about the researchers. But it was extremely hard to reassure some informants, especially during the year 1976 when the Family Planning campaign was at its peak. The informants usually used to identify us with the Family Planning personnel or motivators for sterilization. In a few cases, it happened that even before we entered into the village the young male members stopped working in the fields and hid themselves somewhere. The fear of compulsory sterilization was invariably expressed by the informants, even though they were apparently convinced about the value of our research and were reasonably cooperative. For fear of losing the confidence of the informants and getting unreliable information, we did not ask questions pertaining to the number of children in the subject's family in some cases. So I left these and other related questions to some future visit. Of course, once rapport was established, the informants became, by and large, quite cooperative on our subsequent visits. But it was not possible during the time allotted for data collection for me to visit many cases more than once.

Informants' lack of awareness of value of research. The next factor that posed problems was the ignorance and lack of awareness of the value of such research on the part of the informants. Their understanding of the importance of such research would increase their level of cooperation and help in getting precise information. Those who believed in rebirth felt that research about it was an unnecessary waste of time and money to test such an obvious phenomenon; those who did not believe also expressed a similar opinion but, of course, in a different tone and sense.

Informants' inability to understand importance of firsthand testimony. It is not to be expected that persons who know nothing of the value of research would know how to cooperate in it without some guidance. Many of the informants were unable to distinguish firsthand testimony from something they had learned at second or third hand. Even when I asked them only to say what they had themselves observed, they would usually slip into giving secondhand accounts of events. This was often done with a misguided intention of helping us. They hoped to save time by just giving us the main features of the case. We had to spend considerable time and effort in training the informants to confine their statements only to firsthand testimony. (Occasionally we would admit some secondhand testimony if it seemed reliable, but we would always make a note of its status).

Uncooperative informants. The next problem was posed by the womenfolk of some villages. Since they have less freedom and little or no experience of communication with strangers, they refused to give any information in the absence of male members, and even more when I was accompanied by male investigators. The other problem experienced with these female informants was that once they became cooperative (after some persuasion) they would often go on chattering non- stop and talk whatever came into their minds; and they would sometimes ask more questions from us than they actually answered for us. But in fairness it must be added that some of the women informants were excellent and gave better testimony than many male informants do.

Varied reactions of informants connected with a murder case. Some serious problems also cropped up while dealing with cases in which the previous personalities had been murdered. This posed problems in two ways: First, through the persons who were related with the previous personality (usually his family members). Their expectations from us and revengeful feelings toward their opponents would become stirred up (the case of Bhagwan Das, and another case later investigated). They expected us to do something about the case in the High Courts since the children of the previous personality were very young at the time of the murder and the case was hushed up. Second, through the persons who were conspirators in a murder. They were not only uncooperative but also rude to us for fear of revival of the case by the police or by the courts, which the informants had successfully hushed up. In one case, the previous personality's uncle was said to have murdered her (the case of Pravesh Kumari Singh) and her mother was said to be a co-conspirator. She was quite defensive and did not give us any information. So we had to gather the information from other sources. In the other case (the case of Bhagwan Das), the available headman of the village was said to have been connected with the murder of the previous personality. We unknowingly tried to approach the family of the previous personality through this person. He was not only uncooperative but also extremely rude and even refused to tell the address of the previous personality's sons. Later, we contacted the sons of the previous personality of this case and interviewed them. They told us about their relationship to this headman and his hand in the murder of their father.

Large socioeconomic gaps between the two families concerned. The families of the previous personalities who happen to be much better off socially and economically than the family of a related subject may present special difficulties. Wealthy persons may fear that a hoax is being forced on them in order to exploit their sympathy for some monetary gain. In fact, the subjects' families do not make requests from the families of the related previous personalities. I cannot remember a single instance in which this has happened. (Sometimes, however, they accept offered gifts and even a little monetary assistance.) Nevertheless, the family of a presumed previous personality may fear some demand. This may lead them to an attitude of great skepticism toward the case and a reluctance to appear to endorse the case by cooperating in the investigation. Although I myself was never refused the cooperation of a family of a related previous personality, I had heard of two cases in which families declined to cooperate with an investigation properly for this reason.

Varied attitudes of personnel approached for documents/ records required. Quite often we experienced a different kind of difficulty-small but time consuming. Sometimes when we approached different police stations, hospitals, or municipality offices for various kinds of information related with different cases, the persons in charge of the records have hesitated or refused to cooperate even when we had obtained permission from the higher authorities concerned. In one case, official information appeared to have been falsified since the case was brought to the notice of higher authorities for whom the records may have been altered. In other cases, after spending the whole day the records would not be available with the police stations where the incidents had been reported, and where the records were supposed to be. So we had to make repeated visits at various police stations and hospitals. It was found that sometimes clerks asked to look up records were dilatory, inefficient, or occupied with other work. These impediments to quick searching of records would have caused more trouble than they did if it had not been possible sometimes for us to obtain the record files and make the search directly. (Eventually I myself became quite experienced in searching through files of post-mortem and hospital records.)

The aforesaid were some of the difficulties that came in the way of my data collection during the present investigation of the cases. I have mentioned other problems elsewhere in this book.

Possible Sources of Errors in Recording Information

In the investigation of such cases where large amounts of data are recorded, certain errors are bound to arise. The errors that may arise in recording the information can broadly be classified under two categories: 1) Errors due to the informants; 2) Errors on the part of the investigators.

Errors due to informants. Errors made by informants may be intentional or unintentional. Those that occur due to lapses of memory, poor observation, or poor expression on the part of the informants come under the unintentional category. To reduce these errors, we made an effort to record the testimony of as many informants as were available. We judged intentional falsification of information by assessing devious motivations from the informant's manner of speaking. Or serious discrepancies between what he said and what other, presumably honest and reliable, informants said would provide clues to conscious distortion of information.

Errors on the part of the investigators. Errors that may be attributed to the investigators may arise in several ways. First, the investigators may misinterpret the information given by the informants. This may sometimes occur when the informants make ambiguous statements and an investigator may take the meaning that normally is intended by the majority of informants. On the other hand, he may misperceive information due to his own expectations and bias. Second, the investigator may make errors in recording the information given. While recording the information, the investigator may miss some of it, or, due to the demands of circumstances, such as lack of time or interference from other informants, or an informant's objection to recording something confidential, the investigator may postpone the recording to a later time, at which point he may have forgotten what he wanted to record. It is certainly not possible to check all the possible sources of error, but they can be reduced or minimized by taking certain precautions such as: 1) interviewing multiple informants; and 2) working in a team so that if one person misinterprets a particular meaning some other member of the team may get it correctly. (I exercised both these precautions during the present investigation.)

Techniques for Study of Belief in Reincarnation

In addition to the above-mentioned techniques of

interviewing the informants, I administered a Belief in Reincarnation Questionnaire to one or more members of most of the families of subjects and their related previous personalities. I usually administered the questionnaire, to the mothers of the subjects and to a close relative of the previous personality such as a mother or a spouse. However, occasionally I gave the questionnaire to the male members on either side of the case where female members were not available or not in a position to take up the questionnaire otherwise. I gave the questionnaire mainly to mothers of subjects because they were mostly available and remained with the child most of the time.

Development of the Belief in Reincarnation Questionnaire

There have been general comments and criticisms regarding the cultural influence on belief in reincarnation and occurrence of such cases (Parrinder, 1956). But no systematic study has been reported on different aspects of belief and the patterns reported in rebirth cases. In order to measure the strength of belief and its relationship with various factors, a belief in reincarnation questionnaire was developed. The questionnaire was developed from one originally devised by Thomas (1968) for use in the study of the belief in a life after death and reincarnation among West African natives. Stevenson expanded and adapted Thomas's questionnaire, and he and a colleague administered it (during 1973-1975) to approximately 40 respondents in Turkey where many cases of the reincarnation type occur. The questionnaire— then in a French version— was translated into English, after which I further expanded and adapted it for use in my study after several further revisions.

I discussed the questionnaire among various staff members

in the Department of Clinical Psychology, NIMHANS, Bangalore, and made further necessary alterations and deletions. The developed questionnaire then consisted of 17 items. Wherever the questions were Rely to have more than two responses (other than "yes" and "no" type) I left the items open-ended. The development of the final questionnaire consisted of three stages.

First stage: the pilot study. In the first stage of the pilot study, I administered the questionnaire to some of my colleagues who were training at NIMHANS in different disciplines. The main objective of this pilot study was to ascertain if the items in the questionnaire were difficult to understand, if there were items which were confusing or irrelevant, if additional items should be incorporated, and if the instructions and concepts were clear enough to measure the strength of the belief. The questionnaire administered by an interviewer had obvious advantages over a self-administered one; I could directly observe and clarify the ambiguous or otherwise confusing items, could probe further into questions when responses were unclear or ambiguous, and could get direct insights into related concepts. Some of the respondents particularly disliked the idea of revealing their identity, so I allowed them not to write their names in the identification/demographic section. However, I recorded their age, sex, and educational status. On analysis it was found that three of the items were too technical to be understood by a common man; so I simplified them without changing the sense of the underlying concepts. I added some questions related to the possibility of change of religion, sex, and caste from one life to the next. Also, I incorporated a question related to the belief in a Day of Judgment. One item concerning suffering and rebirth was believed unnecessary by most of the respondents and hence I excluded it. So the revised questionnaire consisted of 21 items.

Second stage. I administered the first revision (March 1975) of the questionnaire to 50 respondents. Most of them were trainees from different parts of India in psychiatric nursing, clinical psychology, and psychological medicine at NIMHANS. A considerable number of respondents were graduate students from Bangalore Medical College who were posted at NIMHANS for orientation training in psychiatry. In addition, three of the respondents were engineering trainees who visited at the Institute. I also administered this questionnaire to 23 respondents in north India. These respondents were relatives of subjects of rebirth cases or their previous personalities. The respondents had no difficulty in understanding the items, but three more items were felt necessary at this stage. I incorporated two of these in the form of multiple-choice questions, and one, a question regarding the approximate age when belief in reincarnation first occurred, left open-ended. I made the second revision in July-August 1975 and administered this questionnaire to 30 more relatives of the subjects or their related previous personalities.

Third Stage. A major revision was made during my first visit to the University of Virginia during April-July 1976. This questionnaire consisted of different sections on identification, socioeconomic status, and the respondent's knowledge of rebirth cases. I categorized the main questions about belief in reincarnation and related beliefs, for example, questions about metempsychosis, intermediate states, and personal preferences under different sections. In consultation with other colleagues, I incorporated several new items without disturbing the contents of the previous items. *We marked all those items that I had previously administered to*

103 respondents with two asterisks, which provided a shorter version of the full questionnaire. Three fresh items were added and four more items related to previous items were incorporated. Some of the earlier respondents had mentioned these items spontaneously. The major change in this revision was in the categorization of responses into forced choice responses. These categories were decided on the basis of responses I had received with previous revisions of the questionnaire. This was mainly done for computer programming for analysis and to determine the direction of responses. I administered a complete version of this revision (April-July 1976) to 16 respondents at NIMHANS. However, uniformity with the previously administered version was maintained by including all the previous items marked with two asterisks in the final analysis.

We also developed a Belief in Reincarnation *Interview Schedule* during the same period (April-July 1976). This is identical with the Belief in Reincarnation *Questionnaire* except that it contained an additional section on "Circumstances and Evaluation of Interview." This was chiefly devised to be used with relatives of the subjects or previous personalities, where it is administered by the field worker, in contrast to the Belief Questionnaire, which can be self-administered. I administered a shorter version (i.e. asterisked items) of this interview schedule to 18 respondents who were related to subjects or previous personalities of cases. In all, the sample for the Belief Questionnaire consisted of 137 respondents. (The reader should note that although the questionnaire was subjected to several revisions and was administered to a number of respondents at each stage, the questions asked of earlier respondents were all retained in the final analysis.)

Analysis of Data

The data derived from the field investigations were analyzed with regard both to individual cases and to the group as a whole. By the latter analysis I intended to show the emergence of any recurrent features or patterns in the cases.

In order to test various hypotheses that have been put forth for claims of recollections of previous lives, I analyzed the data in terms of ratios and proportions of various factors.

In order to facilitate the study of features that seem to be associated with such claims and that have been occurring repeatedly in many cases, the data were subjected to computer analysis.

Depending upon the nature of the distribution of data, parametric and non-parametric tests of significance were computed by means of statistical techniques, programmed in the Statistical Package for the Social Sciences (Nie, Hull, Jenkins, Steinbrenner and Bent, 1975) available at the University of Virginia, Division of Academic Computing.

The chi-square test of significance was computed to detect significant factors that were shared by most of the cases. Also, in order to learn the significance of difference between the features in the two groups of cases (I.S. and S.P.), the chi- square test of significance, and the t test were used as indicated.

The chi-square test of significance was used for non- parametric data. Wherever necessary, Yates' correction for continuity was applied; where the cell frequencies were low and not suitable for a chi-square analysis, Fisher's test of probability was applied. The *t* test was computed for parametric data. The significance of the difference between medians was analyzed because the distribution of scores was skewed.

CHAPTER FOUR

Results

In the hope of introducing a variety of cases of the reincarnation type, in this chapter I will first present some summarized reports of cases from the case material of the present investigation. I will present here typical cases and also some that deviate from the usual ones. However, I have not included these atypical cases in the final analysis of the data.

Following the case reports, I will present the main features of the cases of the present investigation with appropriate data offered in text and tabular forms.

In the next section I will present comparisons between the data obtained by myself and those obtained in a series of cases investigated by Stevenson.

In the final section of this chapter I will present the results obtained from the use of the Questionnaire on Belief in Reincarnation.

Typical Cases - Case Reports

Case Report 1 - Change of Caste

Subject's Name .... Manju Sharma
Subject's Date of Birth .... November 23, 1969
Related Previous Personality's
  Date of Death .... March 6, 1965
Geographical Distance between
  Two Families Concerned .... 5-6 kilometers
Date of First Interview .... December 20, 1973

The subject of this case, Manju Sharma, belonged to a family of Brahmins of modest means. She lived with her mother, father, and two brothers in a small village, Pasauli of District Mathura, U.P. Her parents had lost four daughters before Manju's birth. She was the second in birth order of three living siblings.

When Manju was about two years old, she started saying that she belonged to village Chaumuha (also in District Mathura). She also told the names of her father and brother of the previous life. She said that her father had a "paan shop." She gave a detailed account of events on the day she had died in the previous life. She said that she had gone to school on that day. Her father, after giving her a fee for school, went off to Mathura. After coming back from school she went to the well; while fetching water to bathe the statue of Mahadev she lost her balance, fell into the well, and drowned. She did not say anything about other realms where she might have lived between lives. She gave some other details about the location of her house in village Chaumuha but her parents did not pay much attention to these. They rather ignored her remarks thinking them to be childish talk and imagination.

After Manju started talking about her previous life, one day a man called Babu Ram a money lender of village Chaumuha came to village Pasauli in connection with some business. Manju caught hold of his bicycle saying that he was her uncle. The man was puzzled. He said, "I do not know you, child. Whose daughter are you?" Manju said, "You don't know me, but I know you; you are my 'chacha' (father's brother or friend). My father's name is Ladali Saran." The stranger was startled. He asked her, "How did you get here?" Manju said that she had fallen into the well while drawing water to bathe Mahadev. Babu Ram was puzzled at this, for he knew the family Manju was mentioning, and they did have a daughter who had fallen into a well accidentally. But he did not say anything to Manju. Manju insisted that he take her along to her parents of the previous life. To pacify her he said, "Yes, I shall take you with me, but not today." Then he went back to his village and narrated the whole incident to the family concerned.

On hearing this, the members of that family went to Manju's village. On the first day the mother, on the second day the brother, and on the third day the father of the girl who had drowned went to village Pasauli. On meeting the members of this family Manju wept bitterly. The members of the previous family also wept on meeting her. They asked her certain questions. They became convinced that this girl really was their daughter Krishna, who had fallen into the well while drawing water to bathe the statue of Mahadev. Krishna died on March 6, 1965; she was nine years old at the time of her death.

Krishna's parents requested Manju's parents to send her along with them to village Chaumuha so that others could also meet her. Manju's parents reluctantly accepted the proposal, but said that they would send her with her older brother in case she felt strange or did not want to stay at Chaumuha. In a few days, Krishna's brother went to bring the brother and the sister to stay with Krishna's family. Manju stayed with them without any strange feelings. She was rather happy to be with them. On their way to village Chaumuha Manju recognized a friend of Krishna's. She could also recognize certain articles, such as a pair of anklets, that had belonged to Krishna. After one or two days, Manju's brother became bored over staying in a strange family, so they were sent back to village Pasauli.

Up to the time of my visit in 1977, Manju was still visiting the family of Krishna. She still preferred to stay with the family of Krishna at Chaumuha, and stayed with them whenever they went to take her and her parents permitted her to go. The members of the previous family were Banias. Although they had a *Pukka* house, they did not enjoy a good economic status. They belonged to the low middle socioeconomic class. Krishna's father did not stick to one business after Krishna's death. He kept changing businesses.

The two villages concerned in this case are 5-6 kilometers apart. Although some persons of each village had some business connections in the other village, both the families denied any previous connections with each other.

I interviewed the following informants between December 21, 1973 and October 26, 1977.

On the subject's side	*Number of interviews*
1. Manju - the subject	three
2. Ram Siri - the mother	three
3. Tej Pal Singh - the father	three
4. Chanda Thakur - a neighbor	one
5. O.P. Sharma - a cousin	one
6. Dwarka Prasad - the brother	one
7. Dau Dayal - a villager	one

On the previous personality's side	*Number of interviews*
1. Ladali Saran - the father	three
2. Hansmukhi Devi - the mother	three
3. Kali Charan - the brother	two
4. Babu Lal - a village uncle	two
5. Roop Chand - a neighbor	one
6. Gauma Devi - a friend	one
7. Padma Devi - a school teacher	one
8. Nem Singh - the brother's friend	one

In all, Manju made 23 statements about her previous life, out of which 19 were found to be correct for the life and death of Krishna.

During my interviews, Manju did not show any signs of alteration of consciousness while narrating the events of the previous life. Nor was she said to have shown any such signs on earlier occasions. The informants never noticed any evidence of extrasensory perception on her part. During one of my interviews, Manju did become somewhat serious and sad while narrating the circumstances of the death in the previous life.

Her parents told me that Manju had a fear of going to wells. She preferred to bathe at home.

As far as I could assess, the family of Manju had no apparent motive for contriving a case. The family of Krishna belonged to a caste lower than that of Manju's. (Although caste differences are being eliminated in the cities, they persist among villagers even now.) Manju's parents did not recall having had any knowledge of Krishna's death. Neither did they have any connections in her village, except that Manju's father occasionally passed though it or bought some things there.

I visited Manju and the families concerned again in early December, 1988. She had been married in a middle class Brahmin family in June, 1985 and was living with her husband and his family in Vrindaban since. She had two healthy daughers ages two years, and three weeks respectively. She still exchanged visits with the family of Krishna and her in-laws did not object to it. She has developed normally and has adapted well to the present life.

As regards her memories of the previous life, Manju said that except for the mode of death, she had forgotten most of what she remembered during her childhood. She claimed to remember vividly how she had fallen into a well while fetching water. However, these memories did not interfere with her day to day life and she no longer feared going near the well or drawing water out of one.

Case Report 2 - Change of Religion

Subject's Name .... Lakhan Singh
Subject's Date of Birth ....April 10, 1966
Related Previous Personality's
   Date of Death ....…........ July 10, 1965
Geographical Distance between
Two Families Concerned ....…........…......... 15 kilometers
Date of First Interview ....…..... May 7, 1975

The subject of this case, Lakhan Singh, was fourth among seven living siblings. He lived with his parents and siblings in a small village of Janjari ka Nagla in District Agra. They were Thakurs of modest means.

When Lakhan was about four and one-half years old, his oldest brother, who lived in Etah, U.P., came to visit his family in the village. He asked Lakhan, perhaps a little peremptorily, to get him a glass of water. Lakhan said, "I am not Lakhan; call me Jain Saheb. I am H.L. Jain." Then he gave other details regarding a previous life he was claiming to recall.

He gave the address in Firozabad where he said he had lived and mentioned his previous wife's name, and the number of brothers, sons, and daughters that he had had. He also mentioned a college, a hospital, and a Jain temple to the foundation or support of which he said he had contributed.

Lakhan showed some unusual behavioral features. He wanted to eat his last meal of the day before sunset and drink filtered water. (These are traits all devout Jains show.) His family members did not object to these habits for some time, and more or less tolerated them. Lakhan's attitude toward insects was also

87

different from that of the other family members and other boys of his age in the village. He never killed insects, which is another trait of a devout Jain.

Lakhan also complained of the poor conditions of his present existence. He said he had had a big "pukka" house and now found himself in a "kachcha" one. He said he used to sleep on a cushioned bed, but now had to sleep on a *charpoy*. Formerly he had a chair and now none, and so on. He showed a strong identification with the deceased person whose life he claimed to remember. He preferred to be called by the surname "Jain" and seldom responded to his given name. For some time, his parents and teachers called him by the previous name but they gradually gave this up.

Once the ladies of a neighboring village and Lakhan's village were going somewhere by bus; they casually started talking about the case. The bus driver knew the family of the claimed previous personality. When he heard about the case, he spread the news in Firozabad where the family of H.L. Jain lived.

H.L. Jain's family came to Lakhan's village first. He is said to have correctly recognized the family members. They had also brought some photographs with them to test him. He is said to have correctly recognized the photographs and stated the correct relationships of the people in them. When the previous personality's family became convinced that Lakhan was H.L. Jain reborn, they presented some small gifts and clothes to him.

Both the families concerned denied any direct contact with each other's family. Lakhan's family, however, had purchased cloth from a merchant in a neighboring town who was in some way related to H.L. Jain's wife. A cousin of Lakhan's father was employed as a servant at this cloth shop.

I investigated the case from May 1975 to October 1977 and interviewed the following informants. (Subsequently, I made two more visits between 1979 and 1980 and interviewed nine more informants. I shall present the summary of my later investigation at the end of the report.)

On the subject's side	*Number of interviews*
1. Lakhan Singh - the subject	two
2. Chatur Kumari - the mother	two
3. Durgpal Singh - the father	two
4. Jaipal Singh - the school teacher	one

On the previous personality's side	*Number of interviews*
1. Prakash Chander - the Oldest son	two
2. Bhagwati Devi - the wife	two
3. Navin Chander - the youngest son	two
4. Prabha Jain - the daughter-in-law	one
5. Saroj Jain - the daughter-in-law	one
6. Amar Nath - a friend	one
7. S.P. - a friend	one
8. Nirmal Kumar - the wife's nephew's son	one
9. Kanta Devi - Nirmal Kumar's wife	one

I learned in Firozabad that the person whose life Lakhan was claiming to recall had been a prominent figure in political affairs as well as in business and philanthropy. Lakhan's father had known something about him and had once heard him make a speech at a political meeting. This man's name was H.L. Jain, and he had died in a hospital in Firozabad on July 10, 1965.

I consulted Lakhan's horoscope for his exact date of birth and hospital records for H.L. Jain's exact date of death.

The available history did not suggest any alteration of consciousness when Lakhan recalled the previous life. Nor did it suggest any evidence of extrasensory perception displayed by him at any time. He had shown no adjustment problems except that he asked for meals before sunset and prayed regularly before a portrait of Mahavir Jain that he had obtained from the members of the previous family when he met them.

Lakhan's parents, particularly his mother, did not encourage him to talk about the previous life. She took some measures to suppress his memories of the previous life. She said that she was afraid that if members of the previous family came to know of it, they might claim Lakhan, and he might leave his present family and start living with the previous one.

On the basis of the information available on this case I felt that there was no previous contact between the members of the two families concerned. Nor was it likely that they would have met because of the wide socioeconomic gap between them. H.L. Jain was a rich urbanite, whereas members of Lakhan's family were villagers of modest means. The difference between the religions of the two families would have further diminished the likelihood of social encounters. Lakhan's mother said that she had not even heard about H.L. Jain. His father had once heard him speak from a distance at a public gathering. That was the only occasion when he had seen H.L. Jain.

In October 1977 when I interviewed the family, Lakhan seemed to be adjusting to his present name and situation. Sometime in July or August 1977, all the family members fell ill with the result that they were preparing their meals at odd times. After this, Lakhan started taking his meals after sunset, but he still preferred to eat before sunset. One of his school teachers told me that he (Lakhan) was still bringing his handkerchief to school and filtering the drinking water. The teachers had also started addressing him by his given name and he was responding to it at this time.

In order to complete the investigation of the case I made two more trips between November 1979 and March 1980. In November, 1979 I interviewed three informants in Lakhan's village. During the interviews one of my informants hinted that the case was not genuine and that he did not believe in it. However, he did not offer any reasons for his believing this. Nevertheless, it became exceedingly important for me to pursue the matter further and look for evidence in favor of or against a hoax that I might have missed. Accordingly, I made another visit in 1980 and interviewed six more informants. Three of the informants were neutral informants who lived in a nearby village and knew both the families Lakhan's as well as that of the person who alleged that the case was a hoax. The informants independently agreed that Durgpal Singh was an honest person and would not have hoaxed a case. Moreover, they had all seen Lakhan when he was young and still talking about a previous life. One of these informants was Lakhan's former school teacher who had observed his behavior in school and was particularly impressed by his Jain habits.

In addition, I interviewed three more informants in a nearby town where one of Durgpal Singh's cousin was employed several years ago. One of them was a cloth merchant who was related to H.L. Jain's wife. The other two informants were neutral informants but knew both the families concerned.

On the basis of my interviews with all these informants, I became convinced that the case was authentic and that Lakhan's family would not have contrived it dishonestly. The informant who alleged that the case was a hoax, had made that statement either out of carelessness or out of jealousy perhaps because Lakhan had received some attention outside his own family. Stevenson (1988a) communicated to me that he also has sometimes found informants who make dismissive remarks about a case apparently out of envy at some attention the subject's family may be receiving.

Case Report 3 - Birthmarks

Subject's Name ....Sunita Singh
Subject's Date of Birth ....August, 1967
Related Previous Personality's
   Date of Death ....March 8, 1961
Geographical Distance Between
Two Families Concerned ....2 kilometers
Date of First Interview ....October 2, 1976

The subject of this case, Sunita, was the only child of her parents in a family who lived in a village under Bewar Development Block, District Mainpuri, U.P. She was hardly two and one-half years old when her grand mother went with her to a neighboring village to attend a condolence meeting. Sunita kept playing with other children outside the house. When a certain woman came to the house and joined the condolence meeting, Sunita became frightened. She ran and clung to her grandmother saying, "She will kill me again." So her grandmother brought her back home. The woman who had frightened Sunita was later found to be the daughter-in-law of the person whose life Sunita was just beginning to remember at this time. Sunita's mother said that whenever Sunita happened to see this woman later she would develop a fever.

Before Sunita was taken to the village of the claimed previous personality, she said that she was murdered. She said that her previous daughter-in-law had hired some "goondas" who murdered her. She also described the futile efforts she had made to escape from the murderers.

Initially I investigated the case between October 1976 and October 1977, and interviewed the following informants:

On the subject's side	*Number of interviews*
1. Jagdish Singh - the father	two
2. Savitri Devi - the mother	two
3. Bitto Devi - the grandmother	two

On the previous personality's side	*Number of interviews*
1. Surender Singh - a distant cousin of PP's husband	one
2. Lakhan Singh - a village uncle of PP's husband	one
3. Ram Beti - a village cousin of PP's husband	one
4. Ranbir Singh - the son	one

On verification, I found that a woman called Ram Dulari had been murdered in March 1961 in a village of District Mainpuri, which is about two kilometers from Sunita's village. There was a police case, and the body was sent for a post mortem examination. After the post mortem, the body was taken straight to the cremation ground and was cremated there. It was not washed. Jagdish Singh had heard about this murder but did not see the dead body of Ram Dulari. At the time of the murder, Sunita's parents were not even married; they got married more than five years later.

The two families concerned knew of each other but had no close associations before the development of the case. Sunita's parents belonged to a higher caste than that of Ram Dulari's family.

Sunita's parents, especially an uncle (Sunita's father's elder brother) forbade Sunita to talk of the previous life for fear of losing her. They also feared that Ram Dulari's daughter-in-law might try to kill her. (The family's fear might have induced or increased Sunita's phobia of that woman.) Sunita also had a phobia of darkness and knives.

The available history gave no suggestion of alteration of consciousness or evidence of extrasensory perception on the part of Sunita.

Sunita had prominent birthmarks on her right arm and on the right side of her chest. There were in these areas large "port wine" birthmarks. In addition, she had two prominent linear marks running across the upper part of the right chest. These marks were clearly visible when I met Sunita in 1977. During the same visit we also obtained a report of the autopsy performed on the body of Ram Dulari. This confirmed the date of her death as March 28, 1961 and that she had been murdered by some bladed weapon. The two linear birthmarks across the right upper chest of Sunita corresponded rather closely to two of the wounds inflicted on the murdered Ram Dulari.

In all, Sunita made only six statements about the previous life, far fewer than most subjects of these cases. Most of these pertained to the circumstances and mode of death in the claimed previous life.

Subsequently in October 1979, and November 1988 I made two more visits. In 1979 I interviewed members of both the families concerned. She had shown no problems of adjustment when I interviewed Sunita and her parents. She was studying in fourth standard at the time. Again in 1988, I interviewed Sunita and her parents. She had developed normally and had been married for four years but had had no children. She was visiting her parents for the treatment of "fits" which she had developed after her marriage. From the description they appeared to be epileptic fits with a hysterical overlay. She no longer talked about her previous life but the birthmarks on her body were still clearly visible.

The possibility of normal communication of information to Sunita cannot be ruled out completely, since the two families knew each other slightly and did not live far apart. However, normal knowledge of information alone can not explain the occurrence of birthmarks. The hypothesis of *maternal impressions* may be helpful in understanding the birthmarks in this case. This hypothesis supposes that before or during the pregnancy with a subject, the mother learns about the injuries or wounds on the presumed previous personality either by directly observing or by hearing about them from some one else. (Cases in which the mother-to-be has only heard about the wounds on another person and not herself seen them are rare, but a few have been reported.) With the help of information thus obtained she can then influence the developing fetus and the marks get imprinted on it. It can be thought that although Savitri Devi did not see the injuries on the body of Ram Dulari (she was not even married at the time), after her marriage Jagdish could have described them to her. As I have said earlier, Jagdish had only known about the murder, but had not seen the wounded body of the murdered Ram Dulari. Therefore, it seems extremely unlikely that Jagdish's secondhand information about the murder conveyed to Savitri Devi could have generated in her mental images of the wounds that, in turn, produced in Sunita's body birthmarks that corresponded closely (according to the post mortem report) with the wounds on Ram Dulari.

Case Report 4 - Evidence of Extrasensory Perception

Subject's Name ....Anoop Singh
Subject's Date of Birth ....December 11, 1940
Related Previous Personality's
   Date of Death ....… May 26, 1936
Geographical Distance Between
Two Families Concerned .... 500 kilometers
Date of First Interview ....July 28, 1976

At the time of my investigation, the subject of this case, Anoop Singh, was a married male who lived in Chandigarh with his wife and a widowed aunt. He was born in Mount Gomery (now in Pakistan) and was fifth in order of birth among seven siblings, all of whom were married and well placed. Anoop Singh himself was a double graduate, a government employee and enjoyed an upper socioeconomic status. His parents, aunts, and uncles were highly educated and were in respectable jobs. His father had retired and owned several acres of land in District Gurdaspur, Punjab, where he lived with his wife.

Anoop Singh started talking in coherent phrases at the age of one and one-half to two years and began mentioning a previous life between the ages of two and one-half and three.

It was during a very hot summer day when one of his aunts, who had come to visit them, remarked, "Today it is so hot that I would not like to be burned, even if I am dead." Anoop Singh was playing nearby and said, "Nothing will happen to you if they burn you when you are dead." His parents were surprised when they heard this. They asked him, "How do you know that?" He said, "I know that because nothing happened to me when they burned me." Then he went on giving details of his cremation and other details of the previous life he was remembering. As far as the informants could recall, Anoop had never seen or heard of any cremation at that age. He was hardly three.

He gave his name of the previous life as Kirpal Singh[6] and other details about the place where he had lived, the name of his wife, his possessions, and the nature of his work. Anoop also used some words that were unfamiliar in his family. (The later identified previous personality of the case had lived in Rawal Pindi, now in Pakistan, and the unusual words Anoop spoke were of the dialect of Punjabi spoken in Rawal Pindi.) On seeing his hands, Anoop used to cry saying, "My hands have grown smaller. How will I drive my car?"

Anoop also gave a vivid account of his traveling in the previous life between Lahore and Amritsar in a railway compartment in which his parents were also traveling. He (Anoop) said that he felt attracted (in his previous life) toward them but could not talk with them due to the heavy rush in the compartment. They did not continue the journey together till the end, since one of them had to get down on the way. Anoop correctly told his mother about what particular dress she was wearing then and also that a small child with curly hair was with her at the time of "that" journey. Anoop's mother corroborated this event, and she said that the child mentioned by Anoop was his elder brother who had curly hair at that time.

He kept talking about his previous life and kept worrying about his previous family. He would say, "How will my children go to school? Who will drive them there?" He was particularly fond of the previous personality's wife. Whenever Anoop saw his mother or aunt wearing a nice dress, he urged them to keep that for his wife. He said he would give it to her when he met her. As a result of Anoop's preoccupation with the

6. In keeping with the wish of the informants concerned on the previous personality's side of the case, I have used pseudonyms.

previous life, his health started deteriorating. On his insistence, his parents took him to the place where he claimed to have lived. On the first visit, his maternal grandmother took him to Rawal Pindi but could not get to the place mentioned by Anoop. On the second occasion, when his health started declining, his parents asked him if he could direct them to his previous house. Anoop said that he could. On reaching the station, he is said to have recognized the place and guided the tonga driver to the previous house without any assistance. On the way, he also pointed out the changes that had occurred since the death of Kirpal Singh.

After visiting the place and meeting members of Kirpal Singh's family, Anoop was pacified a good deal. His parents also actively engaged him in other activities to make him forget about his previous life. They thought the memories might affect his mental health. The method they used to suppress his memories was "side tracking."

Anoop stopped talking spontaneously about the previous life around the age of six but he did remember certain things. When he was about ten or 11 years old, studying in class V or VI, a photograph of Kirpal Singh's son appeared in a weekly magazine. Anoop remarked, "Now he has also grown old."

I interviewed the following informants between July 28, 1976 and April 6, 1978 at Delhi, Chandigarh, Ajmer and District Gurdaspur.

On the subject's side	*Number of interviews*
1. Anoop Singh - the subject	two
2. Ratan Kaur - the mother	one
3. Khushal Singh - the father	two
4. Ranbir Kaur - maternal aunt	one
5. Dr. Bhalla - maternal aunt	one
6. Dr. Kulbir - maternal aunt	one

Anoop's father was posted in Rawal Pindi for some time. Kirpal Singh was a well known magistrate, so Anoop's father knew of him but had no close associations with his family. Anoop's mother did not remember having seen Kirpal Singh.

I had great difficulty in tracing the family of Kirpal Singh, since after the partition of India (1947) the two families concerned did not continue their visits. Secondly, most of the members who could furnish some useful information had died, and the exact address of the surviving members of Kirpal Singh's family was not known to the members of Anoop' s family. They thought they knew the general area where the members of Kirpal Singh's family lived in Delhi. But it was insufficient. However, by the end of 1979, I had some more clues about the address of Kirpal Singh's son Suhel Singh. In February 1980 I visited Suhel Singh, a retired, highly placed government official. I interviewed him and his wife. They verified most of the statements made by Anoop. These were essentially correct.

In addition to the usual claims of remembering a previous life, Anoop gave evidence of extrasensory perception, more so with the members of Kirpal Singh's family. I was told that when he was only seven days old, he cried aloud, "Ma." Since this was very unusual for a child of that age, his mother got scared and remembered the episode vividly. Later, when the two families concerned met, it was found that on that particular day (when Anoop had cried out the word "Ma"), Kirpal Singh's mother had passed away. At the age of about four, Anoop had become so sad that he cried the whole day and said, "My Raj ji has died." (Raj was Kirpal Singh's wife's name.) He was upset the whole day. Later, this statement was also found to be correct. This testimony was corroborated by five different informants, related to Anoop Singh, at different places on different occasions.

Apart from this, Anoop said that he had visions of events that were likely to happen. I have not been able to independently confirm this claim. Anoop was so much disturbed by these visions that he even thought of consulting a psychiatrist. However, at the time of my investigation, Anoop did not show any abnormalities of behavior. He was well placed in a government job. (In fact, I conducted my first interview with him in his office.) He got married in 1975, and was quite well adjusted to his family life up to the time of my last visit in 1978.

Although the main events of the case took place several years ago, the informants agreed on the general content of Anoop's statements. All the informants were well educated and I interviewed them separately on different occasions.

Atypical Cases — Case Reports

Case Reports. Possible Fraud[7]

Subject's Name ………….......………………….. Mahesh Shakya
Subject's Date of Birth…………............………….. March 8,1956
Related Previous Personality's
    Date of Death………………………….....……… January 8, 1953
Geographical Distance Between
    Two Families Concerned……………….................……200 Yards
Date of First Interview……………………...... November 29, 1975

The subject of this case, Mahesh Shakya, at the time of my investigation lived in District Farrukhabad, U.P. He was second among four living siblings. He had one older sister, a younger brother, and a younger sister.

According to his mother Leelavati, when Mahesh was about two years old, his aunt took him into her bed, but he refused to

---

7. I have used pseudonyms in this report.

sleep saying, "This is not my house." On being asked where his house was, he pointed at the house of the principal of a college, which is not far away from Mahesh's house. According to Leelavati, Mahesh gave his name in the previous life as Parmeshwar Tiwari, as well as the mode of his death. He said that he was murdered. He gave the names of his wife, sons, and other members of the previous family.

Leelavati claimed that Mahesh had certain birthmarks when he was born. She pointed at the left armpit and back of the neck where she said he had had the marks. However, at the time of my investigation there were no marks visible on the areas pointed to by her.

During the interview with Leelavati, I felt that she was fairly intelligent, but that she had a tendency to say "yes" to all questions that she thought would make a better case for her son. However, Mahesh himself did not tell us much about his claims of recalling a previous life. According to his mother, his memories of a previous life began fading at the age of five or six.

Initially I investigated the case between November 1975 and December 1976 and interviewed the following informants.

On the subject's side	*Number of interviews*
1. Mahesh Shakya -the subject	one
2. Leelavati -the mother	one

On the Previous Personality's Side	*Number of interviews*
1. R.D. Tiwari -an older brother	one
2. C.D. Tiwari -another older brother	one
3. Sunita Tiwari -R.D. Tiwari's wife	one
4. Sanjeev Tiwari -the son	one
5. Sakuntla Tiwari -the widow	one
6. Madhu -the niece	one

As I said earlier, ParmeshwarTiwari's house was in the same locality, about 200 yards away from Mahesh's. I tried to verify whatever information was available regarding Mahesh's statements of a previous life. The older brother of Parmeshwar Tiwari (R.D. Tiwari) said that when the child (Mahesh) had come to visit them he appeared older than his claimed age at the time. R.D. Tiwari said that he asked certain questions of Mahesh which he could not answer. Later he said that he found out from his brother's widow (Parmeshwar Tiwari's wife, Sakuntla Tiwari) that Mahesh's father, Daya Prasad owed some money to Parmeshwar Tiwari.

Parmeshwar's older brother's daughter, Madhu was a firsthand witness to the meeting of the two families. She appeared quite intelligent and had studied up to B.A. Mahesh's family had taken him to the house of Parmeshwar Tiwari. Her observation was that Mahesh could recognize the photograph of Parmeshwar Tiwari from a group of persons, but she felt that some clues were given to him by his father. Some other members of Parmeshwar Tiwari's family asked certain questions about private matter that they said he could not answer. They also said he could not even recognize the wife of Parmeshwar Tiwari. The questions he could answer were very general and the information was well known among the public.

I consulted an autopsy report for the exact date of death of ParmeshwarTiwari and for the correspondence between wounds on his body and the reported birthmarks on Mahesh's body. (The birthmarks did not match with the autopsy report.) No documents were available to verify Mahesh's date of birth.

On analysis the case seems to have mixed features. Some of these go in favor of its authenticity while others go against it.

Points in Favor of the Authenticity of the Case

First, the case had the usual age of onset. Mahesh is said to have started talking of the previous life at the age of two. He narrated some of the incidents connected with the life and death of a person who actually lived in the same general area where the family of Mahesh lived.

Second, Mahesh was said to have shown some behavioral features that were unusual for his family but corresponded well with the behavior of Parmeshwar Tiwari.

Third, Mahesh was said to have given the correct names of persons related to Parmeshwar Tiwari.

Points against the Authenticity of the Case

First, Mahesh was quite old at the time of my investigation, and his mother was the sole informant for his case. I have observed similar situations in other cases where the subjects were quite old at the time of my investigations; but they were usually in a position to say what they used to tell when they were young and still able to remember the previous lives. Most of them frankly acknowledged that at the time of our interviews they no longer recalled the events of the previous life. In the present case, however, Mahesh did not say anything; he did not even repeat the claims that he was said to have made when he was young.

Second, the information given by Mahesh's mother seemed somewhat colored and unreliable. There was no other informant to corroborate her testimony.

Third, unlike most other cases of the reincarnation type Parmeshwar Tiwari's family had not at all accepted the case. However, this may not be a very strong point. Their non-acceptance of the case may be due to their fear of being exploited. Since there was a wide socioeconomic gap between the families, they might not have liked the idea of Parmeshwar Tiwari's seeming rebirth in a lower socioeconomic class.

Fourth, an opportunity of passing information to the child

through the normal means of communication was definitely present. Parmeshwar Tiwari was a well known figure and he lived hardly a few yards from Mahesh's house. Moreover, Mahesh's father also had contact with Parmeshwar Tiwari.

Fifth, there appears to be some motivation for fabricating a case on the part of Mahesh's parents. At the time of Parmeshwar Tiwari's death, Mahesh's father owed him some money.[8] To escape the debt, he might have found out some more details about the life of Parmeshwar Tiwari and credited his son, Mahesh with having the information thus obtained. Since Parmeshwar Tiwari was murdered, news of this fact must have been spread sensationally in the locality, and since Mahesh's father Daya Prasad had some monetary transactions with Parmeshwar Tiwari, and had access to his house, he could easily have picked up some more information regarding the circumstances of his death and other details.

Case Report 6 –Parakayapravesh[9] (Possession)

Subject's Name ………….....……………….. Sudhakar Misra
Subject's Date of Birth………….....………… November, 1959
Related Previous Personality's
  Date of Death ………………….…........…………May 8, 1960
Geographical Distance Between
  Two Families Concerned……………….…..............3 Kilometers
Date of First Interview …………….....…......December 3,1975

8. In order to reassess the case, I made a follow-up visit in 1985 and interviewed the mother and father of Mahesh; and a brother and other members of Parmeshwar Tiwari's family. Daya Prasad said that he had paid back the debt while the members of Parmeshwar Tiwari's family denied having received money. In 1986, I (along with Dr. Stevenson) visited both the families again to resolve the question of debt (whether it was paid or not) and to check some other details. However, the issue of debt remained

The subject of this case, Sudhakar lived in a town near Kannauj, U.P., with his father and older brother. He lost his mother when he was six or seven years old. His father was a businessman and also owned ten to 15 acres of land and other property. They were Brahmins by caste.

Sudhakar was said to have started talking about the previous life following a severe attack of some physical illness. His father was not sure of the boy's age at the time of the illness, since he used to remain away from home most of the time, in connection with his business. But he was sure of this illness because he received a telegram about it. When he came home, the child was quite seriously ill. After some treatment he did not improve. His condition started deteriorating and at one time he was taken as dead. There was no one else available to verify this testimony except one of the maternal aunts who was with Sudhakar's mother during this episode. When we interviewed her in 1976, she did not recall other details but remembered that Sudhakar did suffer from a very serious illness when young.

It was a custom in Sudhakar's family that children below the age of three were not given shoes to wear. Once when Sudhakar saw his older brother wearing shoes, he also asked for them. Since he was not yet three he was not given any. Sudhakar said.

unresolved. Mahesh's father insisted that he had paid the loan through one of the servants of Parmeshwar Tiwari's family while members of Parmeshwar Tiwari's family maintained that they never received it. It may be that Daya Prasad had paid the debt but Parmeshwar Tiwari's family never received it; the servant might have kept the money for himself.

9. The term "Parakayapravesh" has been used in the present context to describe the features of the cases as these have been understood and reported by the informants. Technically, the phenomenon, as it is described in the scriptures, has a slightly different connotation.

"If you don't give me shoes, I will go to my house and get my shoes from there. I have several pairs there." Then he gave other details about the location of his (previous) house. He gave his own name as Vimal[10] in the previous life and that of his wife and daughter. He also talked about his uncles and brothers of the previous life. He said that his wife had covered him with a sheet when he was dying and that he kissed her hand.

Sudhakar's parents were not enthusiastic about searching for the family mentioned by him. His father was too busy with his business, and his mother was scared even to mention his claims for fear of losing him. Sudhakar used to talk about the previous life and sometimes made an attempt to run away from home. To pacify him, his father took him one day to one of his (father's) cousins who had a clinic in the general area where Vimal was supposed to have lived. This cousin's clinic was about halfway between the place of residence of Vimal and that of the Misras. The news reached the family concerned through this cousin and they came to visit the child.

Sudhakar was said to have correctly recognized Vimal's wife, daughter, and some other members of his family. He cried on meeting an old friend of Vimal's, but was somewhat indifferent toward that person's wife. (It seemed that Vimal had been annoyed with her over something that happened before his death; this allegation remained unverified.) He cried bitterly on meeting Vimal's daughter. She also cried and asked Sudhakar's mother to send Sudhakar with her to live with them. But his parents did not agree to this proposal. The visits were discontinued after one or two meetings. Although the uncles of Vimal lived not far off (about three kilometers) they never visited Sudhakar's family. Sudhakar's father occasionally saw them when they happened to

10. Pseudonym

be attending to business at the same place. The members of the previous family also belonged to the Brahmin caste and enjoyed a slightly better social position than that of Sudhakar's family.

Sudhakar's mother took some measures to make him forget the previous life. She had him spun counterclockwise on a potter's wheel.

I investigated the case between December 3, 1975 and November 30, 1976, and interviewed the following informants, all only once.

On the subject's side

1. Sudhakar Misra - the subject
2. Sudhir Misra - the older brother
3. Satish Chander - first cousin
4. Harish Chander - first cousin
5. Prabhu Dayal - the father
6. Siri Devi - maternal aunt

On the previous personality's side

1. Chander Chur - paternal uncle
2. Durga Devi - paternal aunt
3. Shiv Chander - first cousin

I could not interview all the members of the previous family within the stipulated time, since they were scattered all over India. All those members who were available for an interview showed an ambivalent or neutral attitude toward Sudhakar's claims about a previous life. Vimal, although he spent his childhood in Kannauj, had been employed in Rourkela (Orissa) after 1955-56. He had died there of heart failure.

Comments. This case has an unusual feature, namely that the subject was born *before* the death of the claimed previous personality. This type of cases are rare, but not completely unknown. Occasionally such cases have been reported both in the scriptures and scientific literature. The subjects of these cases start talking about their previous lives following apparent death or a near death state. Usually the personality of the subject changes permanently, and he starts talking of events of the life of a different person with whom he identifies himself after his "revival." The literature describes this phenomenon as "Parakayapravesh" or possession.

I started the investigation of the case when Sudhakar was about 18 years old, which is somewhat late. His age would not have proved a weakness of the case if it had been compensated by more informants. Unfortunately, few informants on Sudhakar's side had observed him closely during the period of the development of the case. Hence, some of the details cannot be treated as reliable, although the information on the whole seemed reliable. On the basis of whatever information is available, the following inferences can be drawn.

Although Vimal died in Rourkela, which is many miles away from the place of Sudhakar's birth, some members of his family still lived within 2-3 kilometers of the place of Sudhakar's residence. Therefore, normal communication of some of the information cannot be completely ruled out. There was, however, no acquaintance reported between the two families concerned prior to the development of the case.

As I stated earlier, Sudhakar's parents enjoyed a fairly high economic position, but it was not as high as that of Vimal's family. However, such a difference is probably not a sufficient reason to contrive a case. In addition to what was known in public about the events of Vimal's life, Sudhakar gave other details regarding his private life. This fact had been acknowledged by the members of Vimal's family. Also, Sudhakar's father was a busy person who usually kept away from home (I made three attempts to contact him for the present investigation) in connection with his business. He therefore would not have either the time or the motivation to collect all the information to coach his child for a successful staging. Sudhakar was credited with appropriate recognitions of the members of Vimal's family. Sudhakar's mother, on the other hand, did not even want the other family to know about the case. She took violent measures (spun him counterclockwise on a potter's wheel to suppress his memories.

The reliability of Sudhakar's parents cannot be doubted, or at least they cannot be accused of having cooked up the case, on the basis of information they gave for it. The fact that there was an unusual interval between the death of Vimal and the birth of Sudhakar is in its favor. If Sudhakar's parents were to invent a case, they certainly would have taken this discrepancy into account.

Sudhakar had a history of a severe illness before he started talking of the previous life. The case does not appear to be typical case of the reincarnation type but instead one of "Parakayapravesh."

Case *Report* 7 -*Claims* in a *Psychotic Condition*

Subject's Name ....R.N.Suresh[11]
Subject's Year of Birth...........................1946 (Exact date not available)
Claimed previous personality's
  Year of Death 1930
Date of First Interview ....August 11, 1976

The subject of this case, R.N. Suresh, a 30 year old, single

11. Pseudonym

male, was referred to me by the Psychiatric Out-Patient Department, NIMHANS, Bangalore, since he claimed to recall a previous life. He was brought to the hospital for some psychiatric disturbance, with the following complaints: i) not doing any work, ii) poor memory, iii) not taking any initiative in work, and iv) irritability. He had had these complaints for eight years. In addition, a tendency to wander from home was noticed once.

His illness is said to have begun sometime in 1968. He was returning home, saw some "lights," became scared and then unresponsive. His parents thought that he was possessed by spirits. They performed certain rituals and spells for him. Suresh showed improvement, but never recovered completely. Since then he had been showing psychotic behavior and had been treated with ECT (Electroconvulsive Therapy) and drugs.

A mental status examination was done by a psychiatric resident on July 28, 1976, the day Suresh was brought to the hospital for the first time during the present episode. His orientation was disturbed and evidence for thought disorder was present. His mood was felt to be depressed with blunting of emotions. Hallucinations, delusions, and passivity phenomenon were detected. His memory for recent and remote events was found to be poor, and insight into his condition was lacking. The subject was diagnosed as suffering from schizophrenia and was given treatment for the same.

I interviewed the following informants for Suresh's claims of reincarnation.

On the subject's side	*Number of interviews*
1. The subject	one
2. The Subject's father	two
3. The Subject's sister	two

Suresh said that he remembered his previous life. He gave his name, his father's name, and his daughter's name in the previous life. He also stated the name of a place called Alaharkoil in District Madras where he said that he lived during that life. He said that he used to teach the Ramayana and the Mahabharata to his disciples.

During my interview with Suresh I noticed that most of the time his attention was fleeting and his talk was irrelevant and circumstantial. His account of the previous life also lacked consistency.

The information I received from Suresh was amplified and verified from his father and sister. I was informed that the name (S.N.) he gave as his own name in the previous life was that of his maternal grandfather. The name he gave for his daughter was the name of his present mother; and the name of the place of residence in the previous life mentioned by Suresh was his grandfather's native place.

Suresh, however, made these claims only once during his present illness when he was under medication. His parents observed no unusual behavior, except that Suresh was also, like his grand father, quite "sharp" before the onset of his present illness.

I followed up the case in December 1977. The informants reported that Suresh had improved with medication but never recovered completely. He had made no claims of recalling a previous life before or after the aforesaid claims.

Comments. This case differed markedly from the typical cases of the reincarnation type in certain respects; it also had some features that resemble those of typical cases. The major feature of departure in this case from that of a typical case of the reincarnation type was that of the mental status. With exceedingly rare exceptions, children of these cases show no major abnormalities and they are certainly not psychotics. The present subject (Suresh) made such claims during a psychotic breakdown. In addition, however, his claims to remember a previous life differed from the "typical case" in some other respects that I have mentioned in the Discussion of Chapter Five.

Here I would comment on the features that resemble cases with apparently real memories of a previous life. For example, S.N., whose life Suresh claimed to remember, lived in the place mentioned by him, was a scholar and did teach the Ramayana and the Mahabharata there. Also, before the onset of his illness, Suresh is said to have been "sharp" like S.N. Suresh made his claims at a relatively old age, but that alone does not go against its authenticity. Secondly Suresh's claims to recall the life of his own maternal grand father and other details about his life, were similar to the "same family" cases. I have argued in the Discussion of Chapter Five, the same family cases may be weak from the evidential point of view but they have other important features.

In some of our cases of the reincarnation type, children started or gave abundant details about a previous life when they had a fever. It is possible that the fever changed the brain metabolism enough so that previous life memories could come into consciousness. This may rarely happen also in psychoses. However, in psychoses the memories get distorted and orthodox psychiatrists usually dismiss them as delusions (Stevenson, 1988b). It is quite possible that Suresh had some fragmentary but correct memories of a previous life which were distorted due to his mental illness.

Principal Features of the Cases of the Present Investigation

Status of the Investigation of the Cases

Table 4.01 gives a breakdown of the varying degrees of thoroughness with which I could investigate different cases. It is necessary to say something about the way in which I had characterized "thoroughness of investigation." I did not adopt any formal scale for evaluating thoroughness in the present investigation. (It may be helpful to do so in future research.) Instead, I took a number of factors into consideration, and from weighing these I made an assessment of the thoroughness of the investigation of a case. The factors I included in this assessment were: whether both sides of a case were investigated or only one side; the total number of informants interviewed; the number of informants interviewed who were *not* members of the families immediately concerned with the case; the search for relevant documents; the number of second and third or more interviews with the same informants; whether interviews were conducted (and attended) by one investigator only or by two or more members of a team; the total number of hours spent in the conduct of interviews. Concerning the various factors mentioned above, I had adopted the following standards to assess the degree of thoroughness of the investigation of each case:

Very thoroughly. All possible sources exhausted and all possible information obtained on the case.

Thoroughly. All possible sources contacted and most of the information obtained on the case.

Fairly thoroughly. Most of the possible sources contacted; some relevant information not obtained.

Not too thoroughly. Only some of the possible sources contacted; most of the information still lacking.

Not at all thoroughly. Case study just begun; only a few sources contacted and little information gathered.

TABLE 4.01 Status of the Investigation of the Cases		
Status of the Investigation	**N = 45**	**%**
Very thorough	0	-
Thorough	4	8.9
Fairly thorough	27	60.0
Not too thorough	11	24.4
Not at all thorough	3	6.7

The second and third or later interviews help to test the consistency, and hence the reliability, of the informants. Informants outside the families concerned are apt to be less biased than the family members, but also less well informed. It takes more effort to search them out since they are not as readily available as are family members. Two or more investigators working together can conduct more thorough interviews and also make more accurate recordings of the events of the interview. One investigator may note what the other has missed. Each can check the accuracy of his observations and notes against those of his or her colleague.

Finally, it is necessary to stress that the duration of days spent on a case may have little bearing on the length of interviews conducted for it or on the results achieved. An investigator may spend half a day in a taxi or walking and only have a few hours or less for interviews when he reaches the place for them. Similarly, half a day or repeated half days may be consumed in the search for some pertinent document which, valuable as it may be, contributes only one item of information for the total case.

I have mentioned some of the other difficulties of these

investigations in an earlier chapter (Chapter Three) of this book, and it is necessary for me now to refer to these as a principal explanation for the absence of some items of data for numerous cases. The items of missing data differ from case to case. In some instances, the omissions were due to the inability of the informants to furnish the required data. In other instances, I myself, having only a limited time with informants, chose to inquire about data that seemed most important. And in still other instances, I could not inquire about certain items of data due to unavoidable circumstances. When I discovered such omissions, I often tried to remedy the deficiencies in later interviews, but these were not always feasible. These various factors account for the fact that the number of cases furnishing data for various items analyzed varies widely from item to item.

I shall next present the principal features of the cases in the following section.

Educational level of subjects' parents. The data on the education of subjects' parents was available for 28 fathers and for 29 mothers. The subjects' fathers were illiterate in only three (11 %) of the cases. This rate of literacy (89%) is much higher than that (39%) of the general (male) population of India. Among the literate group of fathers 16 (57 %) had completed high school and nine (32%) had received education up to college level.

The literacy rate among the mothers of the subjects was much lower, being only 48 percent, compared with that of the fathers. However, it was also significantly higher than the literacy rate (19%) for the general (female) population of India *(Times of India Directory and Yearbook,* 1977). Eleven (38%) mothers had had education up to middle school; and three (10%) had completed some college, or had received a graduate degree.

Parental attitudes toward the subjects' memories of previous lives. Information on the matter of parents' judgments about their attitudes toward their children's memories of a previous life was available for 30 fathers and 37 mothers of the subjects. Seven (23%) fathers said that they encouraged their children slightly (two cases) or moderately (five cases) to talk about a previous life; 16 (53%) had more or less neutral or tolerant attitude (13 cases) or an indifferent attitude (three cases); and seven (23%) fathers discouraged their children from talking about a previous life either by scolding (one case), taking nonviolent measures (four cases) or violent measures (two cases) to suppress their memories.

Four (10%) mothers initially encouraged their children (from slight to moderate degree); 23 (62%) were more or less neutral or tolerant (16 cases), ambivalent (two cases) or indifferent (five cases) toward their claims of a previous life. Ten (27%) mothers took nonviolent (three cases) or even violent (seven cases) measures to suppress the memories of previous lives in their children.

I derived the information mainly from statements of the parents themselves. And although naturally observed them as they talked for non-verbal communications of their attitudes, I had no means of reaching an objective assessment of the information provided. Most of the parents claimed that they were more or less tolerant toward their children's claims. This may well have been true at the time of my investigation; but earlier they might have been guiding the child differently to give out more information, for whatever reasons they may have had. Afterward they might have changed and tried to suppress the child's memories because of the widespread superstition that it is harmful to remember a previous life. It is widely believed (at least in northern India) that persons who remember a previous life die young.

Distance (in kilometers) between subject's birthplace and related previous personality's place of death and residence.

The median distance between the place of death of the previous personality and the birthplace of the subject was ten kilometers (the median distance between the subject's birthplace and the main residence of the previous personality was eight kilometers). Five of the subjects were lineal descendants of their related previous personalities, hence were born in the same family and same place (except in one case) where the previous personalities had died. I therefore, took the distance in these cases as zero. The range of distance was 0.2 kilometers to 565.5 kilometers.

Age of subjects when they first spoke in coherent phrases. Information on this variable was available for 40 cases. The age of subjects when they reportedly started talking in coherent phrases ranged from ten months to five years. On the average, they started talking coherently at the age of two.

Age at which subjects first spoke of the previous life. Information for this variable was available on 43 cases. The median age for speaking of the previous life was three years. This finding agrees with one of Stevenson's "universal features" of his cases from eight different cultures. He found that the subjects of these cases usually start talking about the previous life between two and four years of age.

Median age of subjects when memories of previous life faded. Eighteen of the subjects (on whom the information was available) had stopped talking of the previous life spontaneously. They would give information only when questioned and would talk much less than they used to do when they first began to talk about the previous life.

The median age of the subjects was found to be 79 months when they completely stopped talking about the previous life. This information was available on only 14 cases. These figures may not hold good for other cases, since there is a wide variation in the age at fading of memories. This age ranged from 42 months to 132 months.

Principal contents of the subject's statements about the previous life. Table 4.02 summarizes the frequency with which the more frequent themes occurred among the subjects' statements about the previous lives they claimed to remember. (N refers to the total number of cases for which the information was available; *n* refers to the number of cases in which a particular feature was present or absent.)

TABLE 4.02		
Principal Contents of Subjects' Statements			
Regarding Previous Life			
Contents of Statements	*N*	*n*	%
Recall of PP's name	41		
Present		36	87.8
Absent		5	12.2
Insists on being called	26		
by PP's name		3	11.5
Present		23	88.5
Absent			
Recall of mode of death	39		
Present		26	66.7
Absent		13	33.3
Recall of other realms	27		
Some details		5	18.5
Very few details		5	18.5
Absent		17	63.0
Recall of change in	19		
place/person after			
PP's death			
Present		12	63.2
Absent		7	36.8

The contents listed in the table will be readily understood except perhaps the last one. This refers to statements often made by the subjects concerning changes that had taken place in the appearance of persons or places known to the concerned previous personality since his death. On meeting a person or visiting a place known to the previous personality, the subject might comment, for example, that a person known to the previous personality had become bald or lost his teeth; or he might remark that a balcony had been removed from a building or some partition built into it.

Unusual behavioral features in subjects. We are concerned here with behavior that was unusual for the subject's family but that accorded well with the behavior of the related previous personality. In some cases, however, it was not possible to confirm the information that this "unusual behavior" actually corresponded to that of the related previous personality. (See Table 4.03.)

Factors stimulating the subjects' memories. In most (75%) of the cases, the subjects started talking of the previous life spontaneously *before* meeting persons related to the previous personalities. Subsequently, when the subjects met persons or visited places associated with the life of previous personalities, they gave out more information. These memories were often stimulated by meeting persons or visiting places that were important to the related previous personalities.

Behavioral accompaniments of the subjects' statements. Table 4.04 presents in summary form the data obtained from the informants concerning the expressions of emotions or physical symptoms by the subjects as they talked about the previous lives they seemed to remember, or sometimes, as they remembered these lives without talking about them.

Occasionally, I myself could observe emotions in the subjects as they talked. For the most part, however, it was necessary for me to rely on the reports of the subjects' parents and these were naturally liable to bias.

TABLE 4.03
Unusual Behavioral Features of Subjects

Feature	Present			Absent		
	n_1*	n_2*	%	n	%	N
Unusual clothing habits	1	14	46.9	17	53.1	32
Unusual dietary cravings	3	9	41.4	17	58.6	29
Unusual eating habits	2	2	23.5	13	76.5	17
Unusual affections	24	2	86.7	4	13.3	30
Unusual animosities	6	0	46.2	7	53.8	13
Unusual phobias	3	2	55.6	4	44.4	9
Unusual philias	6	2	29.6	19	70.4	27
Unusual skills or apptitudes	1	3	33.3	8	66.7	12
Reliving or mimicry of previous life	15	0	75.0	5	25.0	20
Adult attitude	13**	0	50.0	13	50.0	26
Desire to return to previous family	35	0	100.0	0	-	35
Interest in PP's place of residence	35	0	97.2	1	2.8	36

* n_1 shows unusual feature related to previous personality.

* n_2 represents the number of cases where unusual behavioral features are present but it is not known if these are related to the previous personality or not.

** Three of 13 cases showed extremely adult attitudes 8 moderately adult and 2 slightly adult attitudes tha were more or less present all the time.

TABLE 4.04
Evidence for Behavioral Accompaniments
of the Subjects' Statements

Variable	N	n	%
Evidence of emotions	30		
Extremely emotional		10	33.3
Moderately emotional		10	33.3
No Change		10	33.3
Evidence of physical symptoms	23		
Severe symptoms		1	4.3
Moderate symptoms		1	4.3
No Change		21	91.3
Evidence of ESP	31		
Significant		1	3.2
Slight		2	6.5
Nil		28	90.3
Evidence of ESP with PP's family	24		
Significant		1	4.2
Slight		1	4.2
Nil		22	91.6
Personality change during recall	28		
Moderate		-	-
Slight		2	7.1
Nil		26	92.9
Preoccupation with memories	28		
Considerable		5	17.9
Somewhat		14	50.0
No interference in day-to-day work		9	32.1

Identification of the related previous personalities. In most of the cases, the families of the subjects of these cases usually made efforts to locate and identify the family of the person the child claimed to have been. Sometimes, however, when word reached the families of related previous personalities through any source, they made an attempt to meet the subject and test his knowledge of the previous life in their own ways to their own satisfaction.

It should be noted here that in seven (16%) cases, no person satisfactorily corresponding to the statements of the child had been found. In the autumn of 1977, we (I along with Dr. Stevenson) tried ourselves to trace two of these (presumed) persons. Unfortunately, these efforts were not successful, possibly because the subjects had furnished details that were insufficient in number and specificity.

Mode of death of related previous personality. Information on the mode of death of the related previous personalities was available for 40 cases. The incidence of natural (52%) and violent deaths (48%) was almost equal with a slight tendency toward natural death. However, the frequency of violent deaths in this group was considerably higher than the incidence of violent deaths in the general population (6.7%). For the purpose of analysis, I considered death by any intervention in the normal process of life as a violent or unnatural mode of death. Under this category were included: intentional shooting, accidental shooting, stabbing, drowning, snakebite, suicide, intentional or accidental violent measures such as the use of blunt or sharp weapons (other than mentioned above) and poisoning.

In 26 of these cases I verified the mode of death from the informants who had knowledge of the mode and circumstances of the related previous personality's death. In six other cases, I consulted autopsy reports or other death certificates. In the remaining cases, however, I could not independently verify the mode of death.

Recall of mode of death by the subjects. Information on recall of mode of death was available in 39 cases. Two-thirds of these subjects recalled the mode of death in their related previous lives. However, information on the clarity of recall was available in only 22 cases. Seven (32%) of these subjects recalled most of the details and circumstances of death fairly clearly, 13 (59%) of them recalled these generally clearly, and the remaining two (9%) recalled very slight details regarding the mode of death of their previous personalities.

Verified accuracy of subject's recall of the previous personality's mode of death. Very little information was available on this variable. Out of the 12 subjects, six (50%) recalled the details and circumstances of their related previous personality's death with general accuracy, five (42%) with most details correct, and one (8%) confused some other events of the previous personality's life with the circumstances of his death. The history suggested that the related previous personality in this case was once bitten by a snake, but died as a result of some fever a few years after the snake bite; the subject recalled the mode of death as due to the snake bite.

Median age at death of related previous personality. Information on this variable was available for 33 cases. The median age at death of the related previous personality was found to be 45 years. There was a wide range of age at death (four years to 111 years).

In six (18%) cases I examined the death certificates. In the remaining cases, my information was based on the informant's memories. I made judgments about the reliability of information against the informant's level of education, his memory for other events, general approach to different situations, and his relationship with the previous personality. Hence, of the remaining 27 cases, in seven (21%) cases the information appeared to be precise, in four (12%) cases reliable within six months, and in 11 (33%) cases reliable within one year. In five (15%) cases, the age was given in approximate figures with rough estimations such as,

"He (or she) must have been 30-40 years old or was about my age, and you can write whatever you think about my age," etc.

Although in most of the cases (28 out of 33) information available on the previous personality's age at death was reliable within one year, there were five cases where the exact age was not available. This might have affected the results and the generalization should be made with reservations. However, the average age at death of the related previous personalities in the present group was much below the expected age in the general population (52.6 years).[12]

Intermission between death of related previous personality and presumed rebirth. Information for the interval between the death of the related previous personality and presumed rebirth of the subject was available on 30 cases. The median interval was reported to be 14.5 months. However, data for interval should also be viewed with the same reservations as for age at death of the previous personalities. The interval ranged from one day to 224 months.

Incidence of birthmarks. The information on the incidence of birthmarks was available for 38 cases. The marks present on the body of the subject at the time of birth were usually reported to have been noticed within a few hours to a few days of his birth by the midwife or mother of the subject. They are normally not associated with anything until the subject starts talking about a previous life saying, for example, that he was shot, stabbed, or had a similar mark in his previous life.

The birthmarks were reportedly present on the body of 16 (42%) subjects. One birthmark was reported in 13 (34%) cases, three birth marks in two (5%) cases and five birthmarks in one (3%) case.

12. Times of India Directory and Yearbook (1977).

Information regarding the correspondence of these marks to the fatal wounds on the body of the related previous personality was available only in ten cases. In five of these cases I had consulted autopsy reports.

Announcing dreams. The term "announcing dreams" refers to dreams that are believed to indicate the identity of a deceased person who is being reborn (Stevenson, 1966, 1974b). An announcing dream usually occurs to the expectant mother but sometimes to a relative or a friend in which the deceased personality indicates to the dreamer his intention to be reborn as the baby of the pregnant woman or a woman about to become pregnant. Sometimes the wish is communicated verbally; at other times it may be indicated symbolically. Such symbolic dreams may only be "understood" after the child starts talking about his previous life.

In the present group of cases, information about announcing dreams was available for 30 cases; among these, only six (20%) persons had dreams about the subjects' births. The dream occurred to mothers of the subjects in all but one case; that occurred to another member of the family. In two (7%) cases the announcing dreams occurred prior to the conception, in three (10%) cases during the first eight months of pregnancy, and in one (3%) case during the last month of pregnancy. However, no announcing dreams were reported following the birth of the subjects.

In all these cases in which the announcing dreams were reported, the deceased personalities were related or known to the families of the subjects; hence their identity could easily be established by the dreamers.

Biological relationships between the two families concerned. Of the 45 cases reported here, five (12%) subjects were reported to have been members of the same family in the related previous lives. One of these subjects were related to the previous personality on their mother's side (Neena Tiwari) and four (Prem Chander Gupta, Sanjiv Sharma, Sonu Pachauri, and Shilpa Mehta) on the father's side.

Residential and visiting connections between the two families concerned. Information on this variable was available for 42 cases. In 11 (26%) cases there were no residential or visiting connections, even the remotest, between the two families concerned. In 19 (45%) of the cases, the parents of the subjects had only casually visited the area of the previous personality's residence or passed through his village. Only 12 (29%) parents of subjects lived in the same area of residence as that of the previous personalities.

Social and commercial relations between the families concerned. Information was available on 33 cases. Out of this number, 15 (46%) families on the subject's side had some social relations at the place of residence of the related previous personality. These social relations were not with the family of the previous personality but with distant or close relatives living in the village or area of residence of the previous personality concerned.

Information on commercial relations was available on 19 cases. In 13 (68%) of the cases, the two families concerned had commercial relations in the same area. They used to buy goods from the same market outside their village. It happens that most villages do not have a market. The villagers either go to a neighboring town or city or buy things from a weekly market which is held in a place where customers from nearby villages can approach it. There did not seem to be any other relationship between these families before the development of the case other than this common marketing place. In 21 percent of the cases there were no social or commercial relations in the area of residence of the two families concerned.

Other associations between the two families concerned. Information was available on 42 cases. In 19 (45%) cases, there was no association as far as I could ascertain between the two families concerned; in three (7%) cases, the families knew of each other's existence but had no associations. In ten (24%) cases there was slight association; for example, both the families might have attended a wedding or condolence meeting in the same village. In only ten (24%) cases was there a close association between the two families; for example, the previous personality had visited or had a friendship with the subject's parents or family.

Interactions between the families of the subjects and the related previous personalities after the case had developed. In most of the cases, the two families concerned had already met before I started the present investigation. Five (11%) subjects belonged to the same family (being lineal descendants of the concerned previous personalities.) The families of the related previous personalities had not been traced in seven (16%) cases.

After the two families had met, about half (52%) of them continued to visit each other's family and even exchanged small gifts. In 36 percent of the cases, the visits were discontinued after a few initial visits, either by the subject's family or by the family members of the related previous personalities. In 13 percent of the cases, the two families concerned never visited each other after the first visit. Information on the exchange of visits between the two families concerned was available on 31 cases.

Exchange of gifts between the two families concerned. Information on this variable was available for only 13 cases. In most (eight) of the cases either the family of the previous personality gave some gifts to the subject of some clothes, shoes, sweets, or a small amount of money (when they visited each other); or the gifts were exchanged between both families (four cases). In only one case, the members of the subject's family gave gifts to the family of the previous personality.

Support for the claims of subject's statements from the family of the related previous personality. This varied in range from complete rejection to total acceptance. Information on this aspect was available for 26 cases. In most (73%) cases the statements of the subjects had been accepted by the members of their related previous personalities as indicating to their satisfaction that the subject is, or probably is, the previous personality reborn. However, in five (19%) cases the members of the previous family showed an ambivalent or neutral attitude towards the claims of the subjects; while the claims of another two (8%) subjects were completely rejected by the members of the previous family.

Outside the two families immediately concerned in these cases, the subjects had not received much attention or support for their claims. Information on this aspect was available for 30 cases. Fifteen (50%) of the cases received very little or almost no attention from others; and in another 15 (50%) cases, the subject received some kind of public attention either through newspaper reporters or other visitors from within or outside their villages (or residences) who acknowledged the case. None of the cases was treated as a god or superhuman person by the outsiders.

Factors correlated with previous personality's mode of death. During the analysis of data I found that some of the features in the subjects such as animosities, phobias, and birthmarks etc. showed significant associations with mode of death of the related previous personality. All the factors listed in Table 4.05 were positively associated with a violent mode of death except for the recall of the previous name by the subjects.

Mode of death and sex of related previous personalities. Information about mode of death was available for 28 male and

TABLE 4.05

Relationship between Mode of Previous Personalities'
Death and Presence of other Features of the Cases

Feature	Violent Deaths			Natural Deaths		
	N_1*	N_2**	%	N_1*	N_2**	%
Animosities	7	5	71.4	5	0	-
Phobias	12	6	50.0	12	0	-
Recall of PP's name	17	15	88.2	19	17	89.4
Birthmarks	16	12	75.0	17	3	17.6
Recall of PP's mode of death	19	19	100.0	17	5	29.4

*N_1 - number of cases for which information obtained.

**N_2 - number of subjects in whom features manifested.

12 female previous personalities of the cases. Fourteen (50%) of the related male previous personalities and five (42%) of the female previous personalities had died violently. The incidence of violent deaths was slightly higher among male previous personalities than among female ones.

Summary of the significant findings. I have summarized in Table 4.06 all the more important data from this section of the investigation so that particular items of special interest or importance can readily be found.

Comparison of Results in Two Series of Cases

In this section I shall present a comparison of the results obtained in the present investigation with those obtained by Stevenson. As I have mentioned earlier, the reason for comparing the present results with Stevenson's is that his is the only systematically

TABLE 4.06		
Summary of Significant Findings of Present Investigation		
Factor	*N*	Remarks
Demographic features		
Economic status of S	43	Majority of cases in
Economic status of PP	33	middle class
Population of area of S's residence	45	Most cases from villages or towns
Degree of social difference	24	Small difference observed in many cases
Degree of economic difference	28	Small difference observed in many cases
Principal features		
Recall of mode of death	39	Recall present in most cases
Recall of PP's name	41	Present in most cases
Insistence on PP's name	26	Absent in most cases
Mimicry of PP's life	20	Present in most cases
Unusual affections	30	Present in most cases
Phobias	27	Absent in most cases
Desire to return to PP's family	35	Present in all cases
Interest in PP's place	36	Present in most cases
Evidence of ESP	31	Absent in most cases
Evidence of ESP with PP's family	24	Absent in most cases
Announcing dreams	30	Absent in most cases
Mother's initial attitudes toward S's claims	37	Most mothers showed indifferent attitudes
Commercial relations in area of PP's place	19	Present in many cases

carried out scientific work available on this topic that takes care of all, or almost all of the known factors that result from and influence the phenomenon wherein memories of a previous life are experienced and claimed. A comparison of results in the two series will help toward a better understanding of the factors underlying claims of memories of past lives and also in establishing the authenticity of the cases.

If the differences exceed the similarities in features of these cases in both groups, different interpretations will have to be sought to explain the phenomenon since both the samples were drawn, by and large, from the same geographical area, namely northern India. If, on the other hand, similarities in the two investigations far outnumber the differences, it is likely that the cases of both groups belong to some order of natural, that is, genuine experience. This would add to the knowledge of our understanding of the phenomenon, and could place such claims in a better perspective.

I have denoted the two groups by the letters I.S. and S.P., respectively. I.S. refers to the features of Stevenson's cases; S.P. to the features obtained in the cases investigated by myself. In all, I compared 50 I.S. cases[13] with 45 S.P. cases on 53 features, by using appropriate statistical techniques (mainly *t* test and *chi* square test). However, in some instances information was not available for all items. The number (N) therefore, varied from item to item and I have mentioned these numbers while describing these items or variables. It should be noted that except those features for which I have provided values of the tests of significance, the two groups did not show significant difference with regard to the features compared.

I have presented the results in this section in the following major headings:

13. For criteria of selection of these cases, see Chapter Three, pp.39-40.

A. Demographic Characteristics of Present and Related Previous Personalities of the I.S. and S.P. Cases

B. Principal Features of the Cases of the I.S. and S.P. Groups

Demographic Characteristics of Present and Related Previous Personalities

Sex Distribution

Twenty-seven (54%) subjects of the I.S. cases were males and 23 (46%) were females. Thirty (67%) of S.P. subjects were males and 15 (33%) were females.

On the previous personalities' side the number of males was 28 (56%) and 29 (64%) in the I.S. and S.P. series respectively. There were three cases of sex change in the I.S. series and one case in S.P. series. In the I.S. cases the direction of change was from male to female in two cases and female to male in one case, while in S.P. cases it was from female to male.

Social Status of Present and Previous Personalities

Information on the social status of the subjects was available for 50 I.S. cases and 44 S.P. cases. Ten (20%) subjects of the I.S. cases came from upper, 28 (56%) from middle, and 12 (24%) from the lower social class families. Fourteen (32%) subjects of the S.P. cases came from upper, 18 (41%) from middle and 12 (27%) from the lower social class families.

Information about the social status of the reported previous personalities was available for 44 I.S. cases and 37 S.P. cases. Twelve (27%) previous personalities of I.S. cases belonged to the upper, 24 (55%) to the middle, and eight (18%) to the lower social class. Similarly, eight (22%) previous personalities of

S.P. cases belonged to the upper. 23 (62%) to the middle and six (16%) to the lower social class. In both series the majority of the cases, persons concerned came from middle class families.

Degree of difference in social status between previous and present personalities. Data on this variable were available for 41 I.S., and 37 S.P. cases. In ten (24%) of the I.S. cases and 13 (35%) of the S.P. cases there was *no change* in social status between the claimed previous life and the present life. There was slight change in social status in 12 (29%) of the I.S. and five (14%) of the S.P. cases. In 11 (27%) of the I.S. and 12 (32%) of the S.P. cases a moderate change; and in eight (20%) of I.S. and seven (19%) of S.P. cases a great change in the social status between the two lives was reported, for example, from a sweeper to Brahmin or Kshatriya and vice versa.

Direction of difference in social status between the two personalities. With regard to the change in social status between the two personalities concerned, 12 (29%) of I.S. and nine (24%) of S.P. cases showed an upward movement. That is, the social circumstances of the present life were better compared with those of the previous life. In 19 (46%) of the I.S. cases and 15 (41%) of the S.P. cases a downward movement was reported. As stated above, no change was reported among ten (24%) I.S. cases and 13 (35%) S.P. cases. The subjects were born in the same social class as their reported previous personalities.

Economic Status of Previous and Present Personalities

Information on this variable for the present personalities (subjects) was available for 50 I.S. and 43 S.P. cases; and 45 I.S., and 33 S.P. cases respectively for the related previous personalities.

Only one (2%) subject of the I.S. group and four (9%) subjects of the S.P. group of cases belonged to upper economic status. Therefore, this group was not taken into account for the statistical comparison.

Thirty-seven (74%) subjects of I.S. cases and 29 (67%) of S.P. cases belonged to the middle economic class; 12 (24%) subjects of I.S. group and ten (23%) of S.P. group belonged to the lower economic status.

In the case of the previous personalities, 11 (25%) of the I.S. cases and six (18%) of the S.P. cases belonged to the upper economic class. Twenty-nine (64%) of I.S. cases and 23 (70%) of S.P. cases to the middle; and five (11%) of I.S. cases and four (12%) of S.P. cases belonged to the lower economic class.

Degree of difference in economic status between present and previous personalities. Information on this variable was available for 45 I.S. and 33. S.P. cases. In 11 (24%) cases of the I.S. series and five (15%) cases of the S.P. series no change in economic circumstances from one life to the next was reported.

A small degree of change in the economic status was reported in 13 (29%) of the I.S. cases and nine (27%) of the S.P. cases. A moderate degree of change in 12 (27%) I.S. cases and 12 (36%) S.P. cases; and a great degree of change in nine (20%) I.S. and seven (21%) S.P. cases was observed.

Direction of difference in economic status between the two personalities concerned. From the information on 45 I.S. cases and 33 S.P. cases, a difference in direction of change in the economic status was observed in 34 I.S. cases and 28 S.P. cases. The previous personalities who had lived in better economic conditions were born in poorer economic conditions in 29 (65%) of I.S. cases and 16 (49%) of S.P. cases. The direction of change from poorer to better economic conditions from one life to the next was reported only in five (11%) I.S. and 12 (36%) S.P. cases.

On statistical comparison, the two groups differed significantly ($X^2=6.11$; $df=1$; $p<0.05$). In that, more subjects of I.S. cases remembered lives in better economic circumstances.

Religion of Present and Related Previous Personalities

Most of the subjects and related previous personalities in both the groups were Hindus. Forty-six (92%) subjects of I.S. cases and 41 (91%) subjects of S.P. cases belonged to the Hindu religion. Only four (8%) subjects of I.S. cases belonged to other religions namely, Jain (three subjects) and Sikh (one subject); and four (9%) subjects of S.P. cases (two each from Muslim and Jain) belonged to other religions.

From the information available for 49 I.S. cases and 45 S.P. cases about the religion of the previous personalities, 46 (94%) of I.S. cases and 40 (89%) of S.P. cases belonged to Hindu religion. One each of the three (7%) previous personalities of I.S. cases belonged to the Muslim, Christian and Jain religions whereas two each of the five (11%) previous personalities of S.P. cases belonged to Jain and Sikh religions and one to the Zoroastrian religion. However, for the purpose of statistical analysis, the religious communities had to be divided into two groups, namely Hindus and non-Hindus, since there were too few cases in each of the non-Hindu categories for the statistical treatment.

In both the groups the majority of the subjects and the previous personalities were Hindus.

Difference in religion between the previous and the present personalities. Information on this feature was available for 49 I.S. cases and 45 S.P. cases. A change in religion from one life to the next was reported only among six (13%) I.S. cases and five (11%) S.P. cases.

Population of Area of Residence of Present and Related Previous Personalities

Information about the area of residence of the subjects was available for 50 I.S. and 45 S.P. cases. Nineteen (38%) subjects of I.S. cases and 30 (67%) subjects of S.P. cases lived in the communities with a population up to 10,000 people. Thirty-one (62%) subjects of the I.S. group and 15 (33%) subjects of the S.P. group lived in communities with a population above 10,000 people.

On statistical comparison the two groups differed significantly from each other ($X^2=7.78; df=1; p<0.01$). Most of I.S. cases were from the cities whereas most of S.P. cases came from the villages and towns.

Information on the area of residence of the related previous personalities was available for 45 I.S. cases and 40 S.P. cases. Fourteen (31%) previous personalities of I.S. cases lived in areas with a population of less than 10,000 as compared to 23 (58%) previous personalities of S.P. cases. Thirty-one (69%) previous personalities in the I.S. group and 17 (43%) in the S.P. group lived in areas with a population of more than 10,000 people.

The two groups differed significantly on this feature ($X^2=6.00; df=1; p<0.05$). Most of the previous personalities of the I.S. cases lived in the cities.

Principal Features of the Cases of I.S. and S.P. Groups

Status of Investigation of the Cases

Five (10%) of the 50 I.S. cases and three (7%) of the 45 S.P. cases, were not at all thoroughly investigated. Ten (20%) of I.S. cases were investigated not too thoroughly and 17 (34%) were investigated fairly thoroughly. Eleven (24%) of S.P. cases were also not investigated too thoroughly while 27 (60%) were investigated fairly thoroughly. Eighteen (36%) of I.S. cases were investigated thoroughly, four of which very thoroughly; while only four (9%) of S.P. cases were investigated thoroughly. (For definitions of levels of thoroughness, see pp 113-114.)

On statistical analysis the two groups differed significantly with regard to the thoroughness of investigation of the cases (X^2=12.12; df=4; $p<0.05$). More I.S. cases were investigated thoroughly.

Educational Level of Subjects' Fathers

Enough data with regard to the mothers' education was not available for I.S. cases for a meaningful comparison between the two groups.

Data for the subjects' fathers' education was available for 31 I.S. cases and 28 S.P. cases. Eight (26%) respondents of I.S. group had been educated up to high-school while 16 (57%) respondents of S.P. group were educated up to high-school. Twenty (65%) fathers in the I.S. group had education beyond college as against only nine (32%) in the S.P. group. Only three of the respondents were illiterate in both the groups. (This number being very small, was not taken into account for the statistical comparison between the two groups.)

The statistical analysis revealed significant difference between the two groups with regard to the subjects' father's education (X^2=6.69 ; df=1 ; $p<0.01$). More fathers in the I.S. group had education beyond college level.

Initial Attitude of Subjects' Parents toward their Claims of Previous Life

Information with regard to the initial attitude toward memories of previous life was available for 43 fathers and 31 mothers in the I.S. group; and 30 fathers, and 37 mothers in the S.P. group of cases. The fathers in 14 (33%) I.S. cases and seven (23%) in S.P. cases initially encouraged their children to talk about their previous lives. Twenty (47%) fathers in the I.S. group and 16 (53%) in the S.P. group were indifferent toward the memories, while nine (21%) fathers in the I.S. group and seven (23%) fathers in the S.P. group discouraged their children from talking about the previous lives.

Seven (23%) mothers in the I.S. group and four (11%) mothers in the S.P. group initially encouraged their children (from a slight to a great extent) to talk about the previous life. Seventeen (55%) mothers in the I.S. group and 23 (62%) mothers in the S.P. group remained neutral or indifferent toward these claims; while seven (23%) mothers in the I.S. group and ten (28%) in the S.P. group discouraged their children by ridiculing, deriding, scolding, and even taking violent measures to suppress their memories. The suppression was done to prevent premature death of the subjects because of the prevalent belief in northern India that the children who remember a previous life die young.

Median Distance (in Kilometers) between Subjects' Birthplace and Related Previous Personalities' Place of Residence

Information regarding distance between subjects' birthplace and place of death of the related previous personality was available for 40 I.S. cases and 38 S.P. cases. It was 46.10 kilometers (SD=1402.07) for the I.S. cases and ten kilometers (SD=103.65) for S.P. cases.

Information about the median distance between the subjects' birthplace and the place of residence of the related previous personalities was available on 40 I.S. cases and 37 S.P. cases. It was 45.10 (SD=1404.99) kilometers for I.S. cases and eight (SD=108.86) kilometers for S.P. cases.

Median Age (in Months) of Subjects when They First Spoke in Coherent Phrases

Information on this variable was available for 37 subjects of

I.S. cases and 40 S.P. cases. The subjects of I.S. cases started speaking in coherent phrases at a median age of 18 months (SD=8.20) as against 24 months (SD=11.96) in the subjects of S.P. cases.

On statistical analysis the ages of the subjects at speaking in coherent phrases differed significantly between the two groups (t=2.09;df=75;p<0.05). The subjects of the I.S. cases reportedly attained normal speech earlier than the subjects of the S.P. cases.

Median age (in Months) of subjects when they first spoke of previous life

Data on this variable were available for 48 I.S. cases and 43 S.P. cases. The subjects started speaking about a previous life at 35.8 months (SD=20.26) and 35.7 months (SD=14.75) in the I.S. and S.P. groups respectively.

The subjects of both the groups first spoke about a previous life around the age of three years.

Median age (in Months) of subjects when memory of previous life began fading. The subjects stopped talking spontaneously about the previous life but would give information when questioned. This indicated some fading, unless the subject had gone "underground" because of measures to suppress him. Information about the age when memories of previous life began fading, was available for 22 I.S. cases and 18 S.P. cases. The memory about previous life began fading at 78 months (SD=23.78) in subjects of I.S. cases and 69.5 months (SD=18.86) in S.P. cases.

The memory of the previous life began fading between about six and six and one half years of age in the two groups.

Median age (in months) of subjects when memory of previous life almost completely faded. The subjects when questioned on the matter, reported to their parents or to us that they no longer clearly remembered about the previous life. However, data with regard to their ages at this time were available only for 17 I.S. cases and

14 S.P. cases. The memory about the previous life almost faded at a median age of 108 months (SD=38.81) among I.S. subjects and 79 months (SD=34.91) among S.P. subjects.

Claims of Memory Fading by Subjects

Information with regard to the fading or preservation of memories of the previous life was elicited from 41 subjects of I.S. cases and 29 subjects of S.P. cases. Fifteen (37%) subjects of I.S. cases and ten (35%) of S.P. cases claimed to still have memories of a previous life, while 26 (63%) subjects of I.S. group and 19 (65%) subjects of S.P. group claimed that they no longer remembered the events of a previous life clearly.

The subjects claimed fading of memories (or their preserving them) with more or less the same frequency in both the groups.

Incident After which Subjects Stopped Talking of Previous Life

Information on this variable was available for ten I.S. cases and 13 S.P. cases. Six (60%) subjects of I.S. cases and three (23%) subjects of S.P. cases stopped talking about the previous life as a result of some distraction. The distraction included a visit to the place of residence of the previous personality, meeting persons related to the previous personality, or after the start of school. The parents of four (40%) subjects of I.S. cases and ten (77%) of S.P. cases took definite measures to suppress memories of their children. The measures ranged from mild to severe punishment (tapping on the head of the subject on certain days of the week, to spinning the child counterclockwise on a potter's wheel).

Principal Contents of Subjects' Statements Regarding Previous Life

Most of the terms used here are self-explanatory and for

others I have provided explanations in the preceding section of this chapter. However, in order to maintain the continuity of the subject I shall provide brief explanations of some of the important concepts again at the appropriate places.

Recall of previous name. Information on whether or not the subject's statements included name of his claimed previous personality, was available for 45 I.S. cases and 41 S.P. cases. Thirty-four (76%) subjects in I.S. group and 36 (88%) subjects in S.P. group mentioned their name in the previous life.

In both the groups the statements of most of the subjects included the recall of previous name.

Insistence on being called by previous name. Out of the 41 I.S. cases and 26 S.P. cases for whom the information was available, only three subjects in each group insisted on being called by the previous name. Thirty-eight (93%) subjects of the I.S. cases and 23 (89%) subjects of the S.P. cases did not insist to be called by their previous names.

A majority of the subjects in both groups did not press their parents or others to call them by their previous names.

Recall of mode of death. Information on whether the subjects remembered how they had died in their claimed previous life was available for 46 I.S. cases and 39 S.P. cases. Majority of the subjects 32 (70%) among I.S. cases and 26 (67%) among S.P. cases mentioned how their previous lives had ended.

The recall of mode of death was high in both the groups.

Recall of other realms. Information on how many subjects mentioned about the realms they were in, after the termination of the previous life, was available for 37 I.S. cases and 27 S.P. cases. Fourteen (38%) subjects of the I.S. cases and ten (37%) subjects of the S.P. cases did mention something about the realms where they went after death in the previous life.

A mention of other realms by the subjects occurred with about the same frequency in both the groups.

Recall of associations with present family. Eight (20%) subjects of the 41 I.S. cases and six (15%) subjects of the 39 S.P. cases claimed to recall that in the previous life they were related or associated with members of their present family.

The associations with the present family were reported with about the same frequency in both the groups.

Recall of change in place or person after previous personality's death. On visiting a place or meeting a person connected with previous life, some subjects made references to the changes in the appearance that had occurred after the previous personalities' death. Information on this feature was available for 24 I.S. cases and 19 S.P. cases. Sixteen (67%) of the I.S. subjects and 12 (63%) of the S.P. subjects commented on the change in appearance of the persons or places connected with the previous life.

The subjects in both the groups commented on the change with almost the same frequency.

Factors Stimulating Subjects' Statements of the Previous Life

In most of the cases the subjects had initially started talking about a previous life without meeting the persons or visiting the places connected with the previous life. Subsequent to their initial statements, on meeting the persons or visiting the places connected with the previous life, some subjects gave more information concerning that life.

Data on this variable were available on 30 (for persons) and 28 (for places) for I.S. cases and 29 (for persons) and 26 (for places) for S.P. cases. Memories about a previous life were stimulated for the first time in two (7%) I.S. subjects and eight (28%) S.P. subjects on meeting a person connected with a previous life. Twenty-eight (93%) subjects of I.S. group and 21

(72%) subjects of the S.P. group had already started talking about a previous life before meeting the persons connected with that life but recalled some more events on meeting them.

Only one (4%) subject of I.S. cases and two (8%) subjects of S.P. cases made their statements for the first time on visiting a place associated with the previous life. Twenty-seven (96%) of I.S. subjects and 24 (92%) of S.P. subjects had already started talking about a previous life but recalled some more events or details on visiting places associated with that life.

Memory Stimulation of Subjects by Events Similar to Previous Life

Some subjects started talking about a previous life when they observed events that were similar to the ones in their previous life. For example, cooking of a dish in a particular style.

Information on this feature was available for 29 I.S. cases and 15 S.P. cases. In 23 (79%) I.S. cases and 11 (73%) S.P. cases the subjects started talking for the first time, about a previous life, on observing events similar to the events in a previous life.

Evidence for Behavioral Accompaniments of the Subjects' Statements

The statements of some subjects were accompanied by certain unusual behaviors. For example, they displayed appropriate emotions (of joy, when they spoke of pleasant occasions, of sadness or even crying when they spoke of separation or loss) while describing the events of the previous life.

Evidence of emotions. Information on this variable was available for 35 I.S. and 30 S.P. cases. Twenty-six (74%) subjects of I.S. cases and 20 (67%) subjects of S.P. cases displayed appropriate emotions while speaking about a previous life. The statements of most of the subjects in both the groups were accompanied by appropriate emotions.

Evidence of physical symptoms. Information on this feature was available for 22 I.S. cases and 23 S.P. cases. Only three (14%) subjects of the I.S. group and two (9%) of S.P. group showed physical symptoms while recalling events of a previous life.

In both the groups, very few subjects had displayed physical symptoms when they recalled a previous life.

Evidence of ESP. The information on whether or not the subjects of these cases showed evidence of ESP abilities, was available on 29 I.S. cases and 31 S.P. cases. In 15 (52%) subjects of the I.S. cases and three (10%) subjects of the S.P. cases the presence of ESP was reported.

The two groups differed significantly on the statistical analysis (X^2=10.69;df=1;p<0.01). The subjects of I.S's cases reported ESP more often than those of S.P. cases.

Evidence of ESP with members of previous personality. Information on this variable was available on 16 I.S. cases and 24 S.P. cases. Two (13%) subjects of I.S. cases and two (8%) subjects of S.P. cases were reported to have shown evidence of ESP with members of the previous families.

Evidence of personality change during recall. Information on whether or not any change was observed in their personality while the subjects recalled the previous life, was available for 23 I.S. cases and 28 S.P. cases. Four (17%) subjects in the I.S. group and two (7%) in the S.P. group showed some change in their personality.

A majority of the subjects in both the groups showed no change in their personality during recall.

Unusual Behavioral Features of the Subjects

The subjects sometimes displayed behaviors which were unusual for their present circumstances but corresponded quite well with the behavior of the person whose life they claimed to remember.

Unusual clothing habits. Information on the preference of clothing was available for 27 I.S. cases and 32 S.P. cases. Twelve (44%) subjects of the I.S. group and 15 (47%) subjects of the S.P. group asked for clothes which were not commonly used in their present families.

Nearly 45 percent of the subjects in both the groups showed a preference for unusual clothing.

Unusual dietary cravings. Some subjects showed cravings for particular foods which were not generally prepared in their homes or were not liked with the same intensity by other members of their present families. Information with regard to the dietary cravings was available for 33 I.S. cases and 29 S.P. cases. Twenty- one (64%) subjects of I.S. cases and 12 (41%) of S.P. cases showed intense preference for certain foods.

Unusual eating habits. The information on whether the subjects showed any special eating habits or styles, different from the members of their present family, was available for 25 I.S. cases and 17 S.P. cases. In thirteen (52%) subjects of I.S. cases and four (24%) subjects of S.P. cases some unusual eating habits were reported to have occurred.

Unusual affections. The information on whether the subjects expressed unusual affections toward members of the previous family was available for 33 I.S. cases and 30 S.P. cases. Twenty-seven (82%) subjects of I.S. cases and 26 (87%) subjects of S.P. cases were reported to have shown or expressed strong affections toward members of their previous family.

In both the groups most of the subjects were unusually affectionate toward members of their claimed previous families.

Unusual animosities. Some subjects were reported to have shown feelings of vengeance toward people connected with the previous personality who had harmed them (or were in some way responsible for their death) or had animosity over other issues. Information on this variable was available for 20 I.S. cases and 13 S.P. cases. In 10 (50%) subjects of I.S. cases and six (46%) subjects of S.P. cases such unusual animosities were reported to have occurred.

Unusual philias. These refer to the subjects' attachment to the objects that were of special value or interest to the previous personality. An example would be, a special interest in vehicles on the part of both previous and present personalities. Information on this feature was available for 22 I.S. cases and nine S.P. cases. Eighteen (82%) subjects of I.S. cases and five (56%) subjects of S.P. cases showed unusual philias.

Unusual phobias. Some subjects showed excessive fear (in the absence of a known cause) toward persons or objects. These were generally associated with the termination of the reported previous life. For example a subject, whose previous personality was reported to have been murdered with bladed weapons, showed an unusual fear of bladed weapons (sometimes including knives).

Information about unusual phobias was available for 33 I.S. and 27 S.P. cases. In fifteen (45%) subjects of the I.S. cases and eight (30%) subjects of the S.P. cases such a feature was reported.

Unusual skills or aptitudes. Some children show certain skills or aptitudes for which they have no opportunity to learn during the present life but they claim to have learned in a previous life. For example, knowledge of how to drive automobiles or how to speak a particular language. Information about unusual skills and aptitudes was available for 25 I.S. cases and 12 S.P. cases. Thirteen (52%) subjects of I.S. cases and four (33%) subjects of S.P. cases showed unusual skills.

Reliving or mimicry of previous life. Some of the subjects relive a role of the related previous personality through their play. For example, a child who claimed to have been a doctor in a previous life preferred to play at being a doctor, using sticks (or similar material) as a thermometer or other instruments. Information on this item was available for 20 subjects in each group. Eleven (55%) subjects of the I.S. group and 15 (75%) subjects of the S.P. group were reported to have exhibited mimicry of previous life during play or other activities.

Adult attitude. Information on whether the subjects in their childhood behaved like adults, was available for 29 I.S. cases and 26 S.P. cases. Twenty-two (76%) subjects of I.S. group and 13 (50%) subjects of S.P. group were reported to have displayed this behavior.

On statistical analysis, the two groups showed a significant difference $(X^2=3.93; df=1; p<0.05)$. The subjects of I.S. cases exhibited 'Adult attitude' more often.

Desire to return to the previous personality's family. Information on this variable was available for 35 cases in each group. Thirty-one (89%) subjects of the I.S. group and all (100%) subjects of the S.P. group expressed a strong desire to be taken to the previous personalities' family.

Interest in previous personality's place of residence. Information was available for 32 I.S. and 36 S.P. cases. Thirty (94%) subjects of the I.S. group and 35 (97%) subjects of the S.P. group displayed an interest in visiting previous personality's place of residence.

Most of the children in both the groups showed a desire to return back to the previous family and interest in visiting previous personality's place of residence.

Median Age (in Months) of Persistence of Behavioral Features in Subjects

Information on persistence of unusual behavior in the subjects was available for 22 I.S. cases and seven S.P. cases. The median age of the I.S. subjects was 180.50 months (SD=179.25) and 102 months (SD=42.98) of S.P. subjects upto which they continued to show behavioral features corresponding to the behavior of claimed previous personality.

The behavioral features persisted longer than the imaged memories in both the groups.

Identification of the Related Previous Personalities

Out of 50 I.S. cases and 45 S.P. cases a person corresponding to the subjects' statements was found in 40 (80%) I.S. cases and 38 (84%) S.P. cases.

In most of the cases for both the groups the related previous personality could be identified.

Mode of Death and Incidence of Violent Deaths of the Related Previous Personalities

Information on mode of death of the related previous personality was available for 48 I.S. cases and 40 S.P. cases. Twenty-five (52%) of the related previous personalities in the I.S. group and 21 (53%) in the S.P. group had died nonviolently. The remaining 23 (48%) of the previous personalities of the I.S. cases and 19 (47%) of the S.P. cases had died due to intentional shooting, stabbing, drowning, snakebite, and other intentional or accidental violent modes of death.

For the purposes of statistical analysis I had divided the groups into two categories of modes of death namely, natural and violent. The two groups did not differ significantly. In both the groups the incidence of violent deaths was much higher than reported in the general population.

Verified Accuracy of Mode of Previous Personality's Death

In 21 (42%) of the I.S. cases and 13 (29%) of the S.P. cases the claimed mode of death in the previous life as stated by the subjects, could not be verified independently. However, in 29 (58%) cases of the I.S. group and 32 (71%) cases of the S.P. group it was verified independently which also included examining the certificates in nine (18%) I.S. cases and six (13%) S.P. cases.

Median Age at Death of Related Previous Personalities

Information on the previous personality's age at death was available for 43 I.S. cases and 33 S.P. cases. The median age at the time of death of the previous personalities was 28.9 years or 347 months (SD = 203.71) for the I.S. cases and 45 years or 540 months (SD = 302.20) for the S.P. cases.

On statistical analysis the two groups differed significantly (t=2.52;df=74;p<0.05). The previous personalities in the I.S. group died at a relatively younger age.

Median Intermission Between the Death of the Previous Personality and the Birth of the Present Personality

The information on this feature was available for 39 I.S. cases and 30 S.P. cases. The reported intermission was 19 months for the I.S. cases and 14.5 months for the S.P. cases.

Announcing Dreams Regarding Subject's Rebirth

In some cases, mothers or other relatives of the subjects (generally) or relatives of the related previous personalities (occasionally) had a dream about the birth of the subject. Information on this variable was available for 30 cases for each group. The announcing dreams were reported in ten (33%) cases in the I.S. group and six (20%) cases in the S.P. group.

In the I.S. group, the announcing dreams occurred before the conception in three (10%) cases, during pregnancy in six (20%) cases, and following the birth of the subject in one (3%) case. Similarly in the S.P. group the announcing dreams occurred in two (7%) cases before the conception and in four (13%) during pregnancy. No dreams were reported to have occurred after the birth of the subjects.

Incidence of Birthmarks

Some subjects were born with certain marks on the body which informants said were related to wounds or other marks on the previous personality. Most of these corresponded to fatal wounds inflicted on the body of the previous personality at the time of death.

Information on birthmarks was available for 41 I.S. cases and 38 S.P. cases. In 17 (41%) subjects of I.S. cases and 16 (42%) subjects of S.P. cases birth marks (ranging from one to five) were reported.

The birthmarks were reported with about the same frequency in both the groups.

Correspondence of birthmarks with fatal wounds of previous personality. Information on this aspect was available only for 11 I.S. cases and ten S.P. cases. In six (55%) of the I.S. cases and five (50%) of the S.P. cases the correspondence between the birthmarks on the subject's body and the fatal wounds on the previous personality was verified independently.

Relationships and Associations between the Families of the Present and Previous Personalities

Biological relationship. Information on the biological relationship between the families of the present and the previous personality was available for 44 I.S. cases and 43 S.P. cases. In four (9%) of the I.S. cases and five (12%) of the S.P. cases, the two families concerned were related biologically. However, in both the groups, most of the subjects were not biologically related to the members of the previous personality's family.

Marital relationship. Information on this aspect was available for 46 I.S. cases and 42 S.P. cases. Only in one (2%) of the I.S. cases and two (5%) of the S.P. cases the two families concerned were related by marriage. In most of the cases in both the groups, however, the two families concerned had no marital relationships.

Social relationship. Information on whether the two families concerned had had any social relations with each other prior to the development of the case was available for 31 I.S. cases and 33 S.P. cases. In 16 (52%) I.S. cases and 19 (58%) S.P. cases the two families concerned had had some social contacts between them.

Commercial relations. The information on commercial relations between the two families was available for 24 I.S. and 19 S.P. cases. In 14 (58%) of I.S. cases and 13 (68%) of S.P. cases some commercial contacts were reported. For example, both families may have shopped at the same market.

Other associations. Information on associations between the two families concerned was available for 49 I.S. cases and 42 S.P. cases. It was found that in 14 (29%) I.S. cases and 20 (48%) S.P. cases the two families concerned had some associations in that they either attended the same condolence meetings in the village (slight associations) or the previous personality had a friendship or visiting relationship with the parents of the subject (close associations).

Relationship between Mode of Death of Previous Personalities' Death and Other Features of the Cases

Certain features were reported more frequently among the subjects whose claimed previous personalities had died violently.

I shall now compare these features between the two groups.

Unusual animosities. Information on this aspect was available for 20 I.S. cases and 12 S.P. cases. Ten (50%) previous personalities of the I.S. cases and seven (58%) of the S.P. cases had died violently. In the I.S. group, unusual animosities were reported in eight (40%) subjects whose claimed previous personalities had died violently and two (10%) whose previous personalities had died nonviolently. In the S.P. group the animosities were reported among five (42%) subjects whose claimed previous personalities had died violently and none among the subjects whose previous personality had died nonviolently. In both the groups the animosities were reported more frequently among the subjects whose claimed previous personalities had died violently.

Phobias. Information about the mode of death and phobias was available for 27 I.S. cases and 24 S.P. cases. Fourteen (52%) previous personalities of the I.S. cases and 12 (50%) of the S.P. cases had died violently. In the I.S. group phobias were reported in five (19%) subjects whose claimed previous personalities had died violently and four (15%) whose previous personalities had died nonviolently. In the S.P. group, the phobias were reported among six (25%) subjects whose claimed previous personalities had died violently and none among the subjects whose previous personality had died nonviolently.

On statistical analysis the two groups did not differ significantly although phobias were reported more frequently among the subjects of S.P. group who reported to have died violently in the previous life than subjects of the I.S. group.

Recall of previous personality's name. The information on the mode of death in previous life and recall of previous personality's name by the subjects was available for 43 I.S. cases and 36 S.P. cases. Twenty-two previous personalities of I.S.

cases and 17 (47%) of S.P. cases were reported to have died violently. Twenty-one (49%) subjects of the I.S. cases, whose claimed previous personalities had died violently and 13 (30%) whose previous personalities had died nonviolently, recalled name of that personality. In the S.P. group the recall of previous personalities' name was reported among 15 (42%) subjects whose claimed previous personalities had died violently and 17 (47%) among the subjects whose reported previous personalities had died nonviolently.

On statistical analysis the two groups did not differ significantly although in the I.S. group, recall of previous name was reported more among the subjects who reported having died violently in the previous life than in the subjects of the S.P. group.

Recall of mode of death. Information on this variable was available for 44 I.S. cases and 36 S.P. cases. Twenty-three (52%) previous personalities of the I.S. cases and 19 (53%) of the S.P. cases had died violently. In the I.S. group, recall of the mode of death in the previous life was reported in 21 (48%) subjects whose claimed previous personalities had died violently and ten (23%) whose previous personalities had died nonviolently. In the S.P. group, the recall was reported among 19 (53%) subjects whose claimed previous personalities had died violently and five (14%) among the subjects whose previous personalities had died nonviolently.

In both the groups the recall of mode of death was significantly related with the violent mode of death.

Birthmarks. Information on the birthmarks and mode of death was available for 40 I.S. cases and 33 S.P. cases. Twenty-one (53%) previous personalities of the I.S. series and 16 (49%) of the S.P. series had died violently. In the I.S. group birthmarks were reported in 12 (30%) subjects whose claimed previous personalities had died violently and five (13%) whose previous personalities had died nonviolently. In the S.P. group, the

TABLE 4.07		
Summary of Factors Compared between I.S. and S.P. Cases		
Factors	Level of Significance	Remarks
A. DEMOGRAPHIC CHARACTERISTICS OF PERSONS CONCERNED		
Sex Distribution		
Present personalities	N.S.	
Previous personalities	N.S.	
Social Status		
Present personalities	N.S.	
Previous personalities	N.S.	
Degree of social difference between Previous and Present personalities	N.S.	
Direction of social difference	N.S.	
Economic status		
Present personalities	N.S.	
Previous personalities	N.S.	
Degree of economic difference between Previous and Present personalities	N.S.	
Direction of economic difference	$p < 0.05$	More IS cases have been "demoted" in economic status.
Religion		
Present personalities	N.S.	
Previous personalities	N.S.	
Difference in religion between Previous and Present personalities	N.S.	
Population of area of residence		On both sides of the cases, most of IS's
Present personalities	$p < 0.01$	cases were from
Previous personalities	$p < 0.01$	cities. Most of SP's

TABLE 4.07 (Contd.)		
Factors	Level of Significance	Remarks
		cases came from towns and villages
Educational level of S's father	$p < 0.01$	Fathers in IS's group had, on the whole, a higher education than those of SP's cases.
B. PRINCIPAL FEATURES OF CASES		
Status of investigation of cases	$p < 0.05$	More of IS's cases were investigated thoroughly.
Other significant features of S's parents and their situations		
Attitude of S's parents toward their claims	N.S.	
Distance between S's birth-place and place of PP's residence and death	N.S.	
Period of S's principal statements about Previous life		
Age of first speaking coherent phrases	$p < 0.05$	Subject's in IS's group started talking earlier
Age of first speaking of Previous life	N.S.	
Age when memory of Previous life faded	N.S.	
Incident after which S stopped talking of PL	N.S.	
Claims fading of memories	N.S.	

TABLE 4.07 (Contd.)		
Factors	Level of Significance	Remarks
Principal contents and verified accuracy of subjects' statements		
Recall of previous name	N.S.	
Insists on being called by previous name	N.S.	
Recall of mode of death	N.S.	
Recall of other realms	N.S.	
Recall of association with present family	N.S.	
Recall of change in place/ person after death	N.S.	
Features associated with recall of Previous life		
Factors stimulating memories	N.S.	
Behavioral accompaniments of S's statements	N.S.	
Evidence of ESP	$p < 0.01$	Cases in IS's group exhibited ESP more often.
Unusual behavioral features of S	N.S.	
Adult attitude	$p < 0.05$	IS's subjects showed an adult attitude more often.
Age of persistence of behavioral features	N.S.	
Prominent characteristics of the related Previous personality (PP)		
Identification of related PP	N.S.	
Mode of death of PP	N.S.	
Verified accuracy of PP's death	N.S.	

TABLE 4.07 (Contd.)		
Factors	Level of Significance	Remarks
PP's age at death	$p<0.05$	PPs in IS's group tended to be younger at death.
Interval between PP's death and S's birth	N.S.	
Other important features of S's appearances or circumstances		
Announcing dreams	N.S.	
Birthmarks	N.S.	
Relationships and associations between families of Present and Previous personalities		
Biological	N.S.	
Marital	N.S.	
Social	N.S.	
Commercial	N.S.	
Other	N.S.	
Relationship between mode of death of PP and other features of the cases		
Unusual animosities	N.S.	
Phobias	N.S.	
Recall of previous name	N.S.	
Recall of mode of death	N.S.	
Birthmarks	N.S.	

birthmarks were reported among 12 (36%) subjects whose claimed previous personalities had died violently and three (9%) among the subjects whose previous personality had died nonviolently. In both the groups the birthmarks were reported more often among the subjects whose related previous personality had died violently.

Summary of Factors Compared between I.S. and S.P. Cases

In Table 4.07 I have summarized the findings of the comparisons between the two groups. In all, I compared 53 factors 16 concerned Demographic features and 37 concerned Principal features of the cases. The two groups did not differ significantly except on nine features four related to the Demographic features and five to the Principal features of the cases. I have offered interpretations of these differences (and similarities) in the next chapter on Discussion.

Results Obtained from the Belief in Reincarnation Questionnaire

As mentioned earlier, I had administered this questionnaire to 137 respondents. Of these, 107 (78%) expressed a belief in reincarnation. I did not ask other questions from the section about details of the belief from the respondents who did not express a belief in reincarnation. I did, however, ask them other questions concerning possible modes of life after death apart from reincarnation and about other possible events occurring after death. I allowed the respondents to omit questions about which they did not have definite beliefs or which touched on possibilities in which they did not believe.

The questionnaire itself, also as I mentioned earlier, passed through several stages of revision and enlargement. This fact, together with the variations noted in the preceding paragraph, led to the result that the number of informants for different sections, and even for different items within a section, sometimes differed considerably.

Since one of the main purposes in administering this

TABLE 4.08
Features of Belief in Reincarnation and Associated Concepts

Features	Group I		Group II		Total	
	n	%	*n*	%	*n*	%
Belief in reincarnation	71		66		137	
Present	68	95.8	39	59.1	107	78.1
Absent	3	4.2	27	40.9	30	21.9
Source of belief	46		12		58	
Family	23	50.0	3	25.0	26	44.8
Scriptures	7	15.2	2	16.7	9	15.5
Literature	2	4.3	5	41.7	7	12.1
Influential person	0	-	2	16.7	2	3.4
Personal memory	3	6.5	0	-	3	5.2
Knowledge of persons recalling previous life	8	17.4	0	-	8	13.8
Information about other persons recalling previous life	3	6.5	0	-	3	5.2
Other	0	-	0	-	0	-
Who reincarnates	67		40		107	
Everyone	49	73.1	22	55.0	71	66.4
Some persons only	16	23.9	18	45.0	34	31.8
Do not know	2	3.0	0	-	2	1.8
If "some only", who	2		6		8	
Saints or spiritually advanced	0	-	0	-	0	-
Imperfect persons	0	-	1	16.7	1	12.5
Wicked or evil persons	0	-	0	-	0	-
Who die violently	0	-	0	-	0	-
Who die young	1	50.0	0	-	1	12.5
Who leave "unfinihed business"	0	-	2	33.3	2	25.0
Who die suddenly but not violently	1	50.0	0	-	1	12.5
Anyone	0	-	3	50.0	3	37.5
Other	0	-	0	-	0	-

TABLE 4.08 (Contd.)						
	Group I		Group II		Total	
Features	*n*	%	*n*	%	*n*	%
Possibility of recalling previous life	68		40		108	
Possible	68	100.0	30	75.0	98	90.7
Not possible	0	-	8	20.0	8	7.4
Do not know	0	-	2	5.0	2	1.9
Who can recall	68		30		98	
Everyone	3	4.4	3	10.0	6	6.1
Some persons	65	95.6	27	90.0	92	93.9
Do not know	0	-	0	-	0	-
What facilitates recall	26		7		33	
Spiritual advancement	2	7.7	3	42.9	5	15.2
Imperfectness	0	-	0	-	0	-
Wickedness	0	-	0	-	0	-
Sudden death	14	53.8	0	-	14	42.4
Violent death	3	11.5	0	-	3	9.1
Unfinished business	3	11.5	0	-	3	9.1
Other factors	3	11.5	3	42.9	6	18.2
Do not know	1	3.8	1	14.3	2	6.1
Factors deciding rebirth	45		10		55	
Child's statements	41	91.1	6	60.0	47	85.5
Birthmarks	2	4.4	0	-	2	3.6
Child's behavior	1	2.2	1	10.0	2	3.6
Statements of "mediums"	1	2.2	1	10.0	2	3.6
Statements of "possessed"	0	2.2	1	10.0	1	1.8
Predictions of astrologers	0	-	1	10.0	1	1.8
Dreams	0	-	0	-	0	-
Other factors	0	-	0	-	0	-
Do not know	0	-	0	-	0	-
Time interval	68		39		107	
Same	7	10.3	6	15.4	13	12.1
Variable	49	72.1	28	71.8	77	72.6
Do not know	12	17.6	6	12.8	17	15.9

TABLE 4.08 (Contd.)

Features	Group I		Group II		Total	
	n	*%*	*n*	*%*	*n*	*%*
Possibility of sex change	68		38		106	
Possible	20	29.4	28	73.7	48	45.3
Not possible	44	64.7	7	18.4	51	48.1
Do not know	4	5.9	3	7.9	7	6.6
Why man reborn as woman	19		27		46	
Last thoughts before death	0	-	0	-	0	-
Desire during previous life to change sex	1	5.3	3	11.1	4	8.7
Reward	0	-	1	3.7	1	2.2
Punishment	8	42.1	1	3.7	9	19.6
Enrichment of experience	0	-	5	18.5	5	10.9
Only available choice	0	-	0	-	0	-
Chance	0	-	5	18.5	5	10.9
Other factors	0	-	3	11.1	3	6.5
Do not know	10	52.6	9	33.3	19	41.3
Why woman reborn as man	19		28		47	
Last thoughts before death	0	-	0	-	0	-
Desire during previous life to change sex	1	5.3	3	10.7	4	8.5
Reward	8	42.1	1	3.6	9	19.1
Punishment	0	-	0	-	0	-
Enrichment of experience	0	-	5	17.9	5	10.6
Only available choice	0	-	0	-	0	-
Chance	0	-	5	17.9	5	10.6
Other factors	0	-	3	10.7	3	6.4
Do not know	10	52.6	11	39.3	21	44.7
Possibility of change of religion	68		39		107	
Possible	64	94.1	33	84.6	97	90.6
Not possible	3	4.4	5	12.8	8	7.5
Do not know	1	1.5	1	2.6	2	1.9

TABLE 4.08 (Contd.)						
	Group I		Group II		Total	
Features	*n*	%	*n*	%	*n*	%
Possibility of change of caste/class	67		39		106	
Possible	64	95.5	32	82.1	96	90.6
Not possible	2	3.0	7	17.9	9	8.5
Do not know	1	1.5	0	-	1	0.9
Why birth in higher of caste/class	65		32		97	
Reward	46	70.8	14	43.8	60	61.9
Punishment	0	-	0	-	0	-
Enrichment of experience	1	1.5	7	21.9	8	8.2
Chance	0	-	3	9.4	3	3.1
Other factors	1	1.5	1	3.1	2	2.1
Do not know	17	26.2	7	21.9	24	24.7
Why birth in lower caste/class	65		32		97	
Reward	0	-	0	-	0	-
Punishment	46	70.8	16	50.0	62	63.9
Enrichment of experience	1	1.5	5	15.6	6	6.2
Chance	0	-	3	9.4	3	3.1
Other factors	1	1.5	1	3.1	2	2.1
Do not know	17	26.2	7	21.9	24	24.7
Why birth in same caste/class	65		32		97	
Reward or punishment	41	63.1	10	31.3	51	52.6
To work opportunities of same caste/class	1	1.5	10	31.3	11	11.3
Other factors	3	4.6	5	15.6	8	8.2
Do not know	20	30.8	7	21.9	27	27.8

questionnaire was the hope of learning about the influence that exposure to an actual case would have on the belief in reincarnation, the respondents were divided into two groups according to whether or not they had had such exposure. In the chapter on Present Study I have described how it happened that the group (Group I) of persons having personal experience of a case differed in important features (regional, socioeconomic, and educational) from the group (Group II) that had no acquaintance with actual cases. While studying the results presented in this section, the reader should keep in mind this limitation of the sample.

In Table 4.08 I have summarized the main features of various concepts associated with the belief in reincarnation as elicited by the questionnaire. I shall briefly describe each item listed in the table after its presentation. Readers not interested in the tabular presentation of the information can skip these tables and go on to the text concerning different aspects of the belief.

Concepts Associated with Belief in Reincarnation

Source of Belief

The question for this item was, "What contributed to establishing your belief in rebirth?"[14] The source of knowledge differed significantly in both the groups, namely, those who knew of a rebirth case and those who did not (Groups I and II, respectively). In Group I, 50 percent of the respondents derived their knowledge and belief regarding reincarnation from the family and 30 percent through their personal knowledge of a rebirth case, whereas in Group II, most (83%) of the respondents

14. I included this item after the initial tryout of the questionnaire on 72 persons. Hence this item was administered to 65 respondents, out of which 58 respondents who answered this question were believers in reincarnation. Of these 58 respondents, three were subjects themselves who considered that their own recollections of previous lives were responsible for establishing their belief in reincarnation.

derived their belief from their families or scriptures or other literature pertaining to reincarnation.

Thirty-five respondents had more than one answer to this question.

TABLE 4.09 Other Source of Belief		
Source of Belief	Group I n = 26	Group II n = 9
Family	2	1
Scriptures	7	2
Literature	0	3
Influential Persons	1	1
Knowing other persons recalling Previous life	12	1
Hearing about persons recalling previous life	4	1

Their belief in reincarnation derived from more than one source. Their second source of information is given in Table 4.09.

Who Reincarnates

To the question, "Do you believe that every person reincarnates?" Most (73%) of the respondents in Group I replied that they believed in reincarnation of everyone; in Group II, however, 45 percent of the respondents believed that only some persons reincarnate. Those who opted for "Some persons" were further asked who those persons are; only eight respondents answered this question. Their responses were, "Imperfect persons," "Those who die young," "Those who leave unfinished business," "Those who die suddenly but not violently," "Anyone."

Possibility of Recall of Previous Life

All those respondents who belonged to Group I, felt that it was possible that a previous life can be recalled, whereas in Group II, 20 percent of the respondents felt it was not possible[15]; another five percent of them were not sure.

Those who said that it was possible to recall a previous life felt that only certain persons can recall their previous lives.

What Facilitates Recall

"Who are those some persons who can recall their previous life?" Thirty-three respondents answered this question from Group I and seven from Group II. Most of the respondents in Group I attributed the recall to a premature or sudden death in a previous life; in Group II the recall was attributed to the spiritual advancement of the individual or to some other factors. The "other factors" included, "Who are born after a shorter interval (between the death of the presumed previous personality and the birth of the present one)," "Depends on one's memory," "Any strong impression/incident that acts as stimulant," "Those who are not rotated on a spinning wheel,"[16] "Anyone, no lawful plan," "Those who have special consciousness," "Unnatural death,", "Those who go into deep coma and cannot speak at the time of their death (in previous life)," and "Those who are more attached with money or persons."

15. This response might have been biased by the fact that most of the respondents were trainees at NIMHANS and were aware of my   research and that some cases of the rebirth type had been reported and investigated.

16. One of the measures taken by the parents of subjects of the cases to suppress their memories of previous lives.

Factors that Decide Rebirth

I introduced this question in the second revision and administered it to 56 respondents. The question was: "How do you decide that a certain person is someone else reincarnated?" Fifty-five respondents answered.

Most (91%) of the respondents in Group I attributed the decision regarding rebirth to the statements of the child who narrates the events of his previous life; in Group II, however, respondents gave other responses also, namely, "Child's behavior," "Statements of mediums," "Statements of 'Possessed' persons," and "Prediction of astrologers while casting the horoscope," etc.

Twenty-six respondents had a second choice for this question. Their responses are given in Table 4.10.

	TABLE 4.10	
	Other Choice for Factors Deciding Rebirth	
Factors	Group I n = 21	Group II n = 5
Child's statements	0	2
Birthmarks	4	0
Child's behavior	5	3
Horoscopes	1	0
Dreams	2	0
Other	9	0

"Other factors" were indicated as, "Correct recognitions by the child" (five respondents), "Markedly different behavior of the child in his family" (two respondents), "Overall evaluation of the case" and "If the child can stay with the members of his previous family without any hesitation."

Time Interval

Time interval refers to the interval between death and presumed rebirth. The respondents allowed a range for this interval. There was no fixed interval believed by most of the respondents. Seventy-two percent of them believed that it varies for every person depending upon their karma, circumstances of death, and age of death in the previous life.

Most respondents who opted for a fixed intermission between two earthly lives did not say how long it was; but Jains believe it is nine months for every individual. In the present series of my cases, there were two such cases where the previous personalities were Jains (the cases of Lakhan Singh and Manju Sharma, Appendix B, Nos. 12 and 23). In both these cases, the intermission is reported to have been nine months [17]. During verification, all the informants agreed regarding the month of birth in both the cases. In one of these cases (the case of Lakhan Singh) I checked the date of birth from the horoscope of the subject, and verified the date of death of the related previous personality from the hospital records. The intermission thus calculated came to exactly nine months. In the other case, all the informants, on both sides, agreed regarding the month of the subject's birth and that of the death of the related previous personality, respectively. This intermission was also said to have been nine months although no written records were available in support of this. One of these subjects (Lakhan Singh) lives in Uttar Pradesh and the other one (Manju Sharma) in Rajasthan. In both these cases the mothers said, "I do not know what the fixed intermission is but the subject was born exactly nine months after the related previous personality's death." As I have said earlier, this they

17. Another Jain case was studied by Stevenson (1972) where the intermission was also found to be nine months.

found out from the families of the related previous personalities after the cases had been developed.

Possibility of Change of Sex

Responses varied considerably on this question in the two groups under study. The majority (65%) of the respondents in Group I believed that it is not possible to change sex from one life to the next. Different types of responses were given. Some (mostly illiterate respondents) believed that sex can never change no matter what form (human or sub-human animal) one may get into. Some said, "After seven births sex can change;" on the other hand, 74 percent of the respondents in Group II entertained the possibility of changing sex from one life to the next freely.

Those who believed in the possibility of changing sex from one life to the next thought it was a reward for a woman to be born as a man in her next birth and punishment for a man to be born as a woman. However, one of the respondents in Group II considered that it was a promotion for a man to be born as a woman in his next birth; five of them opined that change of sex was necessary for diversity and enrichment of experience; and three of them said change of sex was due to "Other factors" that included "Natural law," "Heredity" and "Characteristics of the opposite sex in one's previous life."

In Group I, none of the respondents endorsed the idea of sex change for diversity or enrichment of experience. They attributed it to good or bad karma. It was considered as punishment for a man and reward for a woman to be born of the opposite sex in the next birth, respectively. This aspect reflects the existing belief in Indian society that women are always inferior to men. Although the status of women in India has improved considerably in the past few decades, the society by and large appears to be dominated by male members even to this day.

Possibility of Change of Religion

The question whether it was possible for one to change religion from one life to the next was answered by 107 respondents. A majority (91%) of the respondents endorsed the idea of change of religion.

In group I, 94 percent and in Group II, 85 percent of the respondents believed in the possibility of change of religion.

Possibility of Change of Class/Caste

In Group I, the majority (96%) of the respondents agreed with the possibility of change of caste or economic conditions, whereas in Group II, 18 percent of the respondents felt that it was not possible to change caste or class from one birth to the next. However, reasons attributed to this change differed in both the groups. It was believed by respondents of Group I that this change was due to one's good or bad karma in the previous life, whereas some of the respondents in Group II entertained the possibility of change due to "the need for diversity in experience."

Belief in Karma

Out of 107 respondents who believed in reincarnation, 93 percent also believed in the influence of karma on subsequent births. However, 22 percent of them expressed an opinion that, in addition, there could be some other factors, other than karma, that may influence the circumstances of the individual's next births.

To the question of whether the individual's own previous karma is responsible for his next birth or that of his parents, responses varied. More persons in Group I favored the statement that the individual's own karma was responsible for his birth

TABLE 4.11
Features of Belief in Karma and Metempsychosis

Features	Group I n	Group I %	Group II n	Group II %	Total n	Total %
Belief in karma	68		39		107	
Present	66	97.1	34	87.1	100	93.4
Absent	0	-	4	10.2	4	3.7
Do not know	2	2.9	1	2.6	3	2.8
Factors othe than karma	68		39		107	
Possible	12	17.6	12	30.8	24	22.4
Not possible	55	80.9	21	53.8	76	71.0
Do not know	1	1.5	6	15.4	7	6.5
Good karma lead to superior births	68		38		106	
Believers	67	98.5	32	84.2	99	93.4
Non-believers	0	-	4	10.5	4	3.7
Do not know	1	1.5	2	5.3	3	2.8
Bad karma lead to inferior births	68		38		106	
Believers	67	98.5	28	73.7	95	89.6
Non-believers	0	-	9	23.7	9	8.5
Do not know	1	1.5	1	2.6	2	1.9
Whose karma responsible	68		56		124	
Individual's own karma	37	54.4	18	32.1	55	44.4
His parents' karma	1	1.5	1	1.8	2	1.6
Both his own and his parents' karma	25	36.8	14	25.0	39	31.5
Other	0	-	23	41.1	23	18.5
Do not know	5	7.4	0	-	5	4.0
Possibility of birth as sub-human animal	68		55		123	
Possible	63	92.7	28	50.9	91	74.0
Not possible	2	2.9	26	47.3	28	22.8
Do not know	3	4.4	1	1.8	4	3.2

TABLE 4.11 (Contd.)						
	Group I		Group II		Total	
Features	*n*	%	*n*	%	*n*	%
Birth in different forms for working out one's karma	67		32		99	
Believers	61	91.0	28	87.5	89	89.9
Non-believers	1	1.5	4	12.5	5	5.0
Do not know	5	7.5	0	-	5	5.0

compared to Group II.[18]

All those persons who believed in the influence of karma also agreed with the statement that one keeps taking births in upper or lower forms in order to work out his previous karma. These features are summarized in Table 4.11.

Belief in Metempsychosis

The question of whether a human being could be reborn as a sub-human animal or as a plant was answered by 123 respondents. Most (93%) of the respondents in Group I agreed that it was possible, whereas in Group II, 47 percent of them disagreed with this possibility (see Table 4.11).

All those informants who believed in metempsychosis linked it with the individual's own karma in a previous life.

Birth in Intermediate States

The belief concerning the possibility of birth of human beings

18. In addition, in Group II, 41 percent of the respondents also opted for "other factors" responsible for one's subsequent births, as against none in Group I. These were the respondents who did not believe in rebirth and said that "biological reasons" were responsible for one's birth, or it was due to "chance" that one is born to his parents.

in mythological forms such as Sura or Deva or non-godly forms existed more in Group I (78%) than in Group II (34%). All those who entertained this possibility attributed it to one's good or bad karma.

The belief in the existence of heaven or hell was also expressed more by Group I (69%) than Group II (46%).

TABLE 4.12						
Features of Belief in Intermediate States						
	Group I		Group II		Total	
Features	*n*	%	*n*	%	*n*	%
Possibility of birth in	**68**		**53**		**121**	
mythological forms						
Possible	53	77.9	18	34.0	71	58.7
Not possible	8	11.8	34	64.1	42	34.7
Do not know	7	10.3	1	1.9	8	6.6
Belief in Heaven	**68**		**61**		**129**	
Present	47	69.1	28	45.9	75	58.1
Absent	19	27.9	32	52.2	51	39.5
Do not know	2	3.0	1	1.6	3	2.4
Belief in Hell	**68**		**62**		**130**	
Present	47	69.1	28	45.2	75	57.7
Absent	13	19.1	33	53.2	46	35.4
Do not know	8	11.8	1	1.6	9	6.9
Belief in "Day of Judgment"	**68**		**62**		**130**	
Present	5	7.4	31	50.0	36	27.7
Absent	61	89.7	31	50.0	92	70.8
Do not know	2	2.9	0	-	2	1.5

Day of Judgment

Belief in the day of judgment was more freely expressed by Group II, although there were not many Muslims or Christians, respectively, in either group.

These features have been summarized in Table 4.12.

TABLE 4.13 Purpose of Reincarnation						
Features	Group I *n*=68	%	Group II *n*=39	%	Total *N*=107	%
Self-improvement toward perfection	7	10.3	12	30.8	19	17.6
Retribution	12	17.6	6	15.4	18	16.8
To fulfill one's duties	0	-	2	5.1	2	1.9
To fulfill unsatisfied cravings	5	7.4	2	5.1	7	6.5
To complete "unfinished business" of previous life	15	22.1	4	10.2	19	17.8
Natural law	14	20.6	7	17.9	21	19.6
Do not know	15	22.1	6	15.4	22	19.6

Purpose of Reincarnation

In Group I, most of the respondents either opted for "completion of unfinished business of previous life" or "retribution of previous debts," whereas in Group II, the majority of the respondents opted for "self-improvement toward perfection." Other responses were given almost the same preference. (See Table 4.13.)

CHAPTER FIVE

Discussion

The main aim of my present investigation was to study a particular type of experience, that in which subjects, usually children but sometimes adults, claim to recall events of a previous life. The objectives set for the present study and the methodology adapted covered three major areas, namely, alternative interpretations for such claims, comparison of results with other similar studies, and the role of environment in facilitating the expression of such experiences. I have focused attention particularly on the extent to which the evidence justifies such claims. In this chapter of Discussion, therefore, I shall be giving most consideration to the various alternative interpretations available for understanding and explaining claims of remembering previous lives.

After the above-mentioned review, I shall continue the discussion with a comparison of the similarities and differences between the results obtained in my present investigation and those obtained by Stevenson. (As I have said earlier, his is the only scientific study available on the subject.) I shall argue that if the similarities in the two investigations far outnumber the differences, it is likely that the cases of both groups belong to some order of natural, that is, genuine experience. This conclusion will add value to judgments about the authenticity of the cases.

In a following section, I shall briefly mention some important similarities and differences between the cases studied in north

India and those investigated in some other parts of the world.

Throughout this investigation, I have had a continuing awareness of the probable connections between the belief in reincarnation and cases of the reincarnation type. As to whether the belief in reincarnation influences the characteristics of the cases, the present investigation can contribute little information by itself. It does, however, add to the growing body of data showing that the cases have different features in different cultures and are therefore probably influenced — in one way or several ways — by regional beliefs. The present investigation however, does contribute something substantial to the opposite type of influence, namely, the possible influence of a case on the beliefs about reincarnation held by persons acquainted with it. I shall review this important topic in one section of the Discussion.

Demographic Characteristics of the Samples Studied

Consideration of alternative interpretations of data must take account of the special features and particular limitations of the samples studied. It is necessary therefore, to repeat briefly what I have said about the samples investigated.

The cases I have investigated all came from north India or, to be more precise, from Uttar Pradesh, Delhi, Punjab, and Rajasthan. Conclusions drawn from cases in this geographic areas may not be valid for cases even in other parts of India, not to say other parts of the world. (However, respondents for the Belief in Reincarnation Questionnaire came from both north and south India. But this sample had other limitations to which I have already drawn attention in the preceding chapters.)

In my group of cases for the present investigation, the ratio of male to female subjects was 2:1. This ratio differs markedly from that found in Stevenson's group with which I have compared the present one. Stevenson had 27 male subjects and 23 female ones.

I can not offer a ready explanation for the difference in the male/female ratio of the present series. It might be thought that the difference arose from a greater readiness of parents to allow the investigation of boy subjects than of girl subjects. I had learned about one case, but the parents of the girl subject would not agree to an investigation of her case for fear of injuring the girl's chances of marriage. I encountered extremely few such rejections of the investigation and it seems unlikely that this factor alone could account for the skewed male/female ratio of subjects observed.

Stevenson (1970) observed a preponderance of male subjects in a series of Turkish cases that he studied. He attributed some of the preponderance to the higher incidence of violent death among men as compared with women. (There are no cases of the "sex change" type in Turkey.) This seemed to account for some of the imbalance in the male/female ratio of Turkish cases, but an imbalance also occurred in cases in which the subjects recalled a natural death. Violent death in related previous personalities is not the correct explanation for the biased male/female ratio of subjects in my series of cases, or at least does not contribute more than a small part of the observed difference. I can say this because the ratio of violent/natural death was only slightly higher in male previous personalities as compared to female ones.

It is possible that male lives are remembered more often than female ones simply because men lead in general more eventful lives than do women, at least in India. This factor does not explain why Stevenson did not find a biased ratio of male/female subjects in his series. In this connection, it is worth noting that the series of cases that I have studied may be more representative of cases in India than was Stevenson's series. Stevenson, at least in the early days of his investigations, first learned about cases mainly either from newspaper reports or from particular persons who knew about cases and about Stevenson's research. Later, he came to learn about less publicized cases and even about "private" cases that had received no publicity outside the families concerned. On the other hand, my series derived from preliminary information about a wide variety of cases from a wide variety of sources. This makes it possible that the series of cases that I investigated is more representative of the cases as a whole than was Stevenson's earlier series of cases.

The uneven male/female ratio of the subjects was the only obvious feature in the present study in which they seemed an unrepresentative group of the Indian population with regard to demographic features. In all other respects, they appeared to provide a small cross section of Indian society. Poor and well-to-do persons were represented in the group. So were educated persons and illiterate ones. So were villagers and city residents.

I cannot say the same for the related previous personalities of the cases. They showed an incidence of violent death of 47.5 percent, a proportion far exceeding that of the general population of India in which the incidence of violent death is 6.7 percent.[19] Apart from this feature, however, the related previous personalities also seemed to derive from a fairly representative group of the general population in India.

Interpretation of the Cases

Although the cases that I have included in the present analysis have not all been investigated thoroughly, still, they are representative of such cases and present a wide range of features

19. Office of the Registrar General, *Vital Statistics of India 1970* (New Delhi: Registrar General, India [Vital Statistics Division], Ministry of Home Affairs, 1973), pp. 121-159. (Data derived from available surveys in Andhra; Bombay; Goa, Daman, and Diu; Haryana; Mysore; Nagpur; and Rajasthan.)

manifested by them. They illustrate how difficult it is to differentiate this behavior from fantasies, fraud, and other normal and paranormal processes by which a child may obtain information and make such claims.

Stevenson (1966/1974b) has provided an extensive review of the main alternative interpretations of these cases which I shall consider in the present Discussion. I shall first make some reference to the general principles adopted in considering the applicability of a hypothesis to the cases in general; then present the relevance of this hypothesis to the cases of the present investigation with reference to relevant examples from the case material. I have cited the cases by their names or case numbers, or both. However, in keeping with the wish of some informants, I have used only their initials or pseudonyms in certain cases and have indicated at places where I have done this.

Normal Interpretations

Fantasy

Most uninformed critics attribute claims of remembering a previous life to childhood fantasies. This might have been an appropriate hypothesis for such behavior if the claims of these subjects were not verifiable. In 84 percent of the cases I investigated, statements made by the subjects were verified and their respective previous personalities were identified. One can certainly raise questions about how the child acquired the information he had about the deceased person whose life he claimed to remember, and I shall devote much of the later discussion of this chapter to this important question. It is certain, however, that the great majority of the subjects were talking about real persons who had lived and died. The claim to have been that person in a previous life may be wrong, and in that sense the child may be engaging in fantasy; but his numerous correct statements and corresponding behavior cannot be regarded as mere fantasies because they accord with an established reality.

Under this heading, I should also mention of a rather commonly made allegation about the subjects of these cases. This is the suggestion that they are mentally ill and that their claims to remember previous lives are, in effect, psychotic delusions. This suggestion might be a plausible interpretation of such claims if the children who report such experiences had shown other features of behavior disorders or abnormalities. There are very few reports of psychosis of any kind among children. Children do identify themselves with adults in their own family, or outside the family if their emotional needs are not met at home. This identification usually occurs during play and over a shorter period of time. Except for cases of the rebirth type, there have been only a few reports of children claiming continuous identity with a deceased person.

Claims of rebirth or false identification with other persons have been reported more often in adult psychiatric patients. In a psychotic breakdown, the patient sometimes falsely identifies himself with another person or persons — living or dead. During the present investigation a case of this type was referred to me from the psychiatric outpatient department, details of which I have summarized under "Summarized Case Reports." (See Chapter Four, Case Reports.)

This case differed from the typical rebirth case in some respects. First, the subjects of rebirth cases are usually very young when they narrate their experiences of a previous life. The patient in this case had started talking of a previous life at the age of 30 years. Second, the life and other events of the claimed previous personality with whom the subjects identify themselves have been actually verified and found true in most of the rebirth cases. In the psychiatric patient, the information given by him was normally available in the family. The persons whom he mentioned as related to him in his previous life were actually his relatives in the present life. Some were still living. His time concept also appeared to have been disturbed. Third, the subjects of rebirth cases, although their memories may more or less excite them, rarely show any important emotional disturbance; in contrast, this patient showed abundant evidence of serious psychopathology. (For a more detailed report of this case, see Pasricha, Murthy, and Murthy, 1978.)

There are still other reasons for not regarding these cases as mere fantasies or delusions and these reasons deserve some brief review here. First, the subjects of these cases started talking about a previous life between the ages of two and four. Children at this age are said to be highly imaginative and to indulge in fantasies of putting themselves in a different situation in order to avoid stressful situations in their immediate environment. Studies have revealed that children under such circumstances usually identify themselves with their parents or older siblings (Bandura, Ross and Ross, 1963; Mischel and Liebert, 1966; Rosenhan, Frederick, and Burrowes, 1968). If for some reason they fail to do so, they identify themselves with other known living persons who could be emotionally more supportive to them. Contrary to this, the children of rebirth cases have invariably identified themselves with deceased persons.

Second, for most of the subjects no motive for imagining a previous life could be found. It is generally agreed that when children identify themselves with other persons, they do so because they thereby acquire some additional strength or prestige, which is reassuring to them, even if imaginary. This motive may be attributed to cases of the reincarnation type in which the subject is born in a poor family and claims to remember a previous life as a rich person. I certainly had subjects of this type in the present series of cases. For example, Bachan Singh (Case No. 2) was born in a family of appalling poverty who lived in a squalid hovel; he remembered the previous life of a prosperous Thakur. An even more striking example is the case of Lakhan Singh (Case No.12). He was the son of a Thakur, a villager of modest means; he remembered the previous life of a prosperous Jain lawyer and businessman who was wealthy enough to be a noted philanthropist of his community. But these cases and similar ones accounted for less than half the cases of the present study. Many subjects remember the previous lives of persons who had the same economic (and social) status as their own, or a lower one.

In fact, 51 percent of the subjects of the cases I investigated had the same economic status as their claimed previous personalities, or a better one. In other words, the claimed previous personalities were no richer or actually poorer than the subjects themselves were. It is unlikely therefore that such children have indulged in fantasies in order to imagine a change in their material environments.

Fraud

Like the other cases of paranormal claims, fraudulent cases of the reincarnation type are also found occasionally. In the present series of cases, only one such case was identified. This was the case of Mahesh Shakya (see Chapter Four, Case Report 5).

In order to say that a case is a hoax, one should look for some kind of motivation, either on the part of the subject or on that of his parents. As the subjects of these cases are usually very young (so they are reported) at the time of their first utterances regarding the previous life, it seems most unlikely that they themselves could have obtained all the required information about the deceased person with whom they identify themselves. A more probable party to indulge in such a hoax would possibly be one or other of the subject's parents who would collect all the needed information about a deceased person and coach the child to enact the "character" perfectly, so much so that the relatives of the deceased person become impressed sufficiently to accept the child as "that person" reborn. Even if we suppose that parents are clever enough to extract all the required information and supply it to the child, it appears highly improbable that a child of two or three years of age could act it out perfectly. Granting that, the question arises, why would they do all that? A possible explanation is that it satisfies them, both monetarily and psychologically.

Now, about monetary gains, I have pointed out earlier that a large number of subjects enjoy a better socioeconomic status than the related previous personalities, and those who do not might be thought of as indulging in a risky practice. It is risky because higher class people in general are more careful with such matters and test the child and his families in all possible ways before they really accept the claims of such a child. In situations where the parents may somehow succeed in impressing the family members of the claimed previous personality, the child may not stand the tough test because a successful hoax needs more than just knowledge about a person; the whole story also needs to be presented in a perfect way. The tutored child may break down and reveal that his parents coached him.[20] Even if he does not confess, his performance may remain deficient in

20. In the case of Mahesh Shakya cited above, according to one informant, when a member of Parmeshwar Tiwari's family asked him why he was enacting this drama and who had taught him to do this, Mahesh started crying and said, "My father."   Another example of a child (a Tibetan claimant to be a reborn Lama) who was exposed as a fraud has been cited by Norbu and Turnbull (1969).

important respects. It is not enough for him to have knowledge (information) about the previous personality. He must also be able to show appropriate behavior corresponding to that of the person whose life he claims to remember. The subjects are often reported to show such behavior, unusual in their own families, and are said to show strong emotion, such as weeping, when they narrate events of the previous lives or meet members of the previous families. I myself have observed a few of these expressions of emotions and unusual behavior. It is true, however, that in most instances I had to depend on the reports of the informants for knowledge of them. So a critic might say that parents preparing a hoax would naturally add reports of appropriate emotions and other behavior that they say the child has shown. This they could do and may. But quite often the family of the previous personality has also told me about unusual behavior and strong emotions shown by the subject. It is most unlikely that they would falsely report and support such behavior. It seems impossible that a small child can be trained to show such behavior and at just the right moment with the right people.

Let us assume, however, that a subject's parents, and the subject himself, have the motive of obtaining financial gain from the family of which the child says he was a member in his claimed previous life. What are the tangible results for the subject and his family? I have become quite well acquainted with many perhaps most of the families concerned in these cases by reason of having had, with most of them, two or more interviews. I have thus been in a position to know to what extent the subject has received gifts from the family of the related previous personality of a case. If gifts or money had been solicited by the subject or his parents, the members of the previous personality's family would almost certainly have told me about this. No instance came to my attention of a subject or his parents making a request for gifts from a family of a related previous personality. These families sometimes do offer gifts to the child, and in a few instances the gifts may be rather substantial for the means of the subject's family. For example, the prosperous Jain family in which Lakhan Singh claimed to have lived his previous life have given him many gifts of clothes. This has no doubt been helpful to Lakhan Singh's parents. But this case is exceptional. No other cases came to my notice in which such substantial gifts have been given to the subject. In most cases, the related previous family gives a few rupees or some other minor gift, or nothing at all to the child. (I had asked systematic questions about gifts to the informants in 13 cases; it was reported to me that some gifts had been given to the subject by eight of the previous families concerned.)

It may be said that monetary gains are not the only possible motive for contriving a case. Perhaps the gain from a hoax could come from having in the family the reincarnation of some well-known person such as a *Seth* (a wealthy person), a saint, or a great political leader. Association with the family of such a person might bring some publicity to the parents of the subject, or to the subject, or to both. But this again involves a lot of tricks and trouble in gathering the necessary information. In most of the cases, the claimed previous personalities had died under unusual circumstances, if not violently. Why would parents want their children to be identified with such persons? In quite a few cases, murder had been involved and the parents of the subjects had tried to hide their children from public knowledge for fear of another scuffle, which is definitely more a nuisance than an enjoyable experience. In three cases (the cases of Bachan Singh, Ajai Chaudhri, and Mihi Lal Yadav) of the present study, the claimed previous personalities were criminals or debauchees; in one (Case No. 42, the case of Brijesh) probably mentally defective, and in another (Case No. 16, the case of Pramod Sharma) probably an epileptic. These are not the types of persons with whom one would wish to identify publicly. But most of the related previous personalities were not famous or notorious; they were just ordinary people having no special renown, good or bad. Identification with them would confer absolutely no distinction on a subject.

Still another motive for contriving a false case could be the wish for the attention and celebrity that could come from being the subject of a case, or (for the parents) from having a case in the family. There is no doubt that a small number of subjects of cases have become well known as subjects in their own communities and even all over India. The case of Shanti Devi, although it developed in the 1930s, is still famous and often cited all over the world (Gupta, Sharma, and Mathur, 1936; Ducasse, 1961).

A few subjects have made careers, one might say, out of being subjects. (But these are mostly child prodigies who claim to remember scriptures that they learned in a previous life.) But no development of these kinds occurred among the subjects of the present study. Of the 45 cases I have investigated, only nine were reported in newspapers or magazines. These and a few other subjects thus received some attention and some visitors who would otherwise not have come to them. All 45 obviously received visits from us. But this attention, which amounted to little in the first place, quickly subsided and the child and his family were left in the condition of obscurity they were in before. Moreover, reports in newspapers and selection for investigation are rather chancy matters. No one contriving a case would feel confident that the case could be published or would be selected for investigation. If a subject or his parents had invented a case to obtain its fame, one should expect that they would be the persons who would bring the case to the attention of newspapermen and investigators. In the present series, nine cases were reported in the newspapers; but I do not have full information about who inserted these reports. Let us assume, however, that the subject's family did this. In addition, members of the subject's family were the initial informants for five other cases. This makes a total of 14 out of 45 cases in which the subject's family may be assumed to have initiated some outside attention or is known to have done so. For the remaining 31 cases, there was no evidence whatever that the subject's family had sought to bring the case to the attention of people outside the family. My informants for such cases were other persons who had heard of the case by one means or another and who knew of our research; so they furnished us (Dr. Stevenson in many cases) with the preliminary information that eventually led to the investigation. It may be added also that if the subjects' families were expecting attention from an investigation, they often had to wait months or years before receiving any.

By putting forth the above arguments, I do not mean to assert more than that the evidence for fraud was found in only one case (up to the time of submission of my thesis in 1978)[21]; I might have missed evidence of it in other cases. If a fraudulent case is undetected, it may count as an authentic one, and I would not know that I had been taken in. However, on the basis of the information available, I had found no other evidence of fraud and could detect no obvious motive for it in other cases. It can also be said that, with the most insignificant exceptions, there was no suggestion that the subjects or their families had gained from the development of the case. I have argued in the preceding discussion that it would be extremely difficult to train a child for

21. Subsequently we have investigated and reported some more cases of deception and self-deception (Stevenson and Pasricha, 1988).

the successful dramatization of a fraudulent case considering the time and trouble this would involve, and the scanty results if it has ever succeeded. One cannot help remarking that hoaxing a case of the rebirth type must be one of the least profitable ways of acting dishonestly. There are far too many more lucrative and easier ways of gaining from dishonesty. This sort of claim is an unlikely choice for someone willing to cheat his fellowmen.

Genetic or Inherited Memory

Apart from the hypotheses I have discussed above, several other normal hypotheses have been suggested by various critics. One of these is that of "inherited memory." This attributes the claimed memories of the previous life of a child to memories acquired through genetic transmission. This hypothesis can be offered for cases when the subject might be a lineal descendant of the claimed previous personality. For example, Sai Baba of Shirdi is said to have been a reincarnation of Kabir (Osborne, 1975). Because of the long interval between their lives, Sai Baba of Shirdi could, in principle, have been a descendant of Kabir.

But this hypothesis does not seem to be appropriate for most of the cases in the present group of investigations. First, in 88 percent of the cases the two families concerned lived far apart from each other; the subjects of my cases were usually born within a few years (three to five years) of the death of the concerned previous personalities and were not even biologically related to them. Therefore, they could not possibly have descended from the claimed previous personalities. Second, 67 percent of the subjects of the cases recalled the mode of their death in the previous life. Certainly this knowledge could not have been passed to them through genetic memory, since the presumed ancestor of the subject would have been born before, perhaps many years before, the death of the previous personality of the subject.

Among the cases of the present study, five subjects: Prem Chander Gupta, Sonu Pachauri, Shilpa Mehta, Neena Tiwari, and Sanjiv Sharma (Cases No. 7, 18, 21, 28, and 36) were lineal descendants of the persons whose lives they claimed to remember. Of these, two remembered details of the death of the previous personality and these details could not have been conveyed in genetic material. In the other three cases, some "inherited memory" remains a possible explanation for the subjects' correct statements and perhaps also for associated behavior corresponding to that of the previous personality. (Cases in which subject and previous personality belong to the same family are anyway weak evidentially; normal transmission of information to the subject seems a more likely explanation for such cases than "inherited memory.") In the remaining 40 cases, "inherited memory" can be firmly excluded as an explanation. In fact, this hypothesis can be set aside more firmly for these cases than can any other hypothesis.

Cryptomnesia

In cases of cryptomnesia, a "buried memory" erupts into consciousness without the person who experiences this being aware that he has acquired the information normally. Cryptomnesia is an unconscious process. The person may acquire the knowledge through normal means, such as from reading, hearing, or watching a movie. He may later completely forget about his exposure to the information and when it later comes into his consciousness again, he may mistake it for a memory of something that he has lived through himself. Such a person is not being dishonest;

cryptomnesia happens by a simple process of forgetfulness, and should not be confused with pretended forgetfulness. He may or may not be surprised, or have a sense of vague familiarity, when the hidden memories come into his consciousness.

The hypothesis of cryptomnesia supposes that the knowledge the child shows concerning the details about the previous life has reached him through normal means. Since the parents are unaware of the claimed previous personality, the knowledge acquired by the child naturally comes through an outsider without his parents knowing about it. This possibility seems rather unlikely in most cases. Most Indian children (at least in villages) are looked after by their mothers or by their grandmothers (if mothers are working); such children have almost no independent exposure to strangers. Even if they do have some exposure to a stranger, it seems unlikely that this alone would suffice to account for all the knowledge many of these children show about the previous life. The utterances about the previous life almost always first occur at about the time when the child acquires some power of speech; and sometimes he shows his unusual behavior through gestures even earlier.

Most of the children make their first statements about the previous life between the ages of two and three. They not only make correct statements; but also display appropriate emotions.[22] It seems most unlikely that a young child could demonstrate emotions and behavior appropriate for a deceased person solely on the basis of knowledge he has acquired through a stranger who was seen perhaps years before and apparently forgotten.

A type of cryptomnesia may occur in which the parents are the principal actors rather than the subject directly. It may happen

22. Sixty-seven percent of the subjects of my present study displayed extreme and moderate emotions while narrating events of the previous life or on meeting persons figuring in it.

that they know more about the previous personality and talk more about him in the presence of the subject than they realize at the time or remember afterward. Then they may express genuine surprise when, later, the child claims that he was in his previous life the person about whom the parents talked. This type of cryptomnesia is especially likely to occur in cases in which the child claims to have been reborn in the same family. In my series, five of the subjects belonged to the families of the related previous personalities of their cases. Among these subjects, Sonu Pachauri (Case No.18) and Sanjiv Sharma (Case No.36) are particularly relevant examples. The concerned previous personalities in these cases lived and died in the subject's immediate family. They were mourned and naturally talked about, almost certainly in the presence of the subjects.

The literature of parapsychology contains a few reports of cases that appeared at first to include paranormal processes, but which on further examination turned out to be instances of cryptomnesia. Some instances have occurred among mediums. They have been known to claim that they received information from a discarnate spirit; but later it was found that they had acquired the communicated information in a normal way. The information communicated may derive from books or other printed sources, and oral statements by other persons. (This is not necessarily a dishonest process; the medium may have quite forgotten that she had been exposed earlier to the source that furnished the communicated information.)[23]

There is one relevant difference between the known cases of cryptomnesia and the typical case of the reincarnation type. Cryptomnesia seems most apt to manifest in altered states of

23. For a review of instances of proven cryptomnesia in the field of parapsychology, see Stevenson (1980, 1983a).

consciousness such as during hypnosis and mediumistic trances. But the subjects of rebirth cases are nearly always in a normal state of consciousness when they make their statement about the previous life.

Still another difference lies in the amount of detail conveyed in cases of cryptomnesia compared with cases of the reincarnation type. The children subjects of the latter type of case often state numerous details about the previous lives they claim to remember; communications derived in a process of cryptomnesia tend to be short and lacking in detail.

There is one further objection to the hypothesis of cryptomnesia. Even in those cases in which a normal transmission of information to the subject may have occurred, this does not by itself account for the important emotional and other behavioral features so often manifested by the subjects. How can information about someone whom the child has never seen enable him to reproduce that person's characteristic behavior and emotions? And yet just this sort of reproduction is reported for many of the subjects of these cases.

Paramnesia

Paramnesia is a disorder of memory that denotes false recollections. A person suffering from paramnesia (the subject of a rebirth case in the present context) relates with conviction and circumstantiality events that occurred, and claims that he personally experienced them when he did not. In this variety of paramnesia the subject, on seeing a particular place or person for the first time, has a feeling of familiarity with it or him; he thinks that he (or she) has been to this place before, or has seen or met the person before. This phenomenon is technically known as *deja vu*. One of the characteristics of *deja vu* is that a person finds strange places and persons familiar. In order to fulfill this criterion, the subjects of these cases have to be in a new place and meet unknown persons before they claim that they know them or have visited these places or have lived there. But this hypothesis does not cover a large number of the cases I have reported here, since in 94 percent of them the subjects are said to have made statements *before* visiting the places and 75 percent of them before meeting the persons connected with the previous personality. The subjects' memories were stimulated by a meeting with a person known to the previous personality in 25 percent of cases; and a visit to a place with which the previous personality was familiar stimulated memories only in six percent of cases.

Paramnesia may occur in a different way to the parents of a subject and other adult informants for a case. In this type of paramnesia, the informants forget exactly what the subject or someone else said and distort or embellish it with thoughts of their own. Thus it may happen that the two families concerned in a case may, when they meet, mingle their memories of what the child said with the facts about the previous personality's life. Later, both groups of informants may credit the child with more correct information about the previous personality than he actually showed before the families had met.[24] This sort of paramnesia is especially likely to occur when both families enthusiastically endorse the subject's claims; his parents because they are proud to have a subject in the family, the previous personality's family because they welcome the subject as their deceased member returned. It may also occur even in cases in which the observers are more or less detached. Mere passage of time, as well as

24. In the series of cases Stevenson has investigated, it was found in 25 cases (in different countries) that some written statements were made before the verifications were attempted or before the two families concerned had met. The objection here discussed cannot apply to such cases, but they are still rare.

biases, may lead to subtle but important modifications in the reports of events.

Paramnesia on the part of the parents may occur in cases in which the child makes very few statements. It does not, however, seem a probable explanation for other cases in which the child made numerous statements.[25] (In one of the cases [Case No. 10.] of the present series, the subject, Nasaruddin Shah made no fewer than 44 statements.)

The hypothesis of paramnesia does not seem to account adequately for cases in which the subjects have communicated numerous and specific details concerning their previous lives. If it is applied to such cases, it implies a greater fallibility of memory than most persons show. Memories are defective, but they are sometimes remarkably accurate. It must be noted that the subject usually makes the same statements about the previous life over and over again. And he may show the same unusual behavior related to the previous life over several or many years. Such repetitions tend to fix the memories of what the child has said and done in the minds of those who have observed him and later report his behavior to the investigators.

Perhaps the most important argument opposing the hypothesis of paramnesia (and, for that matter, other hypothesis of normal communication) is now developing from the analysis of the recurrent features of large numbers of these cases. It is certain that some of the informants have heard of other cases apart from the one for which they are supplying information; it is also certain that the majority of informants have *not* heard of other

25. The present group of subjects showed a range between four and 44 in the number of statements they made about the previous life. The average number of statements was 14. In all cases, the statements were sufficiently numerous and adequately specific so that the subject's parents could identify the person about whom the subject was talking.

cases. They have therefore no basis whatever for imagining a model case to which they might try to make the case they know about conform. If they lack such a model, however, how is it that many cases show the same features so often?

I have already presented examples of such recurrent features in the preceding chapter on Results. It will be helpful, however, to mention again here just a few of the features that have occurred numerous times in these cases. These include: the age of the subject's first speaking about the previous life between two and four years; the subject's age when he stopped speaking spontaneously about the previous life (on the average at about seven years); the high incidence of violent death in related previous personalities of the cases, far higher than the incidence of violent death in the general population of India; and the frequent mention in the child's statements of the mode of death of the previous personality. These features and numerous others occurred not only in the cases of my series, but with equal, or almost equal frequency in the different series investigated by Stevenson. (I shall discuss the few differences in the results obtained by myself and by Stevenson in a later, separate section of this chapter.)

How can the similarities in widely separated cases be accounted for if it is presumed that the informants have deceived themselves about what actually happened in the cases? Why would all these independent informants make the same errors in telling about different cases? It seems to make more sense to believe that, although the informants certainly do make mistakes in details, they are, in the main, describing the events of a case that really occurred as they say reported them.

The foregoing hypotheses all suppose either that the case is a pure fantasy and consists of nothing worth further study, or that in one way or another, the subject has acquired information about the life he claims to remember by normal means of communication. It has been seen, however, that such hypotheses, although they may account for certain individual cases, and perhaps even for an appreciable number of them, fail to account adequately for the majority of cases. For the interpretation of most cases, acceptance and consideration of paranormal processes is required in order to understand all their aspects. I shall therefore, discuss in the further sections of this chapter hypotheses that include paranormal processes.

Paranormal Interpretations

Extrasensory Perception and Personation

So far, I have considered the hypotheses of normal means of communication of information about the previous personality, to the child or his parents. As I have pointed out earlier, these normal hypotheses may explain the behavior of a few subjects when the two families concerned have already met or knew each other before the development of the case. These hypotheses (of normal channels of communication) do not apply to the large number of rebirth cases in which the two families concerned are widely separated—both genealogically and geographically.

One alternative hypothesis offered to explain these claims under such circumstances of no known normal contact between the families concerned is that of extrasensory perception. This hypothesis presumes that when the subjects do not have normal access to information about a deceased person, they obtain it through extrasensory perception. The main sources of information about the deceased person are his surviving relatives and friends. With the help of the information thus received, the child constructs a new personality that he incorporates into his own and then claims that he himself is that particular deceased person reborn.

This hypothesis supposes that the subject derives his information telepathically or clairvoyantly, or both. Since extrasensory perception appears to transcend all limits of time and space, the subject of a rebirth case is said to slide information back on the time-scale; that is, he attributes the happenings of these events to himself in the past.[26] When the environment in which these claims are reported promotes the belief in rebirth, the claims are accepted as memories of the previous life. Evidence of telepathy has been reported by Schwarz (1961) among young children. Such communications have mostly been with a child's parents and rarely with anyone outside the family, such as seems to occur in cases of the rebirth type.

This hypothesis might explain the informational aspects of those cases in which, although the two families concerned live far away from each other, their members might have had social or commercial relations in each other's area of residence. It supposes that persons known to the deceased, or coming from his area, act as "carriers" (paranormally) of information to the subjects. Technically such persons are known as "psychometric agents." The subjects are said to pick up information from them paranormally (Hill, 1917; Osty, 1923). According to the theory of "psychometric objects" information may be transmitted paranormally if the subject comes into contact with someone having the information (even though they do not speak) or even if he merely handles an object that the person having the information has previously handled.

In the present series of cases, information on connections of the subject's parents to the area of the previous personality was available for 42 cases. In 12 cases, both the families concerned

26. In cases of attested retrocognition, the subject reports that he has seen such and such a thing happening to someone or describes events in someone's life, but he does not confuse events that have happened to other persons with those that have happened to himself (Heywood, 1971).

lived in the same general area (out of this group, five subjects were biologically related to the claimed previous personalities); in 19 cases they had visited the area where the related previous personality lived, but had not met his (or her) family. In 11 cases, they had no commercial or visiting connections in each other's place of residence.

In 57 percent of the cases, the subject's parents had some social relations in the area of the previous personality's residence. They themselves might not have visited the area, but their relatives might sometimes have visited the other family.

The hypothesis of extrasensory perception does not, however, require that the subject has had some contact with the concerned previous family or with an object that a member of that family might have handled. In its more extreme form, known as the "super-extrasensory perception hypothesis," it assumes limitless powers of extrasensory perception on the part of the subject. He is credited with an ability to reach paranormally any physical distance, or to go back for any length of time, in order to gather information that he then includes in the claimed "previous life." It is further supposed that, given these vast paranormal powers, a wish to identify with a deceased person may then, in a culture favorable to the belief in reincarnation, lead to the development of pseudo-memories that appear to justify a claim by the subject that he remembers a previous life. (These processes would occur outside the subject's awareness and without any intention on his part to deceive; according to the hypothesis he would be deceived himself, but would not mean to deceive anyone else, as would the perpetrator of a hoax.)

This hypothesis has a certain appeal, but it also has serious deficiencies when all aspects of the best cases are considered. For example: Why should a child derive information from living persons and identify himself with a dead person whom he has never seen or heard about? In order to do so, he would have to establish telepathic contacts with a person or a number or persons who have some knowledge about the deceased person in question. The subject would have to organize the information thus gathered in bits and pieces from different sources and then construct a personality that closely matches that of the deceased person with whom the subject identifies himself. But supposing that such a selective identification with a deceased person occurs, why does a subject with such remarkable powers of extrasensory perception exhibit this ability only in relation to one particular deceased person? (Except in three cases namely, Manju Sharma of District Mathura, Ghansi, and Anoop Singh, all the parents of the subjects, when I questioned on the matter, said that the subjects show no evidence of extrasensory perception outside the claim to remember a previous life of one particular person.)[27] And they also pick up the information related to the deceased person only *up to the time of his death.* They know nothing of events happening after this person's death or of events unrelated to him. Why do the subjects exhibit such a restricted range of extrasensory perception?

There have been suggestions that the process of deriving information in persons who claim to recall a previous life is similar to the one by which mediums and sensitives derive their information about the living or the dead. It is worth pointing out here that the process of deriving information differs between mediums or sensitives on the one hand, and subjects of rebirth cases on the other hand.

27. In a small number of cases, subjects claim to remember two and occasionally more previous lives. For purposes of this discussion such cases can be ignored. However, in these cases also the subject is identifying with deceased persons, not demonstrating paranormal powers in relation to living ones with whom he identifies.

In order to get information, mediums usually need some sitters, or at least an object, related to the previous person about whom information is sought. The subjects of rebirth cases usually do not need any such assistance, although occasionally their memories have been stimulated by meeting members of the previous personality's family or friends, or by visiting a place familiar to him. Among the subjects of the present sample of cases, in 25 percent the memories of the previous life were stimulated by meeting persons related to the claimed previous personality and in six percent by visiting places where the related previous personality had lived or which were of some importance to him.

Another differentiating feature is that mediums almost always withdraw their attention from the environment and give information only under special circumstances. It has been reported that the whole process is quite demanding and fatiguing for most mediums, which is why most of them do not have many sitters at one time, or engage in frequent sittings. On the other hand, subjects of rebirth cases do not seem to make any conscious effort to obtain the information they demonstrate; it just comes to them like memories of normal events. Except in the cases of Anjali Sood, and Ranjana Tiwari (Cases No. 8 and 40) there was no suggestion of an altered state of consciousness in the subjects during their recalls of previous lives. Also, in most of the subjects who claim to recall previous lives, the process of remembering does not seem to tax them or to interfere with their day-to-day life. (The events remembered may evoke emotion, but that is a separate matter.)

There have been studies on the range of extrasensory perception shown by sensitives and mediums. It was found that some of them have had extraordinary power of obtaining information paranormally without the help of any psychometric agent. Claims to remember a previous life may be attributed to such supernormal powers of deriving information on the part of the subjects. But the cases differ in other aspects. In the present series of my cases, only three subjects have given some evidence of extrasensory perception in addition to their claims to remember of a previous life (the cases of Manju Sharma, Ghansi, and Anoop Singh). Those mediums who have shown extraordinary powers of perception have been able to demonstrate their capacity repeatedly and with a number of persons, certainly with more than a single person (Besterman, 1933). An exceptional case in this regard has been reported by Pratt (1973). In this case, the subject showed a marked degree of extrasensory perception, but only in a particular, restricted situation. Such restricted manifestation of paranormal powers if this is the correct explanation for the present cases occurs as a rule among the subjects considered here.

The hypothesis of extrasensory perception (ordinary or super) also does not explain why and how these children show unusual behavior similar to that of the deceased persons with whom they identify themselves. Behavioral features of this type have been found (quite often) to be peculiar in the subject's family and yet they correspond to the behavior of the person whose life the child claims to remember (see Table 4.03). Stevenson (1980) considered this unusual behavior a type of skill unique for each individual. It has been argued (Ducasse, 1962; Polanyi, 1962; Stevenson, 1974a) that skills cannot be communicated normally or paranormally. One may learn some information about a skill from other persons, but to demonstrate it one has to practice it. It is conjecturable therefore that unusual behavior shown by a subject may have been learned in some previous incarnation. (Here I mean only unusual behavior the child could not have learned since its birth.)

This hypothesis also cannot account for the occurrence, in some cases, of birthmarks and deformities on the body of the subject that are similar to wounds or other marks on the body of the deceased person concerned. In the present group of cases, I inquired about the occurrence of birthmarks in 38 cases. Out of this group, 42 percent of the subjects had one to five birthmarks similar to marks, usually wounds that were found on the body of the deceased person with whom the subject identified himself. The birthmarks usually corresponded to fatal wounds on the concerned previous personality; occasionally they were related to other wounds or marks.

Finally, this hypothesis also does not adequately explain those cases where the environment does not favor the belief in reincarnation and hence a claim to remember a previous life. In such environments, parents are rather unsympathetic and hostile (for religious, personal, or cultural reasons) toward such claims. Cases have been reported in countries where the idea of reincarnation is viewed with contempt or rejected completely.[28] In the present series of cases, only four mothers were reported to have encouraged their children to talk about the previous lives. Twenty-three were indifferent or more or less tolerant toward the claims of their children. Ten of the mothers were quite severe with their children as to these memories, and took some violent measures to suppress their memories of previous lives. Two other subjects of the cases were orthodox Muslims

28. In the collection of cases (1982) at the Division of Parapsychology, University of Virginia, rebirth cases have been reported in the following regions: Asia, 1165; Europe, 253; Central and South America, 22; Africa, 49; Australia and New Zealand, 15; North America, 420 (Native American, 108; Non-native American, 232). These figures represent the cases in countries where the belief in reincarnation is endorsed and also the countries where the belief does not exist or exists only in minority.

whose families did not believe in rebirth and who were rather unsympathetic toward the subjects' claims to remember previous lives; yet the behavioral features of these subjects persisted until the age they usually do in cases where the claims are accepted by the families.

Possession

If it seems reasonable to set aside the interpretations of normal and extrasensory perception for the acquisition of information by the subject regarding a deceased person whose life he claims to remember, there still remains another interpretation that may reasonably account for such claims. This is the hypothesis of possession. It supposes that the body of a person is occupied or possessed (at any stage of life) by a discarnate personality (or spirit) whether devilish, divine, or merely human radically different from his own. Possession implies either a partial influence with the primary personality retaining some control of the physical body (Hyslop, 1909) or a temporary but complete control of the physical body with later return of the original personality (Stevens, 1887; James, 1890).

Cases of possession may present a picture similar to that of cases of the reincarnation type. The distinction may be made on the basis of the relation between the date of death of the previous personality and the date of the subject's birth. When the previous personality dies *after* the subject's birth, the case may be spoken of as one of possession. If the previous personality concerned died before the subject's birth (or conception) the case would be considered one of the reincarnation type.

The hypothesis of possession accommodates better some of the features of the cases that are not well explained by the extrasensory perception hypothesis. These are the theoretical need for "psychometric agents" and the need to explain the occurrence of definite skills in the subjects that correspond to skills the related previous personality had.

Some of the claims of these children can be explained by the possession hypothesis even when the ostensibly possessing personality died *before* the birth of the subject. The hypothesis certainly explains the apparent continuity in personality between subject and related deceased person in these cases. But even so, the hypothesis of possession fails to explain many other features shown by these children.

First, when the children usually begin to give brief statements about a previous life, their remarks are often stimulated by events that strike them as either closely similar to those of the remembered previous life or markedly different. For example, the subjects Prem Chander Gupta, Rakesh Gaur, and Anoop Singh (Cases No. 7, 37, and 45) started narrating their experiences when they were in a situation similar to that of the previous life remembered. Rakesh Gaur started to worry about his children (of the previous life) when there was a heavy downpour of rain. He said, "I am here in a *pukka* house, but what will become of my children who were living in a *kachcha* house. Our house will collapse." And gradually he went on, adding the information in bits and pieces when he remembered other details, not all at once. Other subjects, for example, Lakhan Singh and Santosh Golash (Cases No. 12 and 30), started talking of a previous life when they saw something differently treated in their (present life) situations. Santosh Golash claimed that she was a Parsi in her previous life. Once her mother asked her to pour water on the fire. She showed surprise and said, "We used to worship fire, we never extinguish it." And then she gave other details about a previous life. In a case of possession, one would expect the possessing personality to recall everything at the same time and without waiting for the stimulus of a particular occasion to arise. But perhaps recollections of the possessing personalities also follow the normal principles of memory. It is sometimes said, however, that discarnate spirits transcend all normal laws of memory and are capable of acquiring knowledge of all events and describing them with total accuracy.

Second, among the children who claim to have lived before, additional memories may come to them (after they have already had some spontaneously) when they meet persons or visit places with which the previous personality was familiar. In 75 percent of cases, the subjects in my series started talking about a previous life at home (without meeting persons or visiting places related to the previous personality); but they usually added many more details when they visited the places associated with the previous life. Similarly, in 58 percent of the cases, the subjects gave more details regarding the previous life when they met persons associated with the related previous personality; and 73 percent gave more details on visiting places associated with him. The statements were usually found to be correct.[29] Discarnate personalities, on the other hand, are said to be independent of physical locations.

29. This experience should not be mistaken for paramnesia, which is a different phenomenon. Paramnesia is a disorder of memory. One variety occurs when a person visits a place for the first time, but it seems so familiar to him that he thinks (mistakenly) that he has been there before. In such cases, however, the subject cannot furnish specific verifiable details about the place that would show that he had been there before, or at least that he had some paranormal knowledge of the place. (In some cases of this general type, the subject may show some paranormal knowledge of the place.) When the subjects of rebirth cases visit a place known to the previous personality of a case, however, they usually add additional details of information to those already given before they visited the place. Occasionally a subject of a rebirth case may give his first information about a previous life when he happens to visit, perhaps accidentally, the place where the previous personality of his case lived. I have discussed the topic of paramnesia earlier in connection with normal hypotheses

Their memories do not particularly become affected by visiting places or persons associated with them during their lifetime.

Third, 12 out of 19 subjects (63%) in the present series remarked about changes that they said had occurred in buildings, places, or persons since the previous personality's death. The subjects commented on how these people or buildings looked different from what they claimed to remember from the previous life. In a possession case, the discarnate spirit would be expected to have an up-to-date knowledge of events occurring at least up to the time it became associated with the new physical body. This would be some time (at least) after the death of the related previous personality unless the case is one of instantaneous possession. In the present series of cases, the intermission between the death of the claimed previous personality and the birth of the subjects averaged 14.5 months with a range of one day to 224 months.[30] Except in one case (the case of Anoop Singh) no other subject showed any knowledge of the events that took place after the death of the related previous personality. In this case (Anoop Singh) the subject showed knowledge of events that were mainly related to the members of the concerned previous family.

A similar condition has been studied by some psychologists and psychiatrists. In it the patient is possessed by an imaginary spirit. In most cases of this type, the patient furnishes no evidence of paranormal powers, and although he may seem to be possessed by a real discarnate spirit, the "possession" is that of his own idea of such a spirit. This kind of deviant behavior has

---

30. Cases have been reported with much longer intermissions. In the case of Edward Ryall, the intermission was exceptionally long (217 years) and yet he remembered details that pertained only to the life of John Fletcher whose life he claimed to remember, and nothing outside it (Ryall, 1974).

generally been labeled by psychiatrists and psychologists as "possession syndrome." Instances of it may present a picture similar to that of the subjects who claim to have lived before; but on closer examination the two phenomena are quite different. I shall next describe some of the points of differentiation between the two types of cases.

Subjects who recall previous lives nearly always start narrating their experiences when they are under the age of ten (on average about three years in the present series of cases); cases of the possession syndrome, on the other hand, rarely manifest such behavior when they are under the age of 15, although Varma, Srivastva, and Sahay (1970) and Teja, Khanna, and Subrahmanyam (1970) found some cases between the ages of ten and 15.

The deceased person with whom the patient of a possession syndrome identifies is nearly always someone known to the patient or his family members; in cases of the reincarnation type, the related deceased person is usually a stranger of whom the subject or his family has never heard or has known about only casually. In my series, the information on this aspect was available for 42 cases. Five (12%) cases were biologically related to the claimed previous personalities; in another five (12%) cases, the related previous personalities had friendly relations with the subjects' families; in ten (24%) more cases, there were slight associations between the two families concerned for example, they had some distant relatives in common or had attended the same weddings or condolence meetings; in three (7%) cases, the two families knew about each other but had no direct associations with the other; in the remaining 19 (45%) cases, they *had not known about each other's families at all* before the development of the case. (This pattern of not knowing each other's family does not apply to the cases in Burma, Alaska, and British Columbia.)

In cases of possession syndrome, the motivation for the representation of a deceased person is obvious in terms of gains for the possessed, such as from the ensuing manipulation of the social environment or a stressful situation. Such motivation is usually lacking or is minimal (as far as can be ascertained) in subjects who recall previous lives. In cases of the possession syndrome, the discarnate personality may reappear under further stressful situations, whereas the children with memories of a previous life, once their memories of a previous life cease to occur, do not suddenly begin to talk again about the previously remembered life.

The possession syndrome is nearly always associated with some mental abnormality the signs of which enable a psychiatrist (or a clinical psychologist) to place them under readily recognized categories, for example, schizophrenia or hysteria. In contrast, subjects with claims of previous lives rarely show any evidence of mental illness or other, lesser evidence of psychopathology. The emotions they show on meeting members of the claimed previous family or while recalling events of the previous life seem to be appropriate for the memories associated with it. Sixty-seven percent of the subjects in the present investigation evinced emotions when they met family members related to the previous personality or expressed revengeful feelings on seeing persons who were responsible for the deaths of the related previous personalities (the case of Bachan Singh and of Brijendra Singh).

The subjects of the possession syndrome exhibit unusual behavior in discrete attacks during which a major change of personality occurs, usually for a period of a few days or weeks only. In contrast, in cases with the claim to recall previous life, the unusual behavior remains steady over a period of years. (In the present series of investigations, such behavior lasted from a median age of 36 months [when they began to speak of a revious life] to a median age of 79 months when they had almost stopped talking about the previous lives.) Moreover, there is no abrupt change in personality. Only two subjects (Anjali Sood and Ranjana Tiwari) evinced a slight change of personality while narrating incidents of previous lives. The subject's personality in the usual case of the reincarnation type remains unchanged, or it changes slowly as the traits apparently related to the previous life gradually fuse with others developed since the subject's birth.

Reincarnation

Fraud, cryptomnesia and extrasensory perception (as well as the other processes that may explain these cases) are all known to occur from independent evidence. Reincarnation is not known to occur from evidence independent of the cases of the type I have described in this book. This being so, reincarnation can only be considered favorably as an explanation for the cases provided it is possible to exclude the other interpretations for which independent evidence exists; or provided, at least, that reincarnation seems to cover better than they do _all_ the facts of a case.

I have shown above that explanations other than reincarnation can be reasonably excluded in most cases. Even if it is impossible to rule them out beyond all doubt, it can be seen that they are less probable explanations of most of the cases than is reincarnation itself.

The idea of reincarnation has existed for thousands of years, and still exists in many cultures of the world. This hypothesis supposes that after the death of a person a part of his personality survives, and that later, after variable intervals, it becomes associated with a new physical body. This surviving portion has been called "soul" or psyche by the ancient people, and the modern scientists and philosophers refer to it as "non-physical body" or "psi component" (Broad, 1962/1971). The hypothesis assumes that this surviving component of human personality carries with it some of the characteristic features and impressions from one life to the next.

The hypothesis is called paranormal because it supposes that the person who recalls events of a previous life does not have access to such information through normal channels of communication.

The reincarnation hypothesis is not vulnerable to the various objections raised against other interpretations in the preceding paragraphs. For example, the question as to how a person acquires reasonably accurate information regarding another person whose life he claims to recall remains a puzzle not adequately solved by the other interpretations I have discussed above. Some of them provide an explanation for the transmission of information to the subjects, but they do not adequately account for the unusual behavior shown by so many of them; and they cannot explain birthmarks and physical similarities corresponding between the two personalities of a case.

The hypothesis of reincarnation offers the possibility that a subject who claims to recall a previous life has actually lived and experienced that life. On perceiving certain scenes, or meeting certain persons, his memory of events of that life is stimulated (by associations or contrasts) following the normal laws of memory.

Regarding the birthmarks and other similar physical characteristics in the two personalities, the hypothesis supposes that the "non-physical" body or the surviving component carries these features and they get imprinted on the new physical body with which this non-physical body becomes associated.

This hypothesis is by no means a perfect one, but, compared

with the other hypotheses, it is an adequate one to explain *all* the features that have been found in the present data. I shall discuss the merits and demerits of this hypothesis in the next section after a comparison of my own findings with those of other studies in India and other cultures.

Comparison of Results Obtained in the Present Investigation With the Data of Stevenson's Cases

It is evident from Table 4.07, Chapter Four, that no significant difference was found in 44 out of 53 of the factors compared between the two groups. There were, however, nine factors on demographic as well as on the main features that were found to be significantly different in the two groups under study. I shall now try to explain the nature of these differences.

As I have indicated in Chapter Three, the methods of drawing samples were different in the two groups. Most of Stevenson's sample appears to have been drawn from the urban areas, whereas the cases of my group came mainly from the villages and towns. This difference has also been reflected in some other factors. The fathers of the subjects in Stevenson's group had significantly more years of education than had the fathers of the subjects of my cases. These factors seem to be interrelated. Since the subjects of Stevenson's group mostly came from cities, their fathers had better opportunities, facilities, and needs for higher education compared with the fathers of the subjects in the villages or towns where the usual occupations do not demand a higher education.

The subjects in Stevenson's (I.S.) group acquired speech significantly earlier than the subjects of my (S.P.) group of cases. This factor also appears to have been related to the above-mentioned factors. Since the fathers (much information on the mothers' educational levels in Stevenson's cases was not available) were more educated and mainly dwelled in cities, their environments were more facilitating for their children (the subjects) to acquire speech earlier than those of persons living in villages or towns who would have had less stimulation in their environments. However, the subjects in both groups started talking about the previous lives at almost the same age.

Two other factors in which significant differences occurred between Stevenson's and my cases may also relate to the different educational levels of the parents. (Although enough information is not available about the education of the mothers for comparison, it is reasonable to assume on the basis of information available for my cases that it generally corresponded with that of the fathers, although the mothers would have been, on the whole, less well educated than their husbands.) These factors are the occurrence of extrasensory perception and of adult attitudes in the subjects of the cases. To notice such attributes requires a level of psychological understanding that better educated persons are more likely to have than less well educated ones. Some uneducated persons, for example, do not even understand the concept of extrasensory perception; they are accordingly not able to observe or remember instances of it that may occur in their presence. Such differences between the data of the two series may be considered therefore artifacts of the differing powers of observation shown by the two groups of parents.

Another significant difference between the data of the two series may be an artifact of the different abilities of the investigators to observe features of life in India. When Stevenson first came to India he knew little about the country; and even now, after many years of working in India on these cases, he is less well equipped than myself to make judgments about the socioeconomic status of the families he meets (Stevenson, 1978). Appearances in either direction towards poverty or towards wealth may mislead him in making judgments about a family's socioeconomic status. Stevenson's judgments, moreover, were made impressionistically and without a systematic collection of data bearing on socioeconomic status. On the other hand, I have used scales for evaluating socioeconomic status for urban and rural background, respectively (Kuppuswamy, 1962; Pareek and Trivedi, 1964) in the present study. For these two reasons inexperience of the living standards of India on Stevenson's part and more systematic collection of relevant data in the present investigation of cases it is reasonable to suppose that my data concerning differences in socioeconomic status between subjects and their related previous personalities are more representative than those of Stevenson.

Still another factor may account for the significant differences between the median ages at death of the previous personalities in the two series of cases. Those in Stevenson's series died at a significantly younger age than those in my series. It is not possible for me to give a fully affirmative explanation for this difference, but it may result from nothing more than the different expectations of life of Indian persons in the different generations that comprised the two groups of previous personalities. Most of Stevenson's subjects were born before 1955; most of the subjects of my cases were born after 1960. This means that most of the previous personalities of Stevenson's subjects were born in the first two decades of the century; whereas most of previous personalities of my subjects were born in the third and fourth decades. The expectation of life in India has increased during this century, so that it would be expected that a person born earlier in the century would not live as long as one born near the middle of the century or later.

But the most important outcome of the comparison between

the two groups was the result that no significant differences occurred between them in 44 of the 53 factors compared. I have already explained in Chapter Three (Present Study) that the main data for the two series were collected independently. The close similarity between the characteristics of the two series of cases therefore requires an explanation.

The first possibility is that since I was trained with Stevenson and toured often with him, I might have imitated him in the collection of data. Some unconscious bias in the collection of certain types of data requiring subjective judgments may have occurred. But this hypothesis certainly cannot account for a large part of the data such as of dates, modes of death, and a child's age when first speaking about a previous life. The collection of this sort of data simply requires the investigator to be scrupulously accurate in recording what he is told or learns, quite often by examining reliable written accounts pertaining to the events. It is therefore unlikely that any significant personal bias could enter into the collection of data of this type.

A second possibility is that the informants, both for Stevenson and myself, wanted to please us and so furnished us with information describing what they considered a typical case should be like. But it seems hardly credible that so many different informants would happen to imagine so many different cases with strikingly similar features. The cases occurred in widely separated areas of northern India. Few informants for one case had any acquaintance with informants for another case. To believe in this hypothesis almost requires one to believe in some widespread group extrasensory perception influencing most of the informants.

Another hypothesis actually close to the one I have just discussed is that the informants for the cases of both groups were drawing on their idea of what a typical case should be like.

According to this idea, they were not necessarily trying to please the interviewers, but they were modeling their information on ideas they had picked up here and there about typical cases, or cases that they thought were typical. This raises the question of the extent to which informants had heard about other cases apart from the one for which they were furnishing information. I did not systematically collect data bearing on this important question. Nevertheless, I incidentally acquired much relevant information bearing on this point. Occasionally, I asked informants if they had heard of other cases; some had heard of other cases and others had not. If I did not ask informants about knowledge of other cases, they rarely mentioned any, which suggests that any knowledge they had about other cases was not prominent in their minds when they were giving information about the case immediately known to them. A further relevant point derives from our recent investigations (not part of the present study) which have shown that information about cases rarely travels more than a few kilometers except when a case contains some unusual feature, such as a sensational murder or an unusually prominent person as the previous personality. Also noteworthy is the fact that comparatively few cases are reported in the newspapers and then only brief reports are given. Finally, most villagers do not read newspapers, and a considerable proportion of the informants were illiterate, so that they could not read newspapers even if they had access to them. All these factors support my assumption that few informants knew of other cases apart from the one for which they were furnishing information. It therefore seems reasonable to conclude that the cases were not modeled on each other or on one or several models of which the informants had heard before they encountered the cases for which they were giving information.

If the foregoing argument is accepted, then it seems reasonable to conclude that both series of cases those investigated by myself for the present study and those studied by Stevenson derive from natural phenomena, that is, from cases that have occurred more or less as reported. If this is so, then the similar features that they show are expressions of the processes whereby memories of previous lives occur in some persons. A study of these processes has not been part of the present investigation. But the support, which this investigation gives to the interpretation of the cases as instances of reincarnation, should encourage more intense investigations into the actual processes of reincarnation.

Some Particular Features of Indian Cases Compared with Those of Other Cultures

I did not include cross-cultural comparisons among principal objectives of the present investigation. Nevertheless, I feel the analysis of the data of the present investigation would be incomplete without some reference to the similarities and differences between the cases that I have investigated and those reported from other cultures.

For the purposes of this comparison, I shall combine the 45 cases of the present investigation with the 50 cases investigated by Stevenson. This combination is justified for most comparisons, since the data of my investigation showed no significant differences from those obtained by Stevenson for all except nine of 53 factors. However, I shall make special mention of these while presenting cross-cultural comparisons for factors in which there were significant differences between the cases investigated by myself and those by Stevenson.

The data from other cultures (Tlingit, Alevis of Turkey, Sinhalese of Ceylon, and Haida) have been published elsewhere by Stevenson (1970, 1973, 1974b, 1975b). I shall offer the cross-cultural comparisons principally in the form of tables with short sections of explanatory text. (Figures within parentheses represent percentages.) Sufficient data exist for cross-cultural comparisons for only eight of the 53 factors analyzed for the Indian cases.

Sex of Subjects and Related Previous Personalities in Five Series

There appears to be a preponderance of male subjects in all the five series. This is most marked among the Turkish cases and least among the Ceylonese cases. In Ceylonese cases the sex distribution seems to be almost equal for both sexes. See Table 5.01.

No sex change case was reported among the Turkish, Tlingit,

TABLE 5.01
Sex Distribution of Subjects in Five Series

Sex	Turkish Cases	Ceylon Cases	Tlingit Cases	Haida Cases	Indian Cases
Males	44	15	34	17	57
	(84.6)	(53.6)	(72.3)	(70.8)	(60.0)
Females	8	13	13	7	38
	(15.4)	(46.4)	(27.7)	(29.2)	(40.0)
Total	52	28	47	24	95

and Haida cases. There were, however, six Ceylonese and four Indian cases the subjects of which claimed to recall a previous life as a member of the opposite sex.

Familial Relationships between Subjects and Related Previous Personalities in the Five Series

The familial relationship is presented in Table 5.02. The familial relationship seems to be greatest among Haida and Tlingit cases. Moreover, in these cultures, where the two families concerned were not related to each other, they knew each other's families quite closely. Family relationships and acquaintances were noticed much less frequently among the remaining three series of cases.

TABLE 5.02
Familial Relationships between Subjects and Related
Previous Personalities in Five Series

Status	Turkish Cases	Ceylon Cases	Tlingit Cases	Haida Cases	Indian Cases
Present	4	2	42	18	9
	(8.9)	(16.7)	(97.7)	(75.0)	(10.3)
Absent	41	10	1	6	78
	(91.1)	(83.3)	(2.3)	(25.0)	(89.7)
Not Known	7	16	4	-	8
Total	52	28	47	24	95

Note: Percentages were calculated only for the known familial relationships.

The Tlingits attach a great deal of importance to being in the right family, and the membership comes through the matrilineal line (Stevenson, 1966). Most of the Tlingit cases followed this rule, that is, the relationship between the subject and the related previous personalities was through the mothers of the subjects. For example, the previous personality was father, mother, brother, or sister of the mother of the subject.

The Mode of Death of Related Previous Personalities in the Five Series

Table 5.03 shows the incidence of violent and natural deaths in the related previous personalities. In most instances, the mode of death was verified from informants who had knowledge of it.

In 15 Indian cases we had also consulted reliable certificates.

TABLE 5.03 The Mode of Death of Related Previous Personalities in the Five Series				
Mode of Death	Turkish Cases	Ceylon Cases	Tlingit Cases	Haida Cases	Indian Cases
Vioent					
Male	33	5	19	5	30
	(64.7)	(23.8)	(55.9)	(29.4)	(34.1)
Female	6	5	0	1	12
	(11.7)	(23.8)	-	(5.9)	(13.6)
Total	39	10	19	6	42
	(76.4)	(47.6)	(55.9)	(35.3)	(47.7)
Natural					
Male	11	5	8	8	25
	(21.6)	(23.8)	(23.5)	(47.1)	(28.4)
Female	1	6	7	3	21
	(2.0)	(28.6)	(20.6)	(17.6)	(23.9)
Total	12	11	15	11	46
	(23.6)	(52.4)	(44.1)	(64.7)	(52.3)
Unknown					
Male	0	5	7	-	2
Female	1	2	6	-	5
Total	1	7	13	-	7
Totals	52	28	47	17	95

Note: Percentages are calculated for known modes of death and are given in parenthess.

In a few cases where the related previous personalities had not been identified, we accepted the mode of death claimed by the subjects for the purpose of this analysis.

The incidence of violent death is highest among the Turkish cases and lowest among the Haida and Ceylonese ones. The incidence of violent mode of death seems to have some bearing on the preponderance of male subjects since men die violently more often than women.

Median Age at Death of Related Previous Personalities in the Five Series[31]

Table 5.04 shows the median age (in years) at death of the

TABLE 5.04
Median Age at Death of Related Previous Personalities in the Five Series

	Turkish Cases	Ceylon Cases	Tlingit Cases[1]	Haida Cases	Indian Cases
Median age at death (in years)	30	14	25	-	34
No. of Cases	50	25	9	-	76
Expected life span at birth	48	61.7	69.4	-	52.6[2]

Note: 1. No Data available.
2. Times of India, Directry and Yearbook 1977
(The Times of India Press, Bombay)

31. The previous personalities of Stevenson's cases died at a relatively younger age than those of my cases. But the present comparison will not be affected since in both the groups, the previous personalities died much younger than the expected age for each group, and the expected age at death also differed for both the groups.

related previous personalities for the four series. Information on Haida cases is not available.

Reliable certificates for accurate dates of death were consulted in as many cases as available. However, in a large number of cases the information was obtained from the informants. This was based on their memories, and its reliability naturally varied with the informant's acquaintance with the person in question, and his level of general intelligence. The cases in which informants had known little about the concerned person, but were the only persons available to give information, their testimony was taken. Some of their estimations were vague and approximate only. Therefore, the figures have to be interpreted with caution.

On the basis of the information available on this factor, the median previous personality in Indian, Turkish, and Tlingit cases was a young adult at the time of death. The median related previous personality in Ceylon cases was a youth. The common feature in all four series is that the age at death (irrespective of mode of death) is considerably lower than the expected age at death for their respective cultures.

Median Interval between Deaths of Related Previous Personalities and Births of Subjects in the Five Series

TABLE 5.05				
Median Interval between Deaths of Related Previous Personalities and Births of Subjects in the Five series				
Turkish Cases	Ceylon Cases	Tlingit Cases	Haida Cases	Indian Cases
Median Interval 9 (in months)	21	48	4	18
No. of Cases 34	12	23	17	69

Table 5.05 shows in months the median interval between the deaths of the previous personalities and births of the subjects in the five series under comparison.

The weaknesses concerning the accuracy of information mentioned regarding the age at death of the related previous personalities applies also to the data of Table 5.05. This is especially true for Turkish cases (Stevenson, 1970). The data, therefore, have to be.interpreted cautiously. Here again, on the basis of the information available (with whatever degree of accuracy) the Haida cases have the shortest interval, and there is even a suggestion that in their cases, the subject's conception can occur before the death of the related previous personality.

The Indian cases occupy a middle position between those of Ceylonese and Turkish cases.

Incidence of Announcing Dreams in the Five Series

Table 5.06 summarizes the incidence of announcing dreams in the five series. They occur frequently among the cases of Turkey and among those of the Haida and Tlingit. The occurrence of announcing dreams is considerably lower among the Indian and the Ceylon cases.

TABLE 5.06 Incidence of Announcing Dreams in the Five Series					
Announcing Dreams	Turkish Cases	Ceylon Cases	Tlingit Cases	Haida Cases	Indian Cases
Reported	23	1	22	14	16
	(44.2)	(3.6)	(46.8)	(58.3)	(26.7)
Not	29	27	25	10	44
Reported	(55.8)	(96.4)	(53.2)	(41.7)	(73.3)
Total	52	28	47	24	60

As I have already mentioned, there is a high incidence of familial relationships between the two families concerned among Haida and Tlingit cases, and this may have a bearing on the high incidence of announcing dreams. But this correlation does not occur among Turkish cases. The incidence of announcing dreams among them is disproportionately higher than the reported familial relationships between the present and the previous personalities.

Incidence of Birthmarks in the Five Series

Table 5.07 shows the incidence of birthmarks in the five series considered for cross-cultural comparison. The birthmarks on the body of the subject corresponded to wounds on the body of the related previous personality. The wounds were usually caused by bullets, knives, or blunt weapons, although a few may have resulted from surgical operations or other causes.

	TABLE 5.07				
	Incidence of Birthmarks in the Five Series				
Birthmarks	Turkish Cases	Ceylon Cases	Tlingit Cases	Haida Cases	Indian Cases
Present	28	4	24	5	33
	(53.8)	(14.3)	(51.1)	(20.8)	(41.8)
Absent	24	24	23	19	46
	(46.2)	(85.7)	(48.9)	(79.2)	(58.2)
Total	52	28	47	24	79

The incidence of birthmarks in Indian cases is rather high and close to the incidence in Tlingit and Turkish cases.

Identification of Related Previous Personalities in the Five Series

Table 5.08 presents the number of cases in all the five series in which the related previous personalities have been identified.

In most of the cases in all the series, the previous personalities are usually identified by the parents of the subjects. The mode of identification, however, differs in every culture. In Tlingit cases, for example, a combination of announcing dreams, birthmarks and membership of the two personalities concerned in the same family usually leads to an early identification of the related previous personality. The Haida cases are almost similar to Tlingit cases in these respects. Moreover, among both the Tlingit and the Haida, a living person may select the parents in whose family he hopes to reincarnate after his death.

TABLE 5.08
Identification of Related Previous Personalities
in the Five Series

	Turkish Cases	Ceylon Cases	Tlingit Cases	Haida Cases	Indian Cases
Identified	45	12	45	24	78
	(86.5)	(42.9)	(95.7)	(100.0)	(82.1)
Not	7	16	2	0	17
Identified	(13.5)	(57.1)	(4.3)	-	(17.9)
Total	52	28	47	24	95

All these features—pre-mortem selection of the next parents, announcing dreams, birthmarks, and prior acquaintance of the subject's family with that of the presumed previous personality—tend to weaken the evidence of paranormal processes provided by such cases. These obviously prepare a child's parents to believe that he is a particular person reborn, so that they, quite unconsciously, influence him to assume the role of that person. I am not asserting that this explains all the evidence of cases in these cultures, but most of them are vulnerable to such a criticism.

In Indian and Ceylon cases, these combinations are rather rare. The previous personalities are usually traced or identified only on the basis of the subjects' statements or recognitions.

Turkish cases are somewhat intermediate between Indian and Ceylonese cases on the one hand and Haida and Tlingit ones on the other. Sometimes a combination of an announcing dream and birthmarks may lead the family to a tentative identification with a particular person who is already known to the family, or with another person whose violent death is well known. When the subject starts making statements about his previous life and recognizes members of the family concerned, the parents of the subject may confirm the identification on the basis of their knowledge.

Indications of the Relationships between Belief and Knowledge of Cases

One of the objectives of my present investigation was to study the belief in reincarnation and its relationship with the characteristics of reported cases of rebirth. It is said that the belief influences and promotes the occurrence of these cases. It has also been argued that the occurrence of cases leads to the formation or enhancement of a belief in reincarnation. The strength of one's belief may depend on one's exposure to such a case or to personal experience of recollections of a past life.

During the present investigation, I had prepared a Belief in Reincarnation Questionnaire to measure the strength and various associated concepts of the belief among persons who had direct contact with, or knowledge of, a reincarnation case and those who did not have such experience, but who derived their belief and knowledge of related concepts from their family, scriptures, or other literature on the subject. I undertook the comparative study to learn how the empirical evidence influences and shapes the beliefs and conversely, how the beliefs influence the occurrence and determine the patterns of the actual cases. Most of the informants who were aware of an actual case remarked that they believed in reincarnation, but after seeing this particular case they were convinced. A small number of persons in this group did not even believe in rebirth before coming into contact with such a case. Two of my informants remarked that they believed in rebirth, but they were not convinced about the case known to them.

I shall now discuss the relationship between belief in reincarnation and the patterns observed in children who claim to recall their previous lives. I shall base most of my discussion on the case material gathered during the present investigation with comparison of these features in other cultures where such cases have been reported and studied along with their beliefs (Stevenson, 1970, 1973, 1975b).

On the question of whether everyone reincarnates or some only, there were opinions in favor of both the possibilities. Some of the persons said that only "imperfect persons" or those who leave some "unfinished business" at the time of their deaths are reborn. Others were of the opinion that everyone reincarnates, but only those who die suddenly or violently in a previous life are able to recall their previous lives in a later one. (This last suggestion is also found among some persons in Turkey who believe in previous lives.) The data obtained during the present investigation seems to support the belief in the importance of violent death, but I have also investigated cases in which the related previous personalities died a natural death.

Some of the informants (20%) who did not know of a case at firsthand said it was not possible to recall previous lives.

Regarding the possibility of changing sex from one life to the next, there was a difference of opinion in the two groups. The majority of the informants (65%) in the group with knowledge of a case said that it was not possible to change sex from one life to the next; those who did consider this to be possible thought it was due to one's karma in a previous life. They believed it was a punishment for a man to be born as a woman and a reward for a woman to be born as a man in the next life.

Opinions about "sex change" were almost equally divided among the group who did not have an exposure to a rebirth case. Those who did endorse the idea of sex change attributed it to various factors, such as "a need for enrichment or diversity of experience" or "one's desire during a previous life to change sex."

The ratio of actual sex change cases is rather low in the present series of cases. Only one such case was reported to me that I have investigated. The change in sex was from female to male. From the case material, possible causal relationships for this change could not be ascertained at this stage.

Among some other cultures, the possibility of sex change is completely denied. The Tlingits of Alaska, Alevis of Turkey, and Druses of Lebanon consider it impossible to change sex from one life to the next. Their beliefs agree with the case material of these regions, since no cases of "sex change" have been reported from these areas.

On the question of the interval between a person's death and presumed rebirth, most of my informants in both the groups (72%) said that it varies for every individual. Those who opted for a "fixed interval" did not know how much it was except for three informants, who were Jains. Two of these informants were related to the previous personalities of the rebirth cases and one did not know of any such case. These two subjects themselves were Hindus (Brahmin and Thakur, respectively) and the previous personalities of their cases were Jains. All three Jain informants said that the fixed duration of discarnate existence is nine months. The interval among the present series varied considerably, ranging between one day and 224 months. However, the cases with Jain previous personalities in my series of cases and another Jain case studied by Stevenson (1972) followed the nine-month rule.

Rebirth in animal forms (metempsychosis) was accepted by most of the informants. Ninety-three percent of the informants in the group with a known case and 51 percent who did not know of a case endorsed the idea. However, a small number of subjects have been reported who claimed to recall the lives of animals before they were born in their present families. I have studied none of these cases during the present investigation (nor is it possible at present with the equipment/techniques available to verify such claims directly); therefore, in the absence of empirical evidence it is hard to say whether metempsychosis is possible or not. The idea of rebirth of human beings into animal forms (and vice versa) has been accepted among the Turkish Alevis but completely rejected by Haida, Tlingit, and Druses.

Regarding the question of factors that decide the identity of the claimed person, most of the informants (91%) who knew of a case and most of those who did not know of a case (only ten of the informants in Group II who had no exposure to a rebirth case answered this question) said that on the basis of a child's statements they can decide whether or not this is the same person reborn the one with whom the subject identifies himself. Some of the informants who were acquainted with a case also believed that, in addition to the child's statements, birthmarks and announcing dreams will help to decide whether this is the same person reborn or not. In Group II, however, none of the respondents entertained these possibilities.

The announcing dreams were considered as identifying features in a very few cases compared to the presence of birthmarks.

However, the incidence of announcing dreams in the present study was considerably lower compared with cases in Turkey and Alaska. Haida attach much more significance to announcing dreams than to birthmarks. In fact, some of them found the idea of birthmarks a little strange (Stevenson, 1975b).

All those informants who believed in rebirth also believed in the law of karma, that is, in a moral law which brings about retribution for misdeeds in one life in the form of poor social, economic, and other personal circumstances in another one, not necessarily immediately following that of the bad conduct. The same holds true for meritorious conduct that leads to superior births.

Buddhists also believe in the law of karma. But this belief in karma is not held by Alevis and Druses. They do not believe that God punishes or rewards a person in one life for his sins or virtues in a previous one. They, however, believe in a Day of Judgment, when one is sent to Heaven or Hell according to one's deeds.

From the above presentation, it is clear that people who do not have firsthand knowledge of a rebirth case also believe in reincarnation. But their beliefs regarding concepts associated with the phenomenon differ considerably from those persons who are acquainted with such cases at firsthand. The beliefs of the latter group chiefly derive from the type of case they are exposed to or are familiar with.

CHAPTER SIX

Summary and Conclusions

The phenomena studied by parapsychologists were kept outside the purview of scientific investigations until the late nineteenth century; and claims to remember previous lives did not receive any serious attention until about three decades ago. The claims of some persons that they were able to recall spontaneously the events of previous lives earlier attracted little attention from scientists. In general, the few scientists who became aware of such claims offered conventional interpretations to explain them and dismissed the idea of looking closer by declaring this to be a worthless effort. Even those who proposed normal interpretations for the cases did so without presenting any empirical evidence for their "hunches."

The review of previous work in this area shows that there are hardly any studies prior to the present investigation, except for one single systematic investigation. This is by Stevenson who has objectively and intensively examined the claims of these subjects since 1961. His investigations are still in progress. There have been a few surveys of the belief in reincarnation, but there have been no systematic studies where the belief has been studied in relation to actual cases of the reincarnation type.

Recently there have been increasing reports of persons (mostly children) who claim to recall previous lives. In a period of less than three years available for the data collection of the present investigation, 76 such cases were reported to me. I was ncouraged by the large number of reports and the dearth of scientific inquiries into the claims advanced. I undertook the present investigation with the hope that it would contribute to the existing knowledge of human behavior, both abnormal and paranormal.

I conducted the present study with two main objects in view: First, to verify objectively the claims of the subjects in order to arrive at an interpretation that would adequately explain most of the features of the cases; and second, to learn about the influence of the belief in reincarnation on the occurrence of these cases and, conversely, the influence of the knowledge of such a case in shaping the beliefs of persons.

For the objective verification of the claims of rebirth, I employed the usual clinical methods of case history and interview techniques. Special care was taken in preparing the questionnaires and proformas that would detect the evidence for various plausible hypotheses from the case material available.

In order to learn about the belief in reincarnation and its influence on the occurrence of such cases, I adapted a special questionnaire (I have described the details of its development in Chapter Three). This measured the strength of belief of a person and the related concepts.

Out of the 76 cases with the claims of reincarnation reported to me, I contacted 60 of them in various parts of north India. There were two reasons for my studying the cases in north India. First, the cases were reported to me from that part of the country; and second, I was well versed in the languages spoken there. When I investigated the claims of these 60 subjects, I found that 15 of the cases belonged in some other category, such as fraud, "spiritistic communications," and a category that was described as "Parakayapravesh" by the informants. (This term subsumes instances in which the subject was born *before* the death of the concerned previous personality.) So I excluded all these 15 deviant cases from the final analysis. The final sample therefore consisted of 45 cases.

My sample for the study of the belief in reincarnation consisted of 137 respondents. Seventy-one of these respondents were either related to families concerned in the above-mentioned cases, or they had known another rebirth case at firsthand. The remaining 66 respondents did not know of any specific case. (However, they were aware of my research into reincarnation type cases.) They were living in Bangalore at the time of my interview with them. Although the sample served the purpose of comparing the two groups in terms of their knowledge of a case and its impact on their belief, it had some limitations in other respects. For example, the groups could not be matched with regard to socioeconomic status and education. Despite this weakness the survey produced, in my opinion, some valuable information. It showed that the belief in reincarnation is widely held among persons of different groups drawn from widely differing socioeconomic and geographical sections of India.

In most of the rebirth type cases, the main events had already occurred and the experiences of the subjects had been communicated to all the family members concerned before I could attempt at their verification. This situation resembles that in other clinical manifestations where the clinician mostly does not have an opportunity to observe the onset of a phenomenon. Instead, he must form his opinion on the basis of the information given to him by informants who have observed the patient during the episode or an "attack." Similarly, in the present investigation, I gathered information from various sources in order to understand and reconstruct the events involved in the cases.

I tried to interview as many informants as were available, and interviewed as many as 11 or more informants in some cases. I sometimes interviewed the same persons on different occasions, some of them on three or four occasions. In all, I was able to interview a total of 319 informants; this figure includes 31 subjects of the cases. I interviewed 47 of the informants twice and eight informants on three separate occasions. In all, I conducted 382 interviews during 196 visits that I made at different intervals throughout 51 weeks (April 1975 through March 1978) of fieldwork.

Most of the subjects gave sufficient details regarding the previous lives they claimed to remember. In 38 cases (84%) the respective previous personalities were identified and the subjects' statements verified. Five subjects recalled previous lives as members of their present families. They claimed to be the lineal descendants of the previous personalities. In the remaining 40 cases, the two families concerned were widely separated both geographically and genealogically.

I analyzed the case material obtained from my field investigations both with regard to individual cases as well as with regard to recurrent features that were found in many cases. I shall next summarize the most significant of the latter.

The majority of the cases were reported either from towns or villages. The subjects' ages ranged between three and one-half to 35 years at the time of my first interviews with them. Seventy-one percent of them were under the age of 15.

There was a preponderance of male subjects in the present sample. It might be thought that this arose from a greater readiness of parents to allow the investigation of boy subjects than of girl subjects. But rejections of the investigation had not occurred except in one case, and it seems unlikely that this factor alone could account for the skewed male/female ratio in the present group. It is also possible that male lives are remembered more often than female ones because men in India lead in general more eventful lives than do women. This may be due to the fact that men engage in more dangerous vocational activities and are more inclined than women to use violence in settling their disputes. Therefore, it would be expected that male subjects would preponderate because of the relatively high incidence of violent deaths in male previous personalities.

Apart from the factor of violent death, the other demographic features were more or less representative of the general population. The sample consisted of subjects from all socioeconomic strata, educated and uneducated ones. And the subjects came from all residential areas, namely villages, towns, and cities.

The subjects started talking about the previous lives between the ages of two and four (with the median age of 36 months) and continued to talk about them up to a median age of 79 months. They talked irrespective of the encouragement or discouragement they received from the people in their environment.

Unusual behavioral features were found in most of the cases. Although this behavior was unusual for the subject's family, it was concordant with his statements concerning a previous life. Such behavior might include: unusual likes or dislikes toward food, clothes, persons, and themes of play; phobias of bladed weapons, wells, and guns; and philias, most of them related to the previous personality's mode of death. These behavioral features sometimes persisted in the subjects even when the imaged memories of the previous lives had apparently faded.

The median intermission between death and presumed rebirth was 14.5 months. It varied from one day to 224 months. The data showed some tendency for length of intermission to accord with beliefs about what the length of intermission should be. For example, three of the respondents who were Jains said that the intermission was nine months, and all others said that it varies for each individual. (Other than these three Jain respondents, those who said that it is "fixed for all persons" did not claim to know what the length of the fixed interval was.) In two cases, the related previous personalities were Jains and their intermission was found to be exactly nine months. (In the only one of Stevenson's Jain cases for which he obtained reliable data about birth and death, the intermission was also nine months.)

The related previous personalities of these cases in general died younger than the expected age for persons of their generation. The median age at death was found to be 45 years, whereas the expected life span at birth (for the same generation) was 52.6 years. Another notable feature was that the incidence of violent death was far higher among the previous personalities of these cases than it was in the general population at the time. However, there was not much difference between male and female previous personalities as far as mode of death was concerned. Violent death occurred slightly more often among male previous personalities than among female ones. However, this feature alone should not be taken as responsible for recall of previous lives, since the violent death rate is far higher than the case rate, at least the rate of reported cases. Also, certain features of recall were present in most of the cases irrespective of the previous personality's mode of death; for example, the recall of the name of the related previous personality.

I also made some other observations with regard to the mode of death and its association with other factors.

Subjects who claimed to recall previous lives in the same family almost always remembered lives that ended in natural death. In each of the five cases in the sample in which both personalities concerned belonged to the same family, either on the maternal or paternal side, the previous personality had died at a relatively mature age.

Some factors were found significantly related to a violent

mode of death. These features were: birthmarks, animosities, phobias, and recall of the mode of death and of other events related to the death.

Evidence for extrasensory perception was found in only three subjects.

Since, as I mentioned earlier, Stevenson's is the only available study on the subject, I compared the present findings with his findings on 50 Indian cases. In all, I compared 53 factors. The two series showed significant differences in only nine of these 53 factors. These were: (1) Population of residence of subjects (2) Population of residence of previous personalities (3) Educational level of subject's father (4) Age of subject's first speaking in coherent phrases (5) Evidence of adult attitude in subjects (6) Evidence of ESP in subjects (7) Previous personalities' age at death (8) Status of investigation of cases, and (9) Direction of difference in economic status between previous and present personalities. The first six factors seem to be interrelated. Since the two samples were derived differently, most of the cases in Stevenson's group came from cities and towns compared with the group of my present study which were found mainly in towns and villages. When the subjects' families live in urban areas, they have better opportunities and also more need for higher education in order to qualify for many occupations. Stevenson's subjects started speaking relatively earlier. This also could be attributed to the living conditions of his subjects. The parents in his group were better educated and therefore they could provide more stimuli for their children to learn how to speak. Also, such parents would have taken cognizance more readily of such features as the presence or absence of ESP and an adult attitude on the part of the subject.

Stevenson studied his cases earlier than myself. The life expectancy has increased from what it was two decades ago.

Since he has been studying cases for almost thirty years, most of his cases have been followed-up longer and investigated more thoroughly. The difference in degree of difference in economic status was probably due to Stevenson's not using a standard scale for evaluating the economic status in his cases.

The belief in reincarnation questionnaire revealed that the belief existed even amongst persons who did not know of any actual rebirth case. But such persons' knowledge differed from that of persons who were in some way or other directly associated with such a case. Both knowledge and belief were considerably influenced by firsthand acquaintance with a rebirth case. The respondents with direct knowledge of a case said (usually) that they had believed in reincarnation before, but their belief had been strengthened or weakened depending upon their experience with the case they had observed. Also, their answers regarding other details were based on the features of the cases they knew. For instance, persons who knew about cases with birthmarks said that they would accept cases on the basis of birthmarks, which should correspond with the previous personality's wounds; those who knew of cases whose subjects were born soon after the death of the previous personality said that rebirth occurs instantly; and those who knew of cases with a longer intermission said this varies or is longer for everyone. On the other hand, persons who did not know of a case gave answers based on their knowledge of scriptures or other literature pertaining to the subject of reincarnation.

On the basis of the present findings, it can also be said that the belief in reincarnation does not necessarily produce rebirth cases, since the belief occurs more frequently than the cases. Disbelief in reincarnation, on the other hand, could not quite change the features of the cases. (Yet it might have been responsible for suppression of cases.) I had two Muslim subjects in my group of cases but the features of their cases did not differ from those whose families believed in reincarnation.

Stevenson compared aspects of the belief in reincarnation with the features of the cases found in several different cultures (Stevenson, 1970, 1973, 1974b, 1975b). It seems likely that the belief in reincarnation has a circular relationship with the occurrence of cases. In other words, belief facilitates the recognition and expression of such experiences; and the occurrence of the cases strengthens the belief.

I analyzed the individual cases with regard to possible hypotheses that may account for the subject's claims. The main hypotheses that I considered fall into two groups: those that suppose some normal means of communications between persons knowing the facts about the concerned personality and the subject; and those that suppose the subject acquired his correct information about the concerned previous personality through some other, that is, paranormal process.

To take the first group first, I have considered the following hypotheses on the side of normal communication of the information to the subject about the life of the deceased person who the child claims he has been.

Fantasy. Various critics have suggested that subjects make such claims out of imagination in order to avoid some unpleasant situation, such as an unhappy home. We can set aside this hypothesis since in 84 percent of the cases, the claims of the subjects have been verified and the respective previous personalities have been identified. The subjects of these cases were therefore talking about real persons who had actually lived; they were not just inventing fictional persons. Furthermore, all of the subjects do not claim to have lived before in better socioeconomic situations. In fact, some of them claimed to have been in much poorer situation in the remembered previous lives.

Fraud. I have next considered the hypothesis of fraud. This hypothesis assumes that persons, either the child or his family, fabricate a case to achieve some personal gain. I could identify only one case of a possible fraud during the present investigation. In no other case I could detect any motivation for fraud or other indication of it that seemed strong enough to explain the case.

Genetic memory. The next hypothesis that has been suggested is that the claimed memories of previous life of a child are passed on to him through genetic transmission. In the present series of my cases, only five subjects were lineal descendants of their claimed previous personalities. In the remainder of the cases the subjects were not related—even distantly—to the previous personalities. Therefore the question of genetic transmission does not arise in them. In two cases in which a biological relationship did exist, the subjects remembered the mode of death of the respective previous personalities but, in principle, this could not have been possible by "inherited memory," since the supposedly transmitting parent of the subjects had been born long before the death of the related previous personality.

Cryptomnesia. Another interpretation that has been suggested as an explanation for these claims is cryptomnesia. In this hypothesis the subject's knowledge about a previous life is not in question, but he is thought to have come by it normally. In the absence of information in the child's environment, how can any knowledge be passed on to him? In 21 of the 45 present cases, there were no connections between the two families concerned before the development of the case. This hypothesis has certain other weaknesses and fails to explain various features of the cases. For example, the phenomenon of cryptomnesia (at least in cases of the parapsychological literature) almost always manifests itself in altered states of consciousness; but the subjects of the cases under study here almost always narrated their experiences when in a normal mental condition. Furthermore, the usual subject of a case of cryptomnesia gives few details about his experience and these have usually been traced to some book or some other source. In contrast, the subjects of the present investigation gave many details sufficient (usually) to identify the deceased persons to whom they were referring, and often many others as well. Finally, the hypothesis of cryptomnesia cannot account for the behavioral features shown by the subjects that correspond well with the behavior of the concerned previous personalities.

Paramnesia. Paramnesia is a disorder of memory that of false recollections. A person, on seeing a new place or meeting a stranger feels that he has been to the place or has met the person before. A variant of this phenomenon is also known as *deja vu.* But most of the subjects of the present cases do not come under this category, since they started talking of new places or persons even before visiting or meeting them.

It is possible that informants for the cases had some degree of paramnesia. Many of them possibly—and some of them certainly—gave discrepant testimony on some details. This means assuming their intention to be helpful—that they misremembered some events and therefore had a degree of paramnesia. But a careful review of the testimony makes it most improbable that such errors could account for the main features of the cases. Moreover, confidence in the testimony is increased by the similar features found in so many of the cases. The informants for the different cases did not know each other, except in rare instances. So paramnesia on their part does not account for the similarities among the different cases. It is not reasonable to suppose that separated informants would commit the same errors of memory over and over again.

After having eliminated the hypotheses of normal

communication of the information to the subject, I considered the hypotheses of paranormal interpretations. These will be discussed next.

Extrasensory perception and personation. This hypothesis suggests that the subjects are gifted with ESP and obtain their correct information regarding the concerned deceased person—paranormally most probably by telepathy—from his surviving relatives and friends. Then with this information the subject reconstructs a new personality for himself. In a facilitating environment where the belief in reincarnation exists, his claimed memories are accepted as evidence of reincarnation (Chari, 1962a, 1962b; Murphy, 1973).

This hypothesis has several limitations for explaining the features displayed by the cases in the present investigation. It cannot adequately account for the behavioral features shown by the subjects. Furthermore, the subjects (with three exceptions) showed no evidence of extrasensory perception apart from their claimed memories. This hypothesis also cannot explain birthmarks on the body of a subject that correspond closely with wounds on the body of the deceased person of whom the subject has been talking. I have independently verified the correspondences between these birthmarks and wounds on the concerned previous personalities from the relatives of the deceased persons. In addition, I examined some autopsy reports for more definite confirmation. Finally, I also received reports of and studied cases in the present group where the environment did not facilitate such claims. Cases among Muslims would be examples of this.

Possession. This hypothesis supposes that the body of the subject is taken over or is "possessed" by some spirit, temporarily or permanently. This hypothesis has some appeal, but it fails to explain aspects of the unusual behavior on the part of the subject.

Such behavior often long outlasts the fading away of the subject's imaged memories of the previous life that he earlier remembered. If these memories were due to the influence of a persisting discarnate personality on the subject, one would expect imaged memories and associated behavior to cease together when the presumed possessing spirit withdrew from the subject.

Reincarnation. All the above-mentioned hypotheses are known to exist from independent evidence. But they can be eliminated in the present cases unless particular evidence found in the cases justifies retaining and preferring them. If the cases do not contain adequate evidence for these other hypotheses, one is justified in considering that of reincarnation. It explains most of the features of these cases more adequately than the hypotheses mentioned above. Even if it is impossible to exclude them beyond all doubt, they appear to be less probable explanations than reincarnation itself. Secondly, the comparative study of the present and Stevenson's findings suggests that these cases derive from some natural phenomenon—one occurring more or less as reported by the informants. The similarities between the cases studied by myself and those studied by Stevenson suggest that all the cases derive from some common process, which may be reincarnation.

In conclusion, I must add that the sample had its own limitations. All the cases have flaws, as everything connected with human testimony can have. The cases investigated for the present research were all drawn from a part of north India, namely the states of Uttar Pradesh, Delhi, Punjab, and Rajasthan. Conclusions drawn from cases in this restricted geographic area may not be valid for cases even in other parts of India, not to say of other parts of the world, at this stage.

Implications of the Research and Proposals for Future Investigations

For many studies in psychology and psychiatry, children are the best subjects because an understanding of the child gives insight into the main characteristics of the adult and helps to clarify the foibles and idiosyncrasies of a person's later years. The subjects of my present study started narrating their recollections of previous lives when quite young. This reduced or minimized the possibility of the contamination of their experiences by all the information to which adults are exposed. Young children seem to present the phenomenon of claims to recall a previous life as it manifests under natural conditions.

If the results obtained in the present investigation support the hypothesis of reincarnation, they add to existing knowledge and understanding of human personality. Furthermore, they increase our comprehension of such disorders of personality as unusual and irrational fears, childhood animosities and vengefulness, and gender dysphoria for which there is no satisfactory current explanation.

Orthodox theories of psychology, psychiatry, and criminology emphasize the importance of childhood experiences in the formation of personality. But if we fail to trace the cause of a person's deviant behavior to his genes or to his immediate environment, we may justifiably conjecture that it derives from events even earlier than those of childhood or infancy, namely those of a previous life.

The present study revealed certain physical and psychological characteristics in the subjects that were unusual for their families but that corresponded well with those of the identified previous personalities. Except in five cases, in which the subjects were biologically related to their claimed previous personalities, the hypothesis of genetic transmission cannot adequately explain such unusual behavior on the part of the subjects. Where the genetic theory has failed to explain the inheritance of physical and psychological traits, the hypothesis of reincarnation may offer an explanation for them.

An extensive study of more cases in different geographical areas would be desirable in order to increase the generality of the results obtained. A multivariate analysis might help in mapping out related factors and could throw fresh light on the process of the phenomenon.

Follow-up studies with the subjects would be useful in learning about their development and adjustment in later life. On the basis of retrospective studies, from interviews with older subjects, it appears that—with rare exceptions—these subjects develop normally. They tend spontaneously to forget about their previous lives by about ten years of age. (Systematic follow-up studies with the subjects will aid in an early detection of the rare cases where this does not happen.) This knowledge will help— indeed, has already been helpful—in reassuring the parents of these subjects that the development of their children will not be affected by the recall of a previous life.

The findings of this research will also aid in eliminating or reducing important superstitions associated with the occurrence of previous life memories. It is widely held (in India, particularly northern India) that children who claim to remember previous lives die young. (This belief has no support whatever from the facts of actual cases, so far as their investigation has now progressed.) This leads parents to take measures, sometimes even violent ones, to suppress the memories of children who claim to recall previous lives.

A high incidence of violent death in the concerned previous personalities seems to be associated with the recall of previous lives. It will be helpful to conduct surveys in different parts of India (and eventually in other parts of the world) to determine the incidences of rebirth cases and of violent death in the same areas. It may then be shown that the cases tend to occur with greater frequency in regions having a higher than average incidence of violent death. This correlation, if found, could provide helpful information about factors that contribute to the occurrence of cases of the reincarnation type.

CHAPTER SEVEN

Recent Research

The preceding chapters are based on my work that I had submitted in the form of a thesis for a doctoral degree at Bangalore University in 1978, and the degree was awarded in 1979. Since the project had to be executed within a stipulated period of time, I could not thoroughly investigate all the cases studied. I completed the investigation of some of the cases later. Simultaneously, I have been studying various types of cases— new as well as old—of the reincarnation type. In addition, I have been investigating cases of persons who have had close encounters with death and later report their experiences during the time when they were apparently unconscious. I shall briefly summarize the areas of research that I have been working on for the past ten years, that is after the submission of my doctoral thesis.

Reincarnation

I have continued to investigate cases of the reincarnation type up to the present. Some of the cases recently studied were already under investigation; others were new and reported to me during my investigation of earlier cases. So far, I have investigated nearly 300 cases at various levels of thoroughness. Some of the less thoroughly investigated cases are still under study. I am also following up my cases which I had began investigating several years ago, for learning their further development.

A Systematic Survey

Till the time of the submission of my thesis, I (along with other colleagues) had been studying reincarnation type cases as and when they were reported to us. No systematic studies had been conducted anywhere with the use of standard sampling techniques. We had no idea about the actual (or near actual) incidence or prevalence rate of cases. In order to determine this, we conducted a systematic survey in a region of northern India (Tehsil Fatehabad, District Agra, U.P.) in 1978-1979. The results of this survey, mainly dealing with the methodology and with the incidence of the cases, were published in the *Journal of Asian and African Studies* (Barker and Pasricha, 1979).

During this study we surveyed nine villages selected out of 96 villages, using appropriate sampling techniques in the Fatehabad block. We studied a sample in a population of 8611 persons, and identified 19 cases of persons who claimed to recall a previous life. In other words, one in approximately 450 persons claimed to remember a previous life. However, these figures should be viewed cautiously and no generalizations should be made since the survey was conducted only in a small region of District Agra, Uttar Pradesh, in northern India. It was nevertheless, an important step towards standardizing methodology for the conduct of surveys and determining the incidence of the cases. I hope that more surveys can be conducted in different parts of India (and also in other countries, for cross-cultural comparisons) so that we may have a better estimate of the occurrences of such cases. Such surveys should also throw light on factors associated with the occurrence and reporting of these cases.

In 13 of the 19 cases reported in the Fatehabad survey, a deceased person satisfactorily matching a subject's statements could be identified. We call them "solved cases" (the remaining six cases could not be solved). I investigated these cases further and followed them up between 1979 and 1986. Most of the subjects were already adults when we conducted the survey. On analysis and comparison their cases resembled in important features cases that were investigated when their subjects were still young children.

A Study of Unsolved Cases

Cases where a satisfactorily corresponding deceased person, matching a subject's statements, cannot be found, we designate as 'unsolved cases'. The study of unsolved cases is important for learning about the factors, which are associated with the solvability of a case. As I have stated earlier, cases of the reincarnation type are not unique to India but have been reported from several other countries where they have been investigated by the University of Virginia. These cases have been investigated in Burma, Lebanon, Sri Lanka, Thailand, Europe, and the United States of America. The percentage of unsolved cases varies from culture to culture. In a cross cultural comparison the percentage of unsolved cases was high in Sri Lanka (68%) and the United States (80%) and low in Thailand (8%), Burma (20%), Lebanon (21%), and India (23%). We published a report of these comparisons, in two parts, in the *Journal of American Society for Psychical Research* (Cook, Pasricha, Samararatne, U Win Maung, and Stevenson, 1983). The first part of this report deals with the importance of unsolved cases and presents seven illustrative case reports from different cultures. Three of these cases were from Sri Lanka, two from India, and one each from Burma and Lebanon. The second part of the report deals with a comparative analysis of the features in cases from six cultures; it also included a discussion of possible reasons for failure to solve some of these cases.

Follow-up Studies

In order to learn about the course of development of these children (subjects of the reincarnation type cases), I have been visiting them at various intervals. These visits help in learning about the length of time up to which the subjects continue to talk spontaneously about their previous lives, the age when they cease to talk, and the reasons for their doing so. In addition, follow-up interviews help in understanding the children's developments and adjustments in the physical, psychological, educational, and vocational spheres. Most of the subjects have developed into normal adults.

I have conducted follow-up studies in two series of cases. One series of cases were of fairly recent origin and they were investigated wholly by myself (with or without Dr. Stevenson or other colleagues); the second series was of cases that had been investigated a long time (almost half a century) ago by different investigators. From the follow-up studies of the first series of cases we could learn about the features of the same cases that change (or do not change) over a period of time. From the trends of these studies for example, we found that, in most of the cases, the subjects tend to stop spontaneously mentioning their previous lives between the ages of five and eight years but sometimes continue to manifest behavioral features corresponding to their claims of a previous life for a longer time.

The follow up study of the second series (earlier investigated cases by other investigators) and their comparison with the later investigated cases was intended to show the differences (and similarities) between the two series of cases that occurred at two different points of time. I shall briefly summarize some of the findings of this study under the next heading.

A study of pre-1936 and post-1965 cases. A wish to study the features of cases that may vary from one generation to another, led us to take up this project. We (Dr. Stevenson and myself) collected reports of cases that had been published in the 1920s and 1930s, generally in books, newspaper reports, or small pamphlets. In these sources we found 31 cases; six of them had been reported in newspapers only and the other 25 in several books, journals and pamphlets (Bose, 1959; Sahay, 1927; Sunderlal, 1924). Reports of cases seemed to become less frequent from the mid 1930s until the late 1950s. We chose the year 1936 as an appropriate cut-off point for a comparison of two series of cases which occurred two generations apart.

The addresses given in the reports we had available were not complete for all the cases. It was sometimes an extremely difficult and time-consuming process for us to trace a case. This particularly happened in cases where for an address only the name of a sector in a big town was mentioned, or in cases where the subjects were born in the late 19th or early 20th century. However, in spite of these obstacles, we were able to trace and interview informants for 24 (77%) of the 31 cases. Of the 24 cases traced, we could also interview 14 subjects, the remaining ten subjects having died.

For the later series, we set 1965 as the base year in order to keep the series two generations apart for meaningful comparisons. We compared 54 features but found, surprisingly, that the two series differed significantly only on five of these. We published a detailed report on the discussion of these similarities and differences in the *Journal of the Society for Psychical Research* (Pasricha and Stevenson, 1987).

The Case of Rakesh Gaur

This case, although included in the analysis of data presented in Chapter Four, needs a brief mention here. Before commenting on the importance of this case, I will briefly summarize its salient features. Interested readers can read a fuller report of this case in the European Journal of Parapsychology (Pasricha and Barker, 1981; Pasricha, 1983).

The subject of this case Rakesh Gaur was born in March 1969, in Fateh Nagar, District Udaipur, Rajasthan. At the age of about five years, one night when it was raining heavily, he woke up very disturbed worrying about his children and house in Tonk (also in Rajasthan, about 225 Kilometers away from Udaipur). On being questioned he stated that he had a kachcha house (mud house) in Tonk which would be washed away in such a heavy rain. Regarding his personal details he said that his name was Bithal Das, that he was a carpenter, and that he had died of electrocution while working on an electric pole. In spite of requests from his friends Rakesh's father, S.N. Gaur (a sub-postmaster in Kankroli at the time) made no attempts to go to Tonk for the verification of the claims. However, he did write a letter to the Electricity Board in Tonk asking them to inform him if such an accident had occurred in their department. Failing to get a reply to his letter he did not pursue the matter further, although Rakesh kept on insisting that he be taken to Tonk. Sometime in 1976 a bus from Tonk chanced to stop at Kankroli (where Rakesh was living with his parents at the time) on its way from the pilgrimage place of Nathdwara. Rakesh saw the bus driver, Chhitarji, at a nearby tea-stall, recognized him, and asked him about his (Rakesh's) sons and family of the previous life. From the description the driver could identify the person concerned but did not indicate his knowledge to Rakesh. He however brought back news, of what Rakesh had said, to Bithal Das's sons.

Rakesh's father (S.N. Gaur) encouraged by Rakesh's recognition of the bus driver and urged on by Rakesh himself, finally decided to take him to Tonk. They went there some time in October 1976. Since S.N. Gaur had never before been to Tonk, they took a circuitous route to reach the place. Because S.N. Gaur worked in the post and telegraph department and had no relatives or friends in Tonk, he approached the post office authorities for assistance in tracing the person in question. Gradually a large crowd gathered and someone in the crowd was able to recall one Bithal Das, who had died of electrocution in 1955. They started for the house of Bithal Das but returned back to the post office while they were within 200 meters of his house because the crowd was increasing and it was late in the evening. Rakesh is said to have recognized Bithal Das's son, Bhanwar Lal who was on a rickshaw on his way to the bus station. (He was going to Jaipur for some special medical consultation for his wife.) Radha, Bithal Das's widow, was sent for and she came to the post office where she met Rakesh. After spending nearly six hours altogether in Tonk, Rakesh and his father, returned back to Kankroli by a late night bus.

Two days after their visit, Bhanwar Lal visited Rakesh and his parents in Kankroli and questioned them. After having become convinced that the case was genuine, he returned back to Tonk. Subsequently, the two families continued to exchange visits on important occasions in the family. (I made follow-up visits to Rakesh's family in 1979, 1980. I also obtained some information in correspondence during 1985 prior to my last visit to them in December 1986.)

I, along with Barker (who was assisting me and training in the investigations of such cases) investigated this case between November 1976 (within a few weeks of Rakesh's visit to Tonk) and November 1978. We learned from various informants that Rakesh had made 27 statements about the life and death of Bithal Das. Out of these, 23 statements were found to correspond correctly to the life and death of Bithal Das, whereas four were incorrect.

Although the informants agreed on most of the details, they disagreed on some. Barker and I appraised the discrepancies differently and disagreed to the extent that, in the end, we published different interpretations of the evidence in the same paper (Pasricha and Barker, 1981). Briefly, Barker thought the case might have developed solely from information that could have reached Rakesh normally before he made detailed statements about the previous life; this seemed unlikely to me, and I favored an interpretation including some paranormal process.

The presentation of this case here highlights the need for viewing a case in its totality. It shows how important it is to take all aspects of a case into account at the time of its interpretation; otherwise attention focused only on a few isolated features of a case can distort the picture and impair understanding of the case. In addition, this case highlights the importance of getting to cases quickly before informants' memories have faded, and obtaining corroborating testimony from two or more informants as to what the subject said before the two families had met.

In order to check on certain details and to have a better understanding of the case, I made further visits to Kankroli and Tonk in 1979, 1980 and 1986. I interviewed several old and new informants for this purpose. On the basis of my findings during these and earlier visits I was convinced that Rakesh's statements best referred to the life and death of Bithal Das and that he did not obtain his information normally. I published these observations and interpretations in a later report (Pasricha, 1983).

Unusual or Atypical Cases

During the course of my investigations of the reincarnation type cases I also investigated cases which did not conform to the pattern of 'standard' cases. Here I shall provide reports of two cases which we have investigated as thoroughly as we possibly could do. The first case is a variant of reincarnation type cases with additional feature of Xenoglossy, developed around mid 1970s and we investigated it between 1975 and 1986. We have published a detailed report of this case earlier (Pasricha and Stevenson, 1980), I will provide only a brief account of the case along with a comparison of its features with some other types of cases. The second case comes under the category of possession type cases and has developed quite recently. Although I have included one report of such a case under the case reports of Atypical Cases in chapter Four, for reasons mentioned earlier that case was not investigated as thoroughly as the one I propose to present here. Therefore I shall give a detailed account of the case along with its possible interpretations.

A Case of the Reincarnation Type with Xenoglossy

Xenoglossy is an ability to speak a foreign language without having learnt it normally. Authentic cases of this type are rare in the literature of parapsychology or psychiatry. Almost no such case had been reported from India prior to the one being summarized here.

The subject of this case was Uttara Huddar, an unmarried Marathi woman from Nagpur, Maharashtra. At the age of about 32 years she showed signs of a major change in her personality. On the eighth day of the waning or waxing moon, she assumed the personality of a married Bengali woman who called herself Sharada. During these 'Sharada phases' she conversed only in Bengali (a language not known to Uttara's family or to Uttara herself in her normal state) and spent most of her time in religious rituals and singing devotional songs. Uttara's parents had to arrange for some Bengali-speaking persons in order to converse with her during her Sharada phases.

Sharada stated that she was married and that her husband was a Vaidya (a doctor of the Ayurvedic system of medicine) who used to travel from village to village to attend to his patients. Sharada's married life was mainly spent in what is now Bangladesh, formerly East Bengal. She said that when she was seven months pregnant she was bitten by a snake while plucking flowers, and fell unconscious. She did not remember having 'died' or anything about the period between the times of her falling 'unconscious' and coming to Nagpur. When questioned on this, she said that she came walking in search of her husband.[32]

Sharada gave the names of places and persons connected with her life in Bengal. She gave an accurate account of conditions in the villages of Bengal during the early 19th century. She showed complete unfamiliarity with modern day-to-day utility items such as a fan or an electric switch. In her language she used no English words although the vocabulary of modern Bengali includes about 20 percent of English loan words.

On verification, a family by the name given by Sharada was found in Bansberia, one of several towns in West Bengal that she mentioned. The head of this family has a genealogy, which goes back to the early 19th century, and it has six names of male members in the relationship that Sharada said that she had had to them. This genealogy does not mention any female names but the male names mentioned by Sharada correctly figuring in it, and with the relationships she mentioned, indicate a strong possibility of her membership in this particular family. This

32. Uttara's memories of a previous life first emerged while she was being treated (for some physical ailment) as an in-patient by a Marathi-speaking homeopathic physician of Nagpur. Uttara, during her Sharada phase, claimed that this physician was her husband. He, however, had had no memories of a previous life.

genealogy, Sharada's unfamiliarity with modern technology, and her English-free Bengali indicate that Sharada lived about between 1810 and 1830.

This case is unusual in several ways. First, subjects of the usual reincarnation type cases start talking about their previous lives between the ages of two and four, whereas Uttara started only at the age of 32. Second, the children of the usual reincarnation type cases rarely go into a trance (and almost never one of long duration) while narrating their past experiences; Uttara always went into a trance before changing over to the Sharada personality. Third, the present personality of the usual subject is rarely taken over fully by the claimed previous personality as happened in the case of Uttara. Finally, the intermission between the death of Sharada and the birth of Uttara is much longer (about 110 years) compared with the interval in the usual reincarnation type cases; exceptions do occur but generally the intermission does not exceed three or four years.

This case also presents features of a case of secondary personality, but differs from it in important aspects. For example, the usual secondary personality is generally found to be a contemporary and collocal with the primary personality, whereas Sharada described a life about 150 years earlier and in another part of the country–far removed in time and place from her present life. She also displayed an ability to speak a language that she had not learned during her present lifetime. I (along with Dr. Stevenson) consider that she acquired this knowledge paranormally. In the recent literature almost no cases have been reported of a secondary personality with paranormal abilities.

I first met Uttara in 1975 and have investigated her case mostly with Dr. Stevenson (on some occasions I have visited her without him) over nearly a ten-year period. I last visited her in December 1986. During this last visit I learned from Uttara, her sister and another informant that the frequency and duration of the Sharada phases had diminished but they had not ceased altogether. We first published a brief report of her case in 1979 (Stevenson and Pasricha, 1979) and a year later published a longer version of it (Stevenson and Pasricha, 1980).

A Recent Case of the Possession Type

The subject of this case Sumitra Singh, when I first began studying her case in December 1985, was about 17 years old married woman. She was living with her in-laws in the village of Sharifpura of Farrukhabad District, Uttar Pradesh, India. They belonged to a lower middle economic class and were Thakurs by caste. Sumitra had been married to Jagdish Singh, in 1981, at the age of about 13 years, and gave birth to a male child in December 1984.

Two or three months after the birth of her child she started suffering from fits, characterized by loss of consciousness, rolling up of eyes and clenching of teeth. At times, these fits were followed by a trance-like state during which time she would speak. On some such occasions she claimed that she was goddess *Santoshi Ma*[33] and on two occasions someone else. On one of these occasions she claimed that she was one Munni Devi—a woman of Sharifpura known to the family—who had died of drowning; and on another occasion she said that she was a man of another state, the identity of whom could not be established.

During these episodes of apparent possessions sometimes her condition worsened sufficiently so that her family had to seek

33. Santoshi Ma is a Hindu goddess and is regarded as the special protector of faithful women. Apparently very little was known about her until this century and there is no mention of her in some standard works of reference for Hinduism, such as Walker (1968/1983). Possession by Santoshi Ma is not considered as pathological by the villagers of northern India.

help from local healers. One such healer was one Vishwanath of Sikandarpur who was also distantly related to the family. He was a cultivator by occupation and had been treating some local cases in his village but had no experience in cases like Sumitra's. He himself at times went into trances and would be possessed by the Hindu god *Hanuman*. Vishawanath's intervention, however, did not arrest Sumitra's episodes of possessions although he had a pacifying influence on her.

Sometime around July 16, 1985, during one of her possessions by Santoshi Ma, Sumitra predicted that she would die after three days. On July 19, 1985 she seemed dead to her family members and some villagers who were present. According to the informants she was pulseless, apneic, and her face looked pale, drained of blood, "like that of a dead person." Her family members had started crying and preparing for funeral when she revived after sometime of her apparent death. Different informants estimated the period of her "death" to be between five and 45 minutes. (It is however, possible that some of them considered her dead from the time when her pulse became shallow.) No qualified doctor was available at the time.

Sumitra was confused briefly after her revival, and did not recognize people around. She did not say anything for about a day then began to say that she was Shiva and that she lived in Dibiyapur where she was murdered by her in-laws. She said that during a quarrel, her sister-in-law had hit her on the head with a brick and then the family had carried her to the railway tracks and placed her body there. She refused to recognize Sumitra's husband and child and asked to be taken to her own two children. Gradually she gave many more details about the life and death of Shiva, and about the members of Shiva's parental family. She said that her father was Ram Siya Tripathi, a teacher, who lived in Etawah.

Sumitra's in-laws knew nothing about any Shiva or her death at Dibiyapur, and they made no attempts to verify her statements. They first thought that she had gone mad but when she continued to insist that she was Shiva and refused to recognize them they thought that she was possessed by a spirit. So the members of her in-law's family and other significant persons in the village explained to her that she had died and a new soul has entered into her body. But since the body is same as before her (apparent) death, she should fulfill the duties of Sumitra.

After about two weeks Sumitra resumed normal relations with her husband and also began to look after the child but continued to insist that she was Shiva and that her real family lived in Etawah and Dibiyapur. On hearing about the change in her personality Sumitra's parental family came to visit her but she did not recognize them.

Sometime in the month of August, 1985 Ram Siya Tripathi of Etawah heard about the case and came to visit Sumitra at Sharifpura. I shall describe the details of his visit and other features of the case in a later section of this report.

The case came to my attention in November 1985 within a short time of the first exchange of visits between the families concerned. I began investigation of the case within three weeks of learning about it. On subsequent visits I was joined by Dr. Stevenson and studied it further on five more occasions between February 1986 and December 1988. We interviewed 62 informants at length in different towns and villages (in and out of the Districts of Etawah, Mainpuri, Farrukhabad, and Hardoi). The informants included members of the families concerned as well as those who were not directly related with the families but contributed in establishing the facts of the case. We particularly focused our attention on learning about the nature of illness, apparent death and revival of Sumitra, her education, the possibility for normal communication of information about Shiva's life and death to Sumitra and/or her family; and the circumstances of Sumitra's recognitions of Shiva's family in person or in photographs after the change in her personality.

Change in Sumitra's personality. In addition to her claims that she was Shiva, Sumitra also displayed certain habits that were quite different from her previous ones. She said that she was a Brahmin and behaved like a high-caste educated, urbanized woman. We learned from several informants that Sumitra had never attended a school and had been barely literate and could write a letter and occasionally did so but after her revival she showed marked increase in her ability to read and write Hindi. I had the opportunity of observing her on a few occasions performing both these activities. Considering her educational background, she could perform both these activities with great efficiency and fluency. It should be noted, however, that the change in her literacy was not in her basic knowledge to read and write but in her interest and fluency to do so.

After her revival Sumitra also changed her style of wearing a sari and she put on sandals, which Sumitra had rarely worn. She also addressed her family members differently and with more respect. For example, she addressed Jagdish Singh as Thakur Saheb instead of calling him as Guddi's brother as she used to, before the episode. (One of Jagdish Singh's sisters was called Guddi.) Similarly, she addressed her mother-in-law and father-in-law as *Mataji* and *Pitaji* (respectful way of addressing one's mother and father) instead of *Amma* (as a villager would generally address his mother) and *Chacha* (father's friend or brother).

Meeting of the families concerned. Sometime in the month of August 1985, a lecturer of an intermediate school of Etawah, called Ram Siya Tripathi, whose daughter Shiva had been married and had died in Dibiyapur, heard a rumor that his daughter had been 'reborn' in Sharifpura. For some weeks Ram Siya Tripathi did nothing about this rumor, but eventually learned of a person called Ram Prakash Dube who worked in Etawah and lived in the same general area where the Tripathis lived. He belonged to a village called Murra which was close to Sharifpura. Ram Siya Tripathi requested Ram Prakash Dube to inquire about the rumor. After the necessary inquiries this man reported that Sumitra was indeed giving particulars about the life of Ram Siya Tripathi's daughter Shiva. Stimulated by the news, Ram Siya Tripathi went himself, accompanied by one of Shiva's maternal uncles (Baleshwar Prasad), to Sharifpura sometime in October 1985 i.e. about three months after the revival.

Recognitions by Sumitra at Sharifpura. Ram Siya Tripathi introduced himself to Sumitra's in-laws outside the house and was then allowed to meet her. She is said to have immediately recognized him, called him "Papa" (as Shiva used to), and wept bitterly. She also recognized Baleshwar Prasad who had accompanied Ram Siya Tripathi. Ram Siya Tripathi had taken with him an album of photographs of family members, most of which were taken several years ago. He showed the photographs to Sumitra, and without giving any cues, asked her to identify them which she was able to do. (We interviewed a man from a neighboring village, who had accompanied Ram Siya Tripathi and Baleshwar Prasad to Sharifpura. He confirmed that Sumitra was not given any cues about the persons she named in the photographs.) She correctly recognized 14 persons in the photographs. Sumitra's recognition of these photographs and her answers to his queries convinced Ram Siya Tripathi that she had memories of his daughter Shiva. He requested Sumitra's in-law's to permit her and her husband to visit them in Etawah.

Subsequent to Ram Siya Tripathi's visit, one of Shiva's maternal uncles (Ram Prakash Dixit) went to visit Sumitra wearing a beard that he did not have during Shiva's lifetime. She seemed to recognize him by his voice. (During my first meeting with Sumitra at Firozabad, in November 1985, she was visiting the family of Ram Prakash Dixit. She did not behave like a stranger in that family and seemed to be enjoying their company.)

Recognitions by Sumitra at Etawah. On the following day, Sumitra and her husband accompanied Ram Siya Tripathi to Etawah. She seemed quite familiar with the people and quarter of Etawah where Ram Siya Tripathi's family lived. She recognized other members of Shiva's family whose photographs she had not seen. She recognized, for example, one of Shiva's maternal uncles, gave his name correctly and said that he was from Kanpur (a larger city to the east of Etawah). This uncle had his business in Kanpur and lived there during Shiva's lifetime but had shifted to Etawah since her death. On later occasions she correctly recognized other members of Shiva's family and circle of friends who were not present on the day of her first visit. Altogether Sumitra recognized at least 22 members of Shiva's family or friends in person or in photographs. It is possible that she was aided by cues for certain recognitions but most occurred under satisfactory conditions such as the recognition of Ram Prakash Dixit of Firozabad.

Life and circumstances of death of Shiva. Shiva was the daughter of Ram Rani and Ram Siya Tripathi, a lecturer at an inter college at Etawah. She was born on October 24, 1962 at village Sev of District Etawah; and was brought up and educated at Etawah. She had been educated up to B.A. and had been married and living in Dibiyapur with her husband and his parents and sisters in a joint family. Perhaps due to Shiva's superior education and urban manners a friction developed between Shiva and her in-laws. They grumbled when she returned to Etawah in order to write her final exams for her college degree. A more serious quarrel developed during second half of May 1985 when Shiva wanted to attend a marriage of a member of her sister's family. At first she was permitted by her in-laws to attend the wedding but later they changed their mind and did not allow her to attend it. On the evening of May 18, 1985, Brijesh Pathak, one of Shiva's maternal uncles by marriage, who lived about a kilometer away from Dibiyapur, visited Shiva. She told him about the quarrel at home and how her mother-in-law and sister-in-law had beaten her up. However, Shiva did not seem depressed nor did she talk of suicide. Brijesh Pathak advised the family to contact Shiva's parents to arrange for a peaceful solution.

The next morning Brijesh Pathak and his brothers learned that Shiva had died in an "accident." Her dead body had been found on the railway tracks and her in-laws said that she had thrown herself in front of a train. Brijesh Pathak remembered the quarrel the night before and requested them to wait for Shiva's parents for cremation. However, Shiva's in-laws ignored the request, obtained permission from five local members (filled a *Panchnama*[34] and cremated the body by about 11 a.m. To make it burn quickly they are said to have poured fuel oil on the wood. Ram Siya Tripathi arrived at Dibiyapur around 2 p.m. by which time the body had already been cremated.

At the time of her death Shiva had two young children nicknamed Tinku and Rinku aged one and half years and six months respectively. She died on May 19, 1985 at 22 years of age. She might have committed suicide (out of desperation about

34. The legal formalities for cremation of a body in a village require that five notables of the village sign a document, certifying death of the person, called a *Panchnama* (five names, or names of the chiefs). Although some of the persons in such committees are honest, and incorruptible, many of them may sign a document falsely. A *Panchnama*, however, bears no credence if other evidence points to suspicious circumstances.

her unhappy life with her in-laws); but there were strong suspicions that her in-laws had murdered her and Ram Siya Tripathi instigated a judicial inquiry on the matter.

We interviewed five persons who saw Shiva's body on the morning of May 19, 1985 before it was cremated. When discovered, it lay between two rails of a track at the railway station of Phaphoond (Dibiyapur). The body was intact and therefore had not been run over by the wheels of a train; several trains had passed the station during the night. A firsthand confirmation of this report would have been of immense value but we could not meet a witness in this regard. Therefore, on the basis of available information, we must suspend judgment about circumstances of Shiva's death. However, she died violently after a quarrel with her in-laws on the night of May 18-19, 1985, was established.

Following Ram Siya's complaint, a number of elementary facts about Shiva's death and the legal proceedings were reported in the newspapers of Etawah. However, the newspaper accounts were confined mainly to the facts and conjectures connected with Shiva's violent death. Some newspapers also published some of her recent photographs.

Geographical distances between the families concerned. Sharifpura (where Sumitra's in-laws lived) is a small village about 65 kilometers northwest of Etawah (where Shiva's parents lived). Dibiyapur (where Shiva's in-laws lived) is a small town about 60 kilometers east of Etawah and about 100 kilometers from Sharifpura.

Possible normal means of communication between the families concerned. All the families concerned in the case (Shiva's as well as Sumitra's) denied any knowledge of each other before the development of the case. Considering the separation of the families by socioeconomic status and long geographical distances involved, we have no reason to doubt their testimony in this regard.

The accounts of Shiva's death were published in the newspapers; some of these newspapers had reached Sharifpura and a neighboring place called Sikandarpur (where some relatives of Sumitra's mother-in-law lived and Sumitra had also visited that place from time to time). However, Sumitra could not have learned from newspaper reports about the details she knew about Shiva's private life.

Another possibility of communication of information between the families concerned could have been through certain women of the village of Murra, two kilometers from Sharifpura, who had married and lived in Dibiyapur. They were the ones who first brought to Dibiyapur the news about Sumitra's apparent death, revival and claim to be Shiva. (From there somehow the news reached Shiva's in-laws and during one of Ram Siya Tripathi's visits to Dibiyapur, he was informed that his daughter had been communicating through someone in Sharifpura.) It is possible that the same women might have conveyed information about Shiva back to Murra from Dibiyápur. It may be conjectured that the news somehow got spread from Murra to Sharifpura. However, our inquiries at all these places revealed that these women seldom traveled back and forth between the two villages; but even if they did, they would not have known the details about Shiva's family in Etawah and their private possessions of which Sumitra showed knowledge. This seemed equally true of some persons of Sharifpura who traded in Etawah. They all denied knowledge of Ram Siya Tripathi before the development of the case.

Ram Siya Tripathi himself did not even know about the location of Sharifpura before he learned about the case from Dibiyapur. If he knew the family, he could have immediately visited them but he did not, and that is why it took him nearly three months to reach the case after its development. On the other hand, Sumitra's in-laws had enough clues from her statements to have found Ram Siya Tripathi in Etawah if they had tried to. May be they did not try due to lack of interest or lack of money but if they had already known about the existence of Ram Siya Tripathi, they would have almost certainly tried to communicate with him if not directly then may be through villagers of Sharifpura who traded in Etawah. But since they did not know each other, no attempt was made until Ram Siya Tripathi learned (accidentally) about the rumor and waited for its confirmation.

Evidence of paranormal knowledge. As I have mentioned above, after Ram Siya Tripathi's request for a judicial inquiry into Shiva's death, a number of items, mainly reporting her violent death, were published in the local newspapers of Etawah, and hence they were in public domain. Although we do not know that they were actually available to Sumitra, let us presume they were. There were, however, at least 16 details of knowledge about Shiva and her family given by Sumitra that were not published in the newspapers; nor were they likely to have been known outside her immediate family or close friends.

Possible Interpretations of the Case

It is almost impossible to entertain a definite interpretation in the case presented above. I shall briefly discuss the merits and demerits of several hypotheses which can be considered for understanding the features of such a case.

Hoax. In order to stage a hoax Sumitra would need to collect information about both the families of Shiva including several personal details. This seems virtually impossible because in order to do that Sumitra would have had to leave her village without being noticed; and there was no one in the village who knew the intimate details about Shiva's life. It can be supposed that her husband and some other villagers could have joined her in staging a hoax. Sumitra's husband could have moved around more easily than her to collect the required information. But he was not in a position (nor had any apparent motive) to go to various places to collect unpublished information without the knowledge of anyone. Sumitra and her in-laws might have gained some publicity after the changeover and Sumitra personally would have gained more attention from within and outside her family, but all these gains seem minuscule. Moreover, they had no resources (and possible interest or motive) for making extensive inquiries in Etawah, Dibiyapur, and other places connected with the life and death of Shiva. It has been suggested that the exorcist Vishwanath might have obtained information about Shiva. Later, when he had access to her, would have coached Sumitra before and after her revival. However, this suggestion fails to account for the knowledge Sumitra had about persons and possessions of the Tripathi family.

Shiva's parental family had the information included in Sumitra's statements and it can be conjectured that Ram Siya Tripathi might have collaborated in a hoax. But why did he chose Sumitra for this purpose who lived in a remote village (he did not even know the existence of this village), and belonged to a much lower socioeconomic background than himself? And how could he pass on to her all the required information without having been noticed by others? As he himself said (and we agree to that) that the status of his legal case (against Shiva's in-laws) would not have improved.

Shiva's in-laws at Dibiyapur knew about the circumstances and mode of her death. After her revival, Sumitra had been saying that her in-laws had murdered her (as Shiva). The in-laws could not be suspected in joining Sumitra in a hoax and supplying this information to her. They were already incriminated in Shiva's death and hence would have an interest in Sumitra's silence.

Cryptomnesia. According to this interpretation it is supposed that Sumitra might have somehow obtained information about the life and death of Shiva by normal means through the gossip and rumors of the women of Murra who were married at Dibiyapur, or through the newspaper reports, or both. Although from our investigations we did not find evidence for it, we cannot exclude the possibility that some information, particularly about Shiva's death which was in the public domain, reached Sharifpura by normal means. On the basis of information thus obtained, she would have unconsciously assimilated this information in constructing a secondary personality. She or her family may not be aware that she had gathered the information she later showed. However, the knowledge displayed by Sumitra went much beyond mentioning Shiva's death. Her recognitions of 22 persons known to Shiva cannot be explained on the basis of verbal information, if at all available to her. Moreover, such knowledge cannot be communicated in words; it depends on tacit knowledge (Polanyi, 1966; Stevenson, 1974a; Stevenson and Pasricha, 1979,1980; Stevenson, 1984).

Extrasensory perception and secondary personality. In most of the cases of secondary personalities reported in the literature, the subjects generally do not provide evidence for paranormal knowledge although a few exceptions have occurred for example, the case of Doris Fischer (Prince, 1915-16). However, in Sumitra's case there is no evidence that she had any powers of extrasensory perception before the changeover in her personality. It seems unlikely (but not impossible) that she suddenly acquired such powers to the degree necessary to obtain all the knowledge she showed about the life and death of Shiva and then developed a secondary personality with that information.

Possession. After her apparent death and revival, Sumitra showed a marked change in her behavior that greatly impressed all those who had known her before the changeover. If we set aside the other interpretations (mentioned above) as inadequate to account for all the features of the case, we are justified in considering that a drastic change in her personality had occurred. When the change in personality occurs beyond recognition that the person displays knowledge and behavior of a deceased personality the case may be best interpreted as a type of *Parakayapravesh* (entering into another body) or possession. Although one cannot assert that this is the best interpretation for this case; the weaknesses in other interpretations warrant a serious consideration of this hypothesis at this stage.

On the basis of information so far available, we have published a report on the case (Stevenson and Pasricha, 1989) and we plan to continue our investigations further.

Near-Death Experiences

While investigating cases of the reincarnation type, I learned about individuals who had died or nearly died and then survived after varied periods of time, with or without intervention. After returning back to full life (or regaining consciousness) they narrate experiences they remember having had while they were dead or seemed to be. In addition to the experiences these subjects claim to have had in another realm, some of them show a simultaneous knowledge of events occurring around their physical body or surroundings. In other words, they have access to information about happenings on earth as well as in another realm. The subjects in general report, for example, meeting in another realm some relative about the death of whom they have had no normal knowledge, and simultaneously they can sometimes 'see' from a distant point (located outside the physical body) what is being done to their physical body and that people around it are talking or crying.

I have studied 18 such cases in different parts of India—mainly from the northern regions, such as in U.P. and Rajasthan. I (along with Dr. Stevenson and other colleagues) studied these cases between 1975 and 1983. We could study only 16 of them to a satisfactory level of investigation.

All the subjects were Hindi speakers. Eleven were males and five were females. Here again I should point out that these cases were studied as and when they came to our attention or were reported to us. No systematic sampling techniques were used (although one such study is now underway at NIMHANS); therefore no generalizations about demographic features or other aspects of the cases are warranted at this stage.

We compared the features of 16 Indian cases with 78 American cases. The American subjects generally see their physical body as if from another position in space, whereas Indian cases do not. The Indian subjects are generally taken by messengers of Yama (the god of death); their records are reviewed and a mistake in the name of the person is discovered; the messengers are sometimes reproached for having brought the wrong person (whose life span on earth is not complete) or are simply directed to return the person back and bring someone else.

In many of the cases we were told that a person having the same name as the subject who was generally hale and hearty, had died after the return of the 'wrong' person (our subject). But we ourselves have not been able to verify the detail of another person dying in any case. The subjects of the American cases, on the other hand, do not say they revived because of a mistake. If they say anything about why they returned they might say they did this because of their love for their friends or relatives. Also, some of them report that deceased relatives ask or tell them to go back "as their time has not yet come." Thus the theme that "your time has not yet come or it has not matured" is found among subjects of both cultures, but the way of expressing this differs. The Indian subjects sometimes report meeting relatives or friends or acquaintances in the other realm but these persons seldom tell the subjects that their time has not yet come and that they should continue to live more.

We have discussed the similarities and differences that occur in two cultures in a recent report (Pasricha and Stevenson, 1986).

The preliminary findings suggest that some of the differences between the two groups of cases might have resulted from the differences in culture-engendered beliefs, but others might derive from the subjects' personal beliefs regarding life after death. We need to carry out systematic and detailed studies in this area before we can understand the various factors associated with this phenomenon.

CHAPTER EIGHT

Directions of Future Research

In the preceding chapter, I have briefly summarized the research I have been carrying out since 1978. The study reported in this book has obvious limitations that I have acknowledged in different places. Some of these limitations can be overcome to a great extent if for example, we are informed about the cases as soon as they are developed before any attempt is made at solving a reincarnation type or possession type case by the subjects' parents or any other person concerned.

I have stated earlier that almost all of the cases reported in this book, had already been solved by the members of the subjects' family or others before I (or my colleagues) could reach the scene for investigation. This has meant that for such cases we have had to depend on the observations and memories of persons who, however intelligent they may be, are not trained observers. It is much more satisfactory if we can study a case before anyone has tried to find a family corresponding to the child's statements. Ideally a case should be reported to us as soon as the child starts talking about a previous life. The parents or other relatives should refrain from making any effort at solving the case by themselves. For a better understanding of the phenomenon, I plan to continue to study cases of the reincarnation type and possession type, and also near-death experiences. In the area of reincarnation I am particularly interested in the cases in which:

1. The subject still remembers a previous life and the two families concerned have not met;
2. The subjects have birthmarks or birth defects related to injuries in the claimed previous life;
3. The subjects are twins, at least one of whom remembers a previous life; and
4. The subject remembers having been a member of the opposite sex in a previous life.

I hope to be able to investigate more such cases (particularly of the types mentioned above) and share the results with the readers in subsequent volumes. This will, of course, be possible only with the cooperation of many persons including the informants and families concerned in these cases. Readers are once again requested to write to me about cases of the reincarnation type and possession type, and also about the experiences of persons who have had close encounters with death (near death experiences) as soon as they learn about the development of such cases. The study of such cases at an early stage will perhaps help us discover new facts that will improve our presently limited knowledge of death and what may come after death.

Bibliography and References

Adi Granth. Guru Arjan. *Bavan Akhari* 38, 258.

Adi Granth, Ravidas, 694.

Atreya, B. L. (1957). *An Introduction to Parapsychology.* Banares: The International Standard Publication.

Aurobindo,Sri (1969). *The Problem of Rebirth.* Pondicherry: Sri Aurobindo Ashram. (Originally published in 1952.)

Bandura, A., Ross, D., and Ross, S.A. (1963). A comparative test of the status envy, social power, and the secondary reinforcement theories of identificatory learning. *Journal of Abnormal and Social Psychology.* 67:527-534.

Barker, D.R., and Pasricha, S. (1979). Reincarnation cases in Fatehabad: A systematic survey in north India. *Journal of Asian and African Studies.* 14:231-240.

Barrett, W.F. (1911). *Psychical Research.* London: Williams and Norgate.

Bayer, R. (1970-71). Personal communications cited by I. Stevenson, 1977a.

Beals, R.L., and Hoijer, H. (1965). *An Introduction to Anthoropology.* New Work: Macmillan Company.

Bernstein, M. (1956). *The Search for Bridey Murphy.* Garden City, New York: Doubleday.

Besterman, T. (1933). An experiment in "Clairoyance" with M. Stefan Ossowiecki, *Proceedings of the Society for Psychical Research.* 41:345-351.

Besterman, T. (1968). Belief in rebirth among the natives of Africa (including Madagascar). In T. Besterman, *Collected Papers on the Paranormal.* New York: Garrett Publications.

Bhagavad Gita. 6,43; 4,9;4,9;8,15-16.

Blythe, H. (1957). The *Three Lives of Naomi Henry*. New York: The Citadel Press.

Bose, S. C. (1959). *Jatismar Katha*. Satsang, Bihar. Privately published. (Englih translation [1960] by Edmund J. Spencer, unpublished manuscript.)

Broad, C.D. (1971). *Lectures on Psychical Research*. London: Routledge & Kegan Paul. (First published in 1962.)

Bucke, R. (1961). *Cosmic Consciousness: A Study in the Evolution of the Human Mind*. New Hyde Park, N.Y.: University Books.

Carstairs, M. (1957). *The Twice-Born*. London: Hogarh Press.

Cerminara, G. (1950). *Many Mansions*. New York: William Sloan Associates, Inc.

Chari, C.T.K. (1962a). Paranormal cognition, survival and reincarnation. *Journal of the American Society for Psychical Research*. 56: 158-183.

Chari, C.T.K. (1962b). Paramnesia and reincarnation. *Proceedings of the Society for Psychical Research*. 53: 264-286.

Cohn, B.S. (1959). Changing traditions of a low caste. In M. Singer (Ed.) *Traditional India: Structure and Change*. Philadelphia: American Folklore Society.

Cook, E.W., Pasricha, S., Samararatne, G., U. Win Maung., and Stevenson, I. (1983). A review and analysis of "unsolved" cases of the reincarnation type: I Introduction and illustrative case reports. *Journal of the American Society for Psychical Research*. 77: 45-63.

Cook, E.W., Pasricha, S., Samararatne, G., U. Win Maung., and Stevenson, I. (1983). A review and analysis of "unsolved" cases of the reincarnation type : II Comparison of features of solved and unsolved cases. *Journal of the American Society for Psychical Research.* 77: 115-135.

Dean, D. (1970). Techniques and status of modern parapsychology. AAAS Symposium. *Science.* 170: 1237-1238.

Delanne, G. (1924). Documents pour servir a l'etude de la r'eincarnation. Paris: Editions de la B.P.S. Cited by I. Stevenson, 1977a.

De Rochas, A. (1911). *Les Vies Successives.* Chacornac, Paris. Cited by C.J. Ducasse, 1961.

Dube, S .C. (1955). *Indian Village.* Ithaca, N.Y.: Cornell University Press.

Ducasse, C. J. (1961). *A Critical Examination of the Belief in a Life after Death.* Springfield, Ill.: Charles C. Thomas.

Ducasse, C. J. (1962). What would constitute conclusive evidence of survival after death? *Journal of the Society for Psychical Research.* 41: 401-406.

Durkheim, E. (1965). *The Elementary Forms of the Relgious Life.* New York: The Free Press.

Ebin, D. (Ed.) (1961). *The Drug Experience.* New York: Orion Press.

Elder, J. W. (1959). *Industrialism in Hindu Society: A Case Study in Social Change.* Unpublished dissertation. Harvard University. Press.

Evans, C. (1973). Parapsychology: What the questionnaire reveals. *New Scientist.* 57: 209.

Festinger, L. (1950). Informal social communication. *Psychological Review.* 57: 271-282.

Gallup International (1969). Report of polls concerning the belief in reincarnation in West Europe, Canada, and the United States.

Grof, S., and Grof, J.H. (1976). Psychedelics and the experience of death. In *Life after Death.* Contributed by Arnold Toynbee, Arthur Koestler and others. London: Weidenfeld and Nicolson.

Gupta, L. D., Sharma, N.R., and Mathur, T. C. (1936). *An Inquiry into the Case of Shanti Devi.* Delhi: International Aryan League.

Hall, H .F. (1898). *The Soul of a People.* London: Macmillan.

Hardy, A., Harvie, R., and Koestler, A. (1974). The Challenge of *Chance.* New York: Random House, Inc.

Harper, E. B. (1959). A Hindu village pantheon. *Southwestern Journal of Anthropology.* 15: 227-234.

Head, J., and Cranston, S. L. (1967). *Reincarnation in World Thought.* New York: Julian Press.

Head, J., and Cranston, S. L. (1977). *Reincarnation: The Phoenix Fire Mystery.* New York: Julian Press/Crown Publishers.

Heywood, R. (1971). *The Infinite Hive.* London:Pan Books, Ltd.

Hill, J. A. (1917). *Psychical Investigations.* New York: George H. Doran Co.

Hume, D. (1881). *Essays and Treatises on Various Subjects.* Cited by C.J. Ducasse, 1961.

Humphreys, C. (1943). *Karma and Rebirth* London: John Murray.

Huxley, A. (1954). *The Doors of Perception.* New York: Harper and Bros.

Hyslop, J. H. (1909). A case of vertical hallucinations. *Proceedings of the American Society for Psychical Research.* 3: 1-469.

James, W. (1890). *The Principles of Psychology.* New York: Henry Holt & Co.

Judge, W. Q. (n.d.). *Aphorisms on Karma*. Cited by C. Humphreys. 1943.

Jung, C. G. (1963). *Memories, Dreams, Reflections.* trans. Richard and Clara Winston. London: Collins.

Koestler, A. (1973). *The Roots of Coincidence: An Excursion into Parapsychology.* (Originally published by Random House, Inc., New York, 1972.)

Kolenda, P .M. (1964). Religious anxiety and Hindu fate. In Harper, E. B. (Ed.) *Religion in South Asia.* Seattle: University of Washington Press.

Kuppuswamy, B. (1962). *Manual of the Socioeconomic Status Scale* (Urban). Delhi: Manasayan.

LaBarre, W. (1962). *They Shall Take Up Serpents*. Minneapolis: University of Minnesota Press.

Lewis, O. (1958). *Village Life in Northern India*. Urbana: University of Illinois Press.

Ludwig, A., and Levine, J. (1966). Clinical effects of psychedelic agents. *Clinical Medicine.* 73: 21-24.

McTaggart, J.M.E. (1915). *Human Immortality and Pre-Existence.* London: Edward Arnold.

Makarem, S. (1972). *The Doctrine of the Ismailis.* Beirut: The Arab Institute of Research and Publishing.

Makarem, S. (1973). Personal Communication. Cited by I. Stevenson, 1977a.

Malinowski, B. (1954). Baloma: The spirits of the dead in the Trobriand Islands. *In Magic, Science and Religion and Other Essays.* Garden City, New York: Doubleday.

Marshall, J. (1969). *Law and Psychology in Conflict.* Garden City. New York: Doubleday & Co., Inc.

Marshall, J., Marquis, K.H., and Oskamp, S. (1971). Effects of kind of question and atmosphere of interrogation on accuracy and completeness of testimony. *Harvard law Review.* 84 : 1620-43.

Marston, W.M. (1924). Studies in testimony. *Journal of Criminal Law and Criminology.* 15: 5-31.

Mischel, W., and Liebert, R.M. (1966). Effects of discrepancies between observed and imposed reward criteria on their acquisition and transmission. *Journal of Personality and Social Psychology.* 3: 45-53.

Moody, R. A., Jr. (1975). *Life After Life.* New York: Bantam Books.

Munro, N. G. (1963). *Ainu: Creed and Cult.* New York: Columbia University Press.

Murphy. G. (1973). A Caringtonian approach to Ian Stevenson's *Twenty Cases Suggestive of Reincarnation. Journal of the American Society for Psychical Research.* 67: 117-129.

Nie, N.H., Hull, C.H., Jenkins, J.G., Steinbrenner, K., and Bent, D.H. (1975). *Statistical Package for the Social Sciences.* 2nd Ed., New York: McGraw-Hill Book Co.

Noon, J.A. (1942). A preliminary examination of death concept of the Ibo. *American Anthropoligist.* 44: 638-654.

Norbu, T.J., and Turnbull, C. (1969). *Tibet: Its History, Religion and People.* London: Chatto and Windus.

Office of the Registrar General. (1973). *Vital Statistics of India 1970.* (New Delhi: Registrar General, India [Vital Statistics Division], Ministry of Home Affairs.)

Osborne, A. (1975). *The Incredible Sai Baba.* London: Rider & Co.

Osty, E. (1923). *Supernormal Faculties in Man.* London: Methuen & Co.

Palmer, J. (1979). A community mail survey of psychic experiences. *Journal of the American Society for Psychical Research.* 73:221-251.

Pareek, U., and Trivedi, G. (1964). *Manual of the Socioeconomic Status Scale (Rural).* Delhi: Manasyan.

Parrinder, E. G. (1954). *African Traidtional Religion.* Westport Connecticut: Greenwood Press.

Parrinder, E. G. (1956). Varieties of belief in reincarnation. *Hibbert Journal.* 55: 260-267.

Parrinder, E.G. (1976). Religions of the East. In *Life After Death.* Contributed by Arnold Toynbee, Arthur Koestler and others. London: Weidenfeld and Nicolson.

Pasricha, S.K. (1983). New information favoring a paranormal interpretation in the case of Rakesh Gaur. *European Journal of Parapsychology.* 5:77-85.

Pasricha, S.K., and Barker, D.R. (1981). A case of the reincarnation type in India: The case of Rakesh Gaur. *European Journal of Parapsychology.* 3: 381-408.

Pasricha, S.K., Murthy, H.N., and Murthy, V.N. (1978). Examination of the claims of reincarnation in a psychotic condition. *Indian Journal of Clinical Psychology.* 5: 197-202.

Pasricha, S., and Stevenson, I. (1977). Three cases of the reincarnation type in India. *Indian Journal of Psychiatry.* 19: 36-42.

Pasricha, S., and Stevenson, I. (1986). Near-death experiences in India: A preliminary report. *Journal of Nervous and Mental Disease.* 174: 165-170.

Pasricha, S., and Stevenson, I. (1987). Indian cases of the reincarnation type - Two generations apart. *Journal of the Society for Psychical Research.* 54: 239-246.

Patanjali. Yoga Sutra. 3, 18

Polanyi, M. (1962). Tacit knowing: Its bearing on some problems of philosophy. *Reviews of Modern Physics.* 34: 601-616

Pratt, J.G. (1973). A decade of research with a selected ESP subject: An overview and reappraisal of the work with Pavel Stepanek. *Proceedings of the American Society for Psychical Research.* 30: 1-78.

Prince, W.F. (1915-16). The Doris case of multiple personality. *Proceedings of the American Society for Psychical Research.* 9-10: 1-1419.

Radhakrishnan, S. (1923). Indian Philosophy. London: George Allen and Unwin Ltd.

Radhakrishnan, S. (1953). *The Principal Upanishads.* New York: Harper.

Ranade, R.D. (1926). *A Constructive Survey of Upanishadic Philosophy: Being a Systematic Inroduction to Indian Metaphysics.* Poona: Oriental Book Agency.

Reiff, R., and Scheerer, M. (1959). *Memory and Hypnotic Age Regression.* New York: International Universities Press.

Richardson, S.A. (1960). The use of leading questions in nonschedule interviews. *Human Organization.* 19: 86-89.

Richardson, S.A., Dohrenwend, B.S., and Klein, D. (1965). *Interviewing: Its forms and Functions.* New York: Basic Books, Inc.

Rosenhan, D.L., Frederick, F., and Burrowes, A. (1968). Preaching and practicing: Effects of channel discrepancy on norm internalization. *Child Development.* 39: 291-302.

Ryall, E.W. (1974). *Born Twice.* New York: Harper & Row.

Sahay, K.K.N. (1927). *Reincarnation: Verified Cases of Rebirth After Death.* Bareilly: N.L. Gupta.

Schwarz, B.E. (1961). Telepathic events in a child between 1 and 3½ years of age. *International Journal of Parapsychology.* 3: 5- 47.

Schweitzer, A. (1957). *Indian Thought and Its Development.* Boston: Beacon.

Shirley, R. (n.d). *The Problem of Rebirth.* London: Occult Book Society.

Slobodin, R. (1970). Kutchin concepts of reincarnation. *Western Canadian Journal of Anthropology.* 2: 67-79.

Spencer, B., and Gillen, F. J. (1904). *The Northern Tribes of Central Australia.* London: Macmillan.

Stevens, E. W. (1887). *The Watseka Wonder. A Narrative of Startling Phenomena Occurring in the Case of Mary Lurancy Vennum.* Chicago: Religio-Philosophical Publishing House.

Stevenson, I. (1960). The evidence for survival from claimed memories of former incarnations. *Journal of the American Society for Psychical Research.* 54: 51-71, 95-117.

Stevenson, I. (1966). Cultural patterns in cases suggestive of reincarnation among the Tlingit Indians of Southeastern Alaska. *Journal of the American Society for Psychical Research.* 60: 229-243.

Stevenson, I. (1970). Characterisitics of cases of the reincarnation type in Turkey and their comparison with cases in two other cultures. *International Journal of Comparative Sociology.* 11: 1-17.

Stevenson, I. (1972). Some new cases suggestive of reincarnation. I. The case of Rajul Shah. *Journal of the American Society for Psychical Research.* 66: 288-309.

Stevenson, I. (1973). Characteristics of cases of the reincarnation type in ceylon. *Conributions to Asian Studies.* 3: 26-39.

Stevenson, I. (1974a). Xenoglossy: A review and report of a case. Proceedings of the American Society for *Psychical Research.* 31: 1-268. (Also Charlottesville: University Press of Virginia.)

Stevenson, I. (1974b). *Twenty Cases Suggestive of Reincarnation.* 2nd. Rev. Ed. Charlottesville: University Press of Virginia. (First published in 1966.)

Stevenson, I. (1974c). Some questions related to cases of the reincarnation type. *Journal of the American Society for Psychical Research.* 68: 395-416.

Stevenson, I. (1975a). *Cases of the Reincarnation Type. Vol. I. Ten Cases in India.* Charlottesville: University Press of Virginia.

Stevenson, I. (1975b). The belief and cases related to reincarnation among the Haida. *Journal of Anthropological Research,* 31: 364-375.

Stevenson, I. (1976a). Personal Communication.

Stevenson, I. (1976b). A preliminary report on a new case of responsive xenoglossy: The case of Gretchen. *Journal of the American Society for Psychical Research.* 70: 65-77.

Stevenson, I. (1977a). Reincarnation: Field studies and theoretical issues. In B. B. Wolman, (Ed.) *Handbook of parapsychology.* New York: Van Nostrand Reinhold Co.

Stevenson, I. (1977b). *Cases of the Reincarnation Type. Vol. 2. Ten Cases in Sri Lanka.* Charlottesville: University Press of Virginia.

Stevenson, I. (1977c). The explanatory value of the idea of reincarnation. *Journal of Nervous and Mental Disease.* 164: 305-326.

Stevenson, I. (1978). Personal Communication.

Stevenson, I. (1980). *Cases of the Reincarnation Type. Vol. 3. Twelve Cases in Lebanon and Turkey.* Charlottesville: University Press of Virginia.

Stevenson, I. (1983a). Cryptomnesia and parapsychology. *Journal of the Society for Psychical Research.* 52: 1-30.

Stevenson, I. (1983b). *Cases of the Reincarnation Type. Vol. 4. Twelve cases in Thailand and Burma.* Charlottesville: University Press of Virginia.

Stevenson, I. (1984). *Unlearned Language: New Studies in Xenoglossy.* Charlottesville: University Press of Virginia.

Stevenson, I. (1988a). Personal Communication.

Stevenson, I. (1988b). Personal Communication.

Stevenson, I., and Pasricha, S. (1979). A case of secondary personality with Xenoglossy. *American Journal of Psychiatry.* 136: 1591-1592.

Stevenson, I., and Pasricha, S. (1980). A preliminary report on an unusual case of the reincarnation type with xenoglossy. *Journal of the American Society for Psychical Research.* 74: 331:348.

Stevenson, I., Pasricha, S., and Samararatne, G. (1988). Deception and self-deception: Seven illustrative cases in Asia. *Journal of the American Society for Psychical Research. 82: 1-31.*

Stevenson, I., and Pasricha, S. (1989) A case of secondary personality with evidence of paranormal knowledge. *Journal of Society for Scientific Exploration.* 3:81-101.

Stevenson, I., and Story, F. (1970). A case of the reincarnation type in Ceylon: The case of Disna Samarasinghe. *Journal of the Asian and African Studies.* 5: 241-255.

Story, F., and Stevenson, I. (1967). A case of the reincarnation type in Ceylon: The case of Warnasiri Adikari. *Journal of American Society for Psychical Research.* 61: 130-145.

Sugrue, T. (1974). *There is a River: The Story of Edgar Cayce.* New York: Dell Publishing Co. First published in 1942.)

Sunderlal, R.B.S. (1924). Cas apparents de reminiscences des vies anterieures. *Revue Metapsychique.* 4: 302-307. Trans. I. Stevenson, 1962.

Teja, J. S. Khanna, B. S., and Subrahmanyam, T. B. (1970). Possession states in Indian patients. *Indian Journal of Psychiatry.* 12: 71-87.

Times of India Directory and Yearbook. (1977). Bombay: Times of India Press.

Uchendu, V. C. (1964). The status implications of Igbo religious beliefs. *The Nigerian Field.* 29: 27-37.

University of Virginia: Collection of Registered Rebirth Cases (1982). Personal Communication.

Upanishad, Aitareya. 2,4.

Upanishad, Brihadaranyaka. 1,5,2.,6,2,15.

Upanishad, Chandogya. 5,3,2.

Upanishad, Katha. 1,1,6.

Upanishad, Mundaka. 1,2,7.

Upanishad, Prasna. 1,9.

Van de Castle, R. L. (1973). Personal Communication. Cited by I. Stevenson, 1977a.

Varma, L. P., Srivastva, D. K., and Sahay, R. N. (1970). Possession syndrome. *Indian Journal of Psychiatry.* 12: 58-70.

Walker, B. (1983). *Hindu World: An Encyclopedic Survey of Hinduism* (2 Vols). New Delhi: Munshiram Manoharlal Publishers Pvt. Ltd. (First published in 1968.)

Warner, L. (1952). A second survey of psychological opinion of ESP. *Journal of Parapsychology.* 16:284-295.

Warner, L. (1955). What the younger psychologists think about ESP. *Journal of Parapsychology.* 19: 228-238

Warner, L., and Clark, C. (1938). A survey of psychological opinion on ESP. *Journal of Parapsychology.* 2:296-301.

Appendix-A

Explanation of Terms Used

Informant

Any person related or unrelated to the subject or the previous personality of a rebirth case, who furnished information about what the subject said or how he otherwise behaved in a particular manner in his presence; or any person who knew about the previous personality of a case from direct association with him, and who is therefore qualified to be a firsthand witness about the previous personality.

Intermission

This term has been used interchangeably with "time-interval." This refers to the period between death and presumed rebirth of a person.

Medium

A person who in trance receives messages purporting to come from the deceased and transmits them to the living.

Metempsychosis

This word has generally acquired the meaning of reincarnation of a human personality in the body of a subhuman animal or, conversely, the reincarnation of a subhuman animal in a human body. The term has been used in the same sense in the present context. The word "transmigration" usually has the same meaning.

Parakayapravesh

Technically speaking, this is a voluntary process of leaving one's own body and then entering and functioning in another (dead) body. The power to do this is acquired by certain psycho-physical (yogic) exercises. The phenomenon has also been referred to as "Parasharira-Vivesh" in "Vibhuti-Pada" (sutra 38) of Yoga Sutra. In its expression the outward features may resemble a case of "Bhuta-Cheshta" or "Bhuta-Grah" (possession), and hence can be misidentified by some observers.

Parapsychology

The term "parapsychology" refers to that branch of psychology which deals with the phenomena for which no physical cause has yet been discovered. Basically this refers to the phenomena subsumed under the general term "psi," which in its motor aspect is called "psychokinesis" (popularly known as PK, the direct action of mind over matter) and in its sensory aspect, "extrasensory perception" (generally used in its shortened form as ESP). ESP includes clairvoyance, or the extrasensory awareness of an object or objective event; telepathy, a mental communication between persons without the use of any sensory channels; precognition, non-inferential foreknowledge of future events; and retrocognition, knowledge of the past not based on normal processes of memory.

Reincarnation

The term has been defined in the chapter on Present Study. Among the other words used for the concept of reincarnation by different authors are "palingenesis," "transmigration," "pre-existence," and "metempsychosis." The Greek word "palingenesis" derives from "palin" (back or again) and "genesis" (origin or production) which is equivalent to the

Sanskrit terms "Punarjanma" (again birth) and "Samsara" (the round of births and deaths). According to Head and Cranston (1967), "The word 'transmigration' has been so frequently misused to suggest the birth of humans into animal forms—a complete reversal of the natural evolutionary process—that it is hardly satisfactory for general use". However, it has been observed that the term "transmigration" has been used interchangeably with the term "reincarnation." The term "metempsychosis" seems to derive from "metem" (change) and "psyche" (soul). Head and Cranston interpret this word as meaning the evolution of the soul through a process of rebirth, thus equating change with growth. This concept is in agreement with Sri Aurobindo's ideology (1969).

Revival

This term refers to the concept of "temporary death." The person in question appears to be clinically dead, but regains life after some time. Detailed reports of such cases have been published by Moody (1975), Pasricha and Stevenson (1986).

The concept differs from that of "Parakayapravesh." In the latter case the "soul" of the dead enters into another physical body, whereas in a revival case it comes back to the same body.

Sensitive

Any person who is "psychic," that is, who has frequent paranormal experiences and can at times induce them at will; similar to "medium," except that communications purporting to come from deceased persons are usually not involved. A sensitive derives his knowledge of events and persons through clairvoyant and telepathic abilities.

Soul

This term is used for that portion of a person that is, according to the concept of reincarnation, capable of surviving physical death. In the context of the present study, the words "minds" and "personality" are regarded as approximately synonymous.

Xenoglossy

The term "Xenoglossy" refers to cases in which a person speaks a real language entirely unknown to him in his ordinary state of consciousness. Xenoglossy has been further divided into two subgroups: recitative Xenoglossy and responsive Xenoglossy. In recitative Xenoglossy, the subject can express phrases and sometimes longer passages of a foreign language. Such recitation may occur without the subject having acquired the ability to converse in the language. In responsive Xenoglossy, on the other hand, the subject can converse intelligently in the foreign language. (Stevenson, 1976b).

Appendix-B

Names and Geographical Location of the Subjects

Case No.	Name	District and State
1.	Manju Sharma	Mathura, U.P.
2.	Bachan Singh	Mainpuri, U.P.
3.	Sahdeo Singh	Farrukhabad, U.P.
4.	Ajai Chaudhri	Moradabad, U.P.
5.	Hira Lal	Budaun, U.P.
6.	Bhagwan Das	Bareilly, U.P.
7.	Prem Chander Gupta	Budaun, U.P.
8.	Anjali Sood	Delhi, U.T.
9.	Pravesh Kumari Singh	Budaun, U.P.
10.	Nasaruddin Shah	Shahjahanpur, U.P.
11.	Mihi Lal Yadav	Budaun, U.P.
12.	Lakhan Singh	Agra, U.P.
13.	Jagmohan Lal	Budaun, U.P.
14.	Brijendra Singh	Mainpuri, U.P.
15.	Naresh Kumar Verma	Delhi, U.T.
16.	Pramod Sharma	Mainpuri, U.P.
17.	Sangeeta Srivastva	Lucknow, U.P.
18.	Sonu Pachauri	Delhi, U.T.
19.	Krishna Sharma	Bulandshahar, U.P.
20.	Harchand Singh	Sangrur, Punjab
21.	Shilpa Mehta	Jhalawar, Rajasthan

Case No.	*Name*	*District and State*
22.	Ramesh Sharma	Jhalawar, Rajasthan
23.	Manju Sharma	Jhalawar, Rajasthan
24.	Prithvi Raj Sharma	Jhalawar, Rajasthan
25.	Sunita Khandelwal	Alwar, Rajasthan
26.	Daulat Ram	Jhalawar, Rajasthan
27.	Jai Kishan	Jhalawar, Rajasthan
28.	Neena Tiwari	Farrukhabad, U.P.
29.	Sohan Lal	Ajmer, Rajasthan
30.	Santosh Golash	Ajmer, Rajasthan
31.	Ghansi	Jhalawar, Rajasthan
32.	Satyanarain Minna	Bundi, Rajasthan
33.	Chothmal Sharma	Jhalawar, Rajasthan
34.	Parmanand	Jhalawar, Rajasthan
35.	Noor Bano	Kota, Rajasthan
36.	Sanjiv Sharma	Delhi, U.T.
37.	Rakesh Gaur	Udaipur, Rajasthan
38.	Ramvir Singh Yadav	Mainpuri, U.P.
39.	Kishore Agarwal	Agra, U.P.
40.	Ranjana Tiwari	Mainpuri, U.P.
41.	Sunita Singh	Mainpuri, U.P.
42.	Brijesh Kumar	Mainpuri, U.P.
43.	Anita Shastri	Etah, U.P.
44.	Kirpal Singh	Etah, U.P.
45.	Anoop Singh	Chandigarh, U.T.

Name Index

General Index

Abnormal behavior, 230
Adi Granth, 28
Adjustment problems in subjects, 90
Adult attitude among subjects, 211
Affections, unusual, 97
Age at death of previous personality, 234
  among Ceylon cases, 219
  among Indian cases, 219
  among Tlingit cases, 219
  among Turkish cases, 219
Age of the subjects
  at fading of memories, 95, 117, 139
  at first interview, 41, 232
  of first speaking about previous life, 117, 139
  of first speaking in coherent phrases, 117, 138
  of persistence of behavioral features, 148
Agra, 246
Ainu, 23
Ajai Chaudhri, case of, 184
Alaska, 18
Altered states of consciousness, 10
  among subjects during recall, 86, 90, 94
Alevis, 23
American Association for the Advancement of science, 9
Animosities, unusual, 145
Anjali Sood, case of, 199, 208
Anklets, 84

Announcing dreams, 125, 221, 228
  among Ceylon cases, 221
  among Haida cases, 221
  among Indian cases, 221
  among Tlingit cases, 221
  among Turkish cases, 221
Anoop Singh, case of, 96, 200, 203
Aphorisms of Karma, 34
Approaches to the evidence of reincarnation, 10
  use of drugs, 10
  life readings by Yogis and mediums, 12
  use of hupnosis, 13
  philosophical reasoning, 24
Artifacts of observation, 211
Associations, See relationships between the families concerned
Attitudes unusual
  of subjects, 88, 120
  of others towards suubject's claims, 91
Austrialia, central, 23
Authenticity of cases
  points in favor and against, 102-103
Autopsy, see post-mortem examination
Avatar, 34

Bachan Singh, case of, 181, 184
Bangalore University, 245
Bania, 85

Paperbacks also available from
White Crow Books

Jesus of Nazareth with Simon Parke—
Conversations with Jesus of Nazareth
ISBN 978-1-907661-41-9

Thomas à Kempis with Simon
Parke—*The Imitation of Christ*
ISBN 978-1-907661-58-7

Julian of Norwich with Simon
Parke—*Revelations of Divine Love*
ISBN 978-1-907661-88-4

Allan Kardec—*The Spirits Book*
ISBN 978-1-907355-98-1

Allan Kardec—*The Book on Mediums*
ISBN 978-1-907661-75-4

Emanuel Swedenborg—*Heaven and Hell*
ISBN 978-1-907661-55-6

P.D. Ouspensky—*Tertium Organum:
The Third Canon of Thought*
ISBN 978-1-907661-47-1

Dwight Goddard—*A Buddhist Bible*
ISBN 978-1-907661-44-0

Michael Tymn—*The Afterlife Revealed*
ISBN 978-1-970661-90-7

Michael Tymn—*Transcending the
Titanic: Beyond Death's Door*
ISBN 978-1-908733-02-3

Guy L. Playfair—*If This Be Magic*
ISBN 978-1-907661-84-6

Guy L. Playfair—*The Flying Cow*
ISBN 978-1-907661-94-5

Guy L. Playfair —*This House is Haunted*
ISBN 978-1-907661-78-5

Carl Wickland, M.D.—
Thirty Years Among the Dead
ISBN 978-1-907661-72-3

John E. Mack—*Passport to the Cosmos*
ISBN 978-1-907661-81-5

Peter & Elizabeth Fenwick—
The Truth in the Light
ISBN 978-1-908733-08-5

Erlendur Haraldsson—
Modern Miracles
ISBN 978-1-908733-25-2

Erlendur Haraldsson—
At the Hour of Death
ISBN 978-1-908733-27-6

Erlendur Haraldsson—
The Departed Among the Living
ISBN 978-1-908733-29-0

Brian Inglis—*Science
and Parascience*
ISBN 978-1-908733-18-4

Brian Inglis—*Natural and
Supernatural: A History
of the Paranormal*
ISBN 978-1-908733-20-7

Ernest Holmes—*The
Science of Mind*
ISBN 978-1-908733-10-8

Victor & Wendy Zammit
—*A Lawyer Presents the
Evidence For the Afterlife*
ISBN 978-1-908733-22-1

Casper S. Yost—*Patience
Worth: A Psychic Mystery*
ISBN 978-1-908733-06-1

William Usborne Moore—
Glimpses of the Next State
ISBN 978-1-907661-01-3

William Usborne Moore—
The Voices
ISBN 978-1-908733-04-7

John W. White—
The Highest State of Consciousness
ISBN 978-1-908733-31-3

Stafford Betty—
The Imprisoned Splendor
ISBN 978-1-907661-98-3

Paul Pearsall, Ph.D. —
Super Joy
ISBN 978-1-908733-16-0

**All titles available as eBooks, and selected titles available in Hardback
and Audiobook formats from www.whitecrowbooks.com**